The Knowledge Tornado

Bridging the Corporate Knowledge Gap

About the Author

Marcus Goncalves is currently the CEO of iCloud, Inc. (www.icloudinc.com), a topware technology developer tapping into the pervasiveness of web services. He is the former CTO and earlier on CKO of Virtual Access Networks, a startup that, under his leadership and with the use of the Knowledge Tornado concept, was awarded the best enterprise product at the International Comdex Fall 2000 after only thirteen months of company's inception. He is a Sr. Partner/ Consultant at Marcus Goncalves Consulting (www.marcusgoncalves.com), with an international consulting practice spanning for more than fourteen years in North and Latin America, Europe, and the Middle East. He is known for his dynamic expertise in managing early stage companies targeting the software industry. Marcus also lectures at Boston University's (MET) graduate program in CIS on subjects including Program and Project Management, and Information Systems Management, among others. He holds a master degree in Computer Information Systems, a BA in Business Administration, and a BA in Psychology. He is also the author of more than 28 books in the areas of information systems and technology, knowledge management and management of early stage companies, many of them translated into several idioms. In 1989, Marcus was simultaneously awarded *Who's Who* in the US Executives and in the Computer Industry. Marcus can be contacted at marcusg@marcusgoncalves.com

PRAISE FOR *THE KNOWLEDGE TORNADO: BRIDGING THE CORPORATE KNOWLEDGE GAP*

"In the coming tidal wave of web services, knowledge management will be crucial to competitiveness in the global economy. Marcus Goncalves defines the role of the Chief Knowledge Officer (CKO) whose purview is knowledge management in the post-industrial corporation. The role of the CKO will be critical in closing the gap between 'know-how' and 'how-to' in the contemporary corporation, in the understanding of the technology and its immediate relevance to the corporation's business. How quickly this gap is bridged internally will determine the measure of profitability and competitiveness of the corporation in a global economy where business is done in web time. Mr. Goncalves makes the case that one of the crucial tasks of tomorrow's CEO will be selecting the right CKO and ensuring that there is a synergistic interplay between the two roles at the highest levels in the corporation. Speaking from actual experience he describes how the CEO could select and develop the corporate cultural machinery to achieve this goal. A must read for the globally oriented executive."

Richard Paradies, President, Micromuse Inc.

"*The Knowledge Tornado* guides you in the challenge of bridging the knowledge gap. Companies all over the world have built large databases with all sorts of information. This book is about how to transform information into useful knowledge, in corporate learning, and finally into action. Marcus Goncalves provides in his new book a multi faceted view of the knowledge problem and develops an experienced analysis on how to succeed exploring a new collaborative oriented enterprise environment. Read this book before your competitors...

"During the last [few] years we were dealing with filling the gap between business systems and the plant shop using Collaborative Production Management technologies. This new book from Marcus Goncalves dives on the next level abyss: the knowledge gap. How to transform information into useful knowledge, in corporate learning, and finally into action? *The Knowledge Tornado* is a survival guide on this new arena."

Constantino Seixas Filho – R&D Director – ATAN Automation Systems – Brazil

"*The Knowledge Tornado* brings knowledge management into detailed focus and distinguishes it from mere technology. Transferring knowledge into action, the key to the enormous productivity and competitive gains that knowledge management can bring, is emphasized throughout and examined from multiple viewpoints including the ethical. Written by someone who has navigated the shoals and seen the good and bad, this book will not just answer your questions but also the questions you didn't know to ask."

Donald Eastlake III, Principal Staff Software Engineer, Motorola

"Marcus Goncalves's *The Knowledge Tornado*...will assist you understanding all aspects of Knowledge Management. It gives you an excellent vision on how KM will change the business culture and the human behaviour. A much needed book to be read by everybody who wants to stay on the leading edge of the changing world."

Uwe Grundmann, General Manager,
North Europe, ARC Advisory Group

"*The Knowledge Tornado* does an excellent job at outlining the various aspects of Knowledge Management and the role of the knowledge manager. Particularly of interest is the emphasis on the need for people, organizations and governments to strategically manage and utilise their historical and constantly evolving knowledge to put them ahead of the pack in a turbulent and uncertain economy."

Lakshman Ratnapala, President Emeritus & CEO,
Pacific Asia Travel Association (PATA) and Chairman, Enelar International

"In an era in which the only constant is change, the ability of organizations to constantly adapt is the key to success. Marcus' book is a hands-on guide on change management through knowledge. The book is refreshingly different in that it views knowledge well beyond the precincts of technology and information systems and addresses 'softer' issues such as culture and organization design which are critical to success of knowledge based strategy, yet are most often ignored. A must read for all those in the business of knowledge."

Bharat Salhotra, Sloan Fellow 2002,
MIT Sloan School of Management

"The next generation of business leaders will be organizations who are able to harness their inherent collective knowledge to leapfrog the competition. Marcus does an outstanding job of identifying the steps today's company must take to achieve this leadership."

Gary Logie, Chief Financial Officer,
Corporate Software & Software Spectrum

"In the industrialized world, knowledge is the source of all profitability. The extent to which enterprises can harness, leverage and extend its knowledge 'core' will ultimately drive its competitive stance into the future. As value chains disperse geographically, and the 'corporate memory' is either transferred, relocated or down-sized, Knowledge Management (KM) and the New Breed of CKOs – as defined by Goncalves – will play a greater role in maintaining continuity, forming strategy and providing the intellectual scalability necessary for today's organizations. For most executives, the fact that 'knowledge is king' comes as no surprise, what Goncalves' Knowledge Tornado provides is an evangelical 'what, how, where, when' to the topic. His ability to summarize facts with explicit, real-life examples that serve to reinforce his advice and guidance will provide the basis and validation of the CKO's role as it evolves and moves forward. A must read for both those who recognize the need of KM or those who've wondered what it's all about.

Mark L. Withington, President, PLM Research

"Rapidly evolving technology is providing companies and their top executives with a confusing array of new tools to better manage the breadth of their supply chains. Avoiding the trap of simply explaining these new technologies, Marcus Goncalves' latest book, *Knowledge Tornado*, provides the intellectual tools to understand the changing dynamics of the market. Goncalves provides the higher perspective of knowledge management, its issues, its challenges, and the way it impacts companies."

Edward W. Bassett, Editor, ARC Advisory Group

"Marcus Goncalves is an IT visionary extraordinaire; he's 'been there, done that!' His intimate, first-hand experience on bridging the gap between know-how and how-to clearly defines the path of turning knowledge into action. In the past several years, corporate IT has spent incalculable resources in nurturing and cultivating multi-headed knowledge monsters that have become more and more untenable. With *Knowledge Tornado*, Marcus Goncalves clearly puts a stake in the ground for the importance of visionary knowledge leadership, but more importantly, its criticality for corporate survival. This book should be read by CKOs and CEOs alike; it sets them on a no-fail course for KM co-leadership success."

Vic Marcus Muschiano, President, Vortex Advisory Group, Inc.

"There are not many books written on this topic and Marcus Goncalves' book *The Knowledge Tornado: Bridging the Corporate Knowledge Gap* serves to fill this vacuum. Marcus, with many years of experience as a CKO of successful business ventures, is ideally placed to author a book on this subject. I found the book very readable and complete with many interesting case studies. It presents a concise view of the knowledge industry, and amply demonstrates the many challenges faced by the knowledge managers of today. I am sure this will prove to be an essential reference to everyone who is associated with the knowledge industry and responsible for managing change."

Abhaya Induruwa, Technical Advisory Unit, University of Kent at Canterbury, UK

"The concept of 'knowledge is power' continues to evolve as an insightful benchmark in business process refinement. It is no longer adequate to empower knowledge workers with information, nothing less than empowerment with understanding is acceptable. *The Knowledge Tornado: Bridging the Corporate Knowledge Gap* displays this understanding and offers a roadmap for a successful transition."

Dave Woll, VP Consulting, Automation Research Corporation

"In all organizations, processes are changed or reengineered frequently due to fluctuation in the number of employees, some new crisis, new board directives, or the results of a marketing survey. Out with the old and in with new. As a result corporations forego the experience gained previously in order to embrace change. Marcus Goncalves' book, *The Knowledge Tornado*, effectively documents this phenomenon and describes solutions for the prevention of this costly loss of knowledge. The most valuable take away was the realization that this endeavour,

Knowledge Management, will be required of all companies in order to have a competitive advantage and utilize resources efficiently. This book does an exceptional job of identifying the path that every company will be forced to take in the near future...to survive."

Kerri Holt Apple, VP Product Management & Development,
bTrade, Inc.

"Marcus Goncalves' *The Knowledge Tornado* is one of the most dynamically relevant books written during and about the new economy. It has become very difficult for Americans, as well as others in the global community, to make sense out of the rapid pace of change and information overflow, both cultural and economic, that has ensued since the advent of the Internet revolution. For the first time, X, Y and Z generation Americans are facing an economic downturn – and companies are encountering the reality of having to report consecutive quarters of falling revenues and profits. The latter prospect has not occurred since the Depression. The 'Knowledge Tornado' thoughtfully and insightfully assesses the current, seemingly chaotic environment of the global economy, takes a deep look at the paradoxical nature of the kind of radical change being forced upon businesses and their desire for stability (risk aversion), and then proposes a knowledge management-based solution that embraces continuous change as the only means to advancing innovation and ensuring survival. Those businesses that have collective corporate ears will 'hear' what Mr. Goncalves is expounding in this must-integrate business guide for the generation. If you didn't understand why you needed to develop, implement and measure a knowledge management system before, or hire or develop the right CKO built for this post-Internet world of change, 'Knowledge Tornado' can help build the roadmap that will keep you from the typical pitfalls of incorporating knowledge management into your business culture. Some people conceive of knowledge management as a great collective of enterprise technologies, but as Mr. Goncalves so persuasively explains: 'Knowledge management is a business practice, not a technology-based concept ... through which organizations generate value from their intellectual and knowledge-based assets.' Bottom line: In order to derive value from knowledge, one must make sure that this knowledge is shared throughout an organization. One of the most resonating, yet perplexing conclusions Mr. Goncalves makes is that currently our businesses reward the exact opposite: the hording of information by individuals within businesses who have been told their value and relevancy is a growing function of their ability to personally control proprietary information. With these kinds of insights and wisdom, you are entreated to go deep into the eye of the 'Knowledge Tornado' and to learn and apply what you can. It will benefit your competitive, creative and ethical well being."

John Howard, Vice President of Porter Novelli Convergence Group

"A must read for anybody that wants to understand the insights to knowledge management and how to use it to improve the success of your company."

Andy J. Funk, CEO & Founding Partner Funk Ventures, Inc.

"Marcus Goncalves goes beyond the technology of knowledge management systems to explore the organizational and strategic issues involved in any successful implementation. Drawing on the experiences of KM-savvy organizations such as Staples and The World Bank, he lists the essential strategies a CKO can employ to bridge the gap from Know-How to How-To. These strategies can be used effectively in organizations of any size, and in sectors as diverse as banking, retail, and government. If your responsibilities include KM, you should read *The Knowledge Tornado*. It will help you make the most from the investment your organization has already made (or is about to make) in KM technology and systems."

Ken Skier, President, SkiSoft, Inc.

The Knowledge Tornado

BRIDGING THE CORPORATE KNOWLEDGE GAP

Marcus Goncalves

BLACKHALL
Publishing

This book was typeset by Gough Typesetting for

Blackhall Publishing
27 Carysfort Avenue
Blackrock
Co. Dublin
Ireland

e-mail: blackhall@eircom.net
www.blackhallpublishing.com

© Marcus Goncalves, 2002

ISBN: 1 842180 42 8 (HB)
ISBN: 1 842180 48 7 (PB)

A catalogue record for this book is available from the British Library.

Printed in Ireland by
ColourBooks Ltd

Contents

Foreword

Successful business leaders have always known that their accomplishments depend on managing the knowledge of their "circle of innovation." Their circle is their organization; no matter if they are referring to their staff, their division or their extended enterprise, the same basic principles apply. Promoting innovation through collaboration, assuring that information is easily attainable. Finding the right person at the right time is paramount to providing the decisive synergy to get the task accomplished effectively and efficiently. The successful business leader understands not only the metrics of the general ledger, but also the metrics of business intelligence. The successful business leader knows how to effectively measure and evaluate his or her organization's intelligence, and constantly takes the right steps to "make things happen."

How intelligent is your organization? Do you consider your organization a circle of innovation? What are the right steps? Up until now, leaders have had to rely on their instincts alone in making this evaluation. If you are reading this book, chances are you too are such a leader – always attempting to harness and align the factors for success. Leveraging your experiences, you attempt to fit past scenarios to today's information-intensive environment to create analogies to better understand one aspect or another, and thus, how best to exploit your organization's position for the future. You are always attempting to find the right tools to make better intelligence decisions. However, you have found that the past does not always fit as nicely as we would like into present requirements. Knowledge management, though closely related to prior sciences, has become a science in its own right. *The Knowledge Tornado: Bridging the Corporate Knowledge Gap* treats the subject as a science, and provides ample subject matter in a straightforward style, building a broad base of common sense – in short, this book is a great tool of reference.

Never has there been a better time for putting into place knowledge management principles in your organization. The time is now, the technology is maturing, the economic climate is ripe, and recently customers are demanding it. Based purely on finances, corporate drivers are both internal as well as external. Internally as organizations seek to be more agile, and externally as organizations seek to be more responsive to their customers' needs. Because of these prime drivers, knowledge management plays a prominent role in our new global economy, where collaboration is not an afterthought in our e-business implementations but instead is architected to be one of the critical foundational components. Marcus Goncalves' creative approach connects e-business, KM, and collaboration together to meet the organization's strategic requirements and create the winning mindset to making your organization world-class.

The Knowledge Tornado: Bridging the Corporate Knowledge Gap provides us with a roadmap detailing the best routes to take on our journey, providing us with a wealth of information on what it takes to be a successful Chief Knowledge Officer. How rare it is to find a book that informs us on the "How-to" and at the same time identifies in a thorough manner the potential roadblocks to success. Marcus Goncalves is unique in that not only does he identify critical obstacles but also takes it up a notch and provides tried-and-true solutions to overcoming the barriers that have plagued previous initiatives. Perhaps you have learned these lessons the hard way, and wished you had the chance to read this book. No matter if you are just beginning your journey or if you are an experienced knowledge manager, there is much valuable information here for you. The insights that Marcus Goncalves advances in this book are a necessary read for everyone – organizations must build on this model to be successful in today's volatile marketspace.

Bruce T. Peat
President of eProcess Solutions,
Cofounder XML/edi Group,
Coauthor of "Professional ebXML Foundations,"
and "Professional XML"

Acknowledgements

I have been incubating this book in my mind for quite some time. A lot of it is a result of my own curiosity throughout my professional life of why professional people and common people alike typically know the answer to their own problems and challenges, yet seem to be immobilized in resolving those issues. Thus, I read a lot about the subjects, talked to a lot of people, and learned from many people as well.

To thank every single one of them here would be impossible, so if I miss some of their names, please forgive me. I would like to start by thanking Vijay Gummadi, for his great friendship, and excellent contribution on chapter twelve, of which he is the author; my gratitude goes to Paul Strassmann, acting NASA's CIO, for sharing with me his views of IT investment in the US; Verna Allee (www.vernaallee.com), author of *The Knowledge Evolution*, for so kindly sharing with me valuable material used in this book; Harry Rabin, of Miramar Systems, for his valuable feedbacks; Lee Barberie, of Stata Venture Partners; Michael Useem, Dept. of Management, Wharton School, University of Pennsylvania, author of *Leading Up*, for his contribution and many valuable insights; Yogesh Malhotra, Ph.D., Founding Chairman and Chief Knowledge Architect of BRINT Institute (www.brint.com); David A. Galper; Douglas K. Brockway and Frederick M. Joseph at SG Cowen for their collaboration in allowing me to use some of their insightful market data; Dorothy Leonard, from Harvard Business School, author of *Wellsprings of Knowledge*, for her insightful feedback and permission to use some of her references; professor Kip Becker, Ph.D., Chairman, Department of Administrative Sciences at Boston University.

I would also like to express my appreciation to many corporate leaders that shared their views and experiences with me about management in the knowledge economy, the importance of KM for learning organizations and simply common sense. My special thanks go to the following leaders: Steve Fisch, of Virtual Access Networks; Kerri Apple, of bTrade; Gregory Baletsa, of Stata Venture Partners; Nick Lurowist, of iCloud; Andy Chatha, or ARC Advisory Group; Vijay Kanabar, Ph.D., of Boston University; Dan Bathon, of WindSpeed Ventures; Mark Lukoviski, of Microsoft; Carla Dimond, Sun Microsystems; Gerry Lynch, Founder of Virtual Access Networks; Donald Eastlake III, from Motorola; Jeremy Epstein, from WebMethods; Joe Ferlazzo, from CMGI; Luis Ferro, SAP Brazil; Jack Genest, from YankeeTek Ventures; David Webber, from XML Global; David Mellor, from Oracle; Tarek Makansi, from IBM; Hans Holmstrom, from ABB; Arthur Butt, from AOL; Steve Carpenter, from BAAN; Susan Osterfelt, from Bank of America; Jeffrey A. Studwell, from BASF; Bill Kirkey, from Dupont; Mark Mueller, from DynCorp; and many others.

I would like to thank Gerard O'Connor, my publisher, and Ruth Garvey, my editor, at Blackhall, for their confidence, expert advice, and most of all, patience with me. Many thanks also go to my spiritual leader at the Boston Church of Christ, Jerry Hollister, for his continuous support and friendship. Last but not least, my deepest gratitude to my wife Carla and kids Samir, Andrea, and Joshua for their unconditional support during the many hours it took to write this book. Glory be to God!

To my forever beautiful wife Carla, my son and friend Samir, my princess and daughter Andrea, and my little prince and young son Joshua. These are the real treasures of my life.

Eternal gratitude goes to my brother in Christ John Howard, for his friendship, advice, love, and support in many ways.

To God be the glory.

Introduction

As corporate America strives to do more of what it already knows it should be doing, but isn't, Chief Knowledge Officers (CKOs) emerge to show that it is not the lack of smarts or strategies within the company that prevents success, but rather it is how business professionals utilize and apply their expertise. By bridging the gap between know-how and how-to, CKOs today must stretch themselves beyond data-mining and "knoware" activities to help companies to do what they already know how.

In addition, CKOs must become proficient in knowledge technologies, and take advantage of them to extend the benefits of quasi-legacy data-mining approaches. The reality is that ordinary databases and full text queries, as well as simple profiles, do not provide the expected level of service in churning intelligent information that can be useful. Knowledge technologies can fuel intelligent searching, personalized feedback dialogs, and sophisticated knowledge navigation, allowing knowledge managers and CKOs the kind of access to data necessary to make sense of much-needed information about business processes, supply chain and distribution channels, as well as customer relationship management for this new economy.

It is becoming evident that CKOs, the right breed of CKOs that is, along with knowledge technologies, are becoming essential in empowering organizations in dealing with the new economy and bridging the gap between the knowledge necessary to adapt to the constant new market moves and new trends, and acting upon those new business and customer requirements.

Setting the stage, the table below provides a sample[1] of the challenges corporations face today in adapting and competing in the new economy, in Internet time:

Providers	79% of all retailers and 28% of manufacturers have e-business in place
Revenue	Revenue is about 9.3% (retailers) and 7.3% (manufacturers)
Interaction	50% of communication/interaction is already purely by electronic media
Content	58% of catalogs worldwide are already on electronic media

---

1. Sources: Ernst & Young, Forrester Research, Boston Consulting Group, IDC, Bank of America, Meta Group 1999, 2000.

Quantity	e-business applications hold about 131,000 information entities, increasing by 35% per year
Interactions	Company/Customer Interactions will increase from $4 billion in 1999 to $23 billion in 2003
Success	1,000 contacts turn into 18 buyers. Loss of $6 billion during last Christmas season
Self-confidence	66% of managers said their current search functionality is sufficient
Reality	76% of the customers said they had difficulties with the provided search functionality of the respective sites

This book is about a much-needed new breed of CKOs. Today's CKO, must be able to develop and deliver a rich set of action-oriented tools and procedures that help companies to transition from learning into action, so they can deal with the realities and challenges outlined in the previous table. In the process, CKOs must be able to tap into not only their corporate employees' facts and observations, but also their hopes, fears, dreams, and feelings, so they can then use them to break the major obstacles to action that confront business professionals and organizations.

In addition, this book provides a broad range of information about a much-needed, revised, and revamped new CKO role in the organization, the need for co-leadership with the CEO and co-partnership with the executive staff. It describes the vital role of CKOs in turning knowledge into action, developing and nurturing enterprise systems, capturing and transforming knowledge into corporate learning, fostering this learning into action, and becoming the corporate lead evangelist inside and out.

Ask a room full of IT-minded executives what a CKO is and what defines its role, and you will probably hear as many definitions as you see Palms, Visors, and iPaqs in the room. Those more in sync with the industry may venture to define a CKO as the professional responsible for the practice of finding, organizing, and managing people's knowledge. But as other IT professionals, namely chief information officers (CIOs), try their hands at knowledge management, the definition of a CKO, and therefore the expectations surrounding the role, can be very blurry and will vary according to the environment these *pseudo CKOs* are in and the challenges they have ahead of them.

Chapter one, "Knowledge Officer's Challenges in the Fast-Paced Global Economy," addresses the challenges CKOs face, where their role is not often well defined and many times confused, as of a CTO with business and information systems skills, or, from a different angle, a CIO with business and information technology expertise.

Chapter two, "The New Breed of CKOs," focuses on the importance of knowledge management (KM) initiatives and how essential a new breed of CKOs are, given the increasing dependence of most companies on information and technologies within a business environment of radical, discontinuous change, often at global levels. This chapter shows that twenty-first century CKOs must extend their KM initiatives beyond simply setting up mailing lists between workers with specific interests, which can very well be executed under the CTO/IT umbrella, or even building intranets empowered with collaboration tools. Although CKOs are, and will continue to be, very important in multibillion-dollar KM and customer relationship management (CRM) projects, as well as smaller ones directly targeted at the bottom line, such as sales force automation projects, these professionals should not let the technology dominate their attention.

Focusing on database and data mining systems, the time-honored technique for transferring knowledge, does not always work well and very seldom delivers to expectations. Such best-practice techniques work very well for the discrete environment, but, for the most part, the quantifiable performance of these systems is very modest, at best. Chapter two shows that traditional CKOs (can the profession be called traditional and yet be so new?!) tend to be very single-minded in their efforts to derive competitive advantage from explicit knowledge, the kind of information one can capture, write about and distribute to anyone via brownbags, automated systems, or a database. Today's CKOs (or should I say yesterday's?) do not realize that more than ever before, knowledge is a living entity, it has always been, thus making information a living thing. By capturing and making knowledge a structural capital, an intellectual property, they are actually killing it. Thus, in order to be effective, this practice must change; otherwise, the gap between knowledge and capital knowledge, which directly translates into successful business actions, will widen.

Chapter three, "Identifying, Capturing, and Transferring Learning into Action," focuses on transferring learning into action. Of course, KM databases and other sophisticated systems will continue to exist, but in order to bridge the knowledge gap (the gap between know-how and how-to) CKOs must be able to identify, capture, and transfer not data, not information, but learning into action. This is all that chapter three is focused on. CKOs must be able to identify the knowledge to be captured, by breaking up a great percentage of its processes. They should then be able to capture and transfer it to others. But a certain amount of any knowledge, about anything, always remains tacit, and cannot be read or taught. At this level, knowledge is transferred by learning, watching, and experiencing, as tacit knowledge is always deeply embedded in the person who performs the task.

Chapter three also addresses the difficult task of transferring, not turning, learning into action. One of the main reasons first-generation KM software and systems are inadequate in this process is exactly because you cannot turn knowledge into action; it is not a two-step deal, an input and an output process. Tacit knowledge is already difficult to disseminate and apply throughout the organization.

Chapter four, "Learning Organizations: Striving by Transferring Knowledge," draws upon learning to learn, and an effective element of such organizations is the transferring of the knowledge learned. Here, a healthy perspective of a learning organization is placed in a coherent framework, which is brought to life by an array of engaging and practical examples. Organizations can only achieve performance by constant learning and refocus of its business strategies and actions. This chapter shows how important it is for CKOs to help knowledge managers, and themselves, to dissociate the technology from KM. Technology and document management is only part of the knowledge-transferring program so necessary to extract capital knowledge.

Chapter four shows how knowledge should be seen as socially constructed through the organization, and even its interacting partners. CKOs must leave room for social aspects, and make sure to organize knowledge and know-how in order to get expected results. CKOS and knowledge managers must no longer rely on human resources methods, as they are anathema to knowledge. Instead of codifying tacit knowledge, they must concentrate their efforts in connecting the individuals who have the knowledge to others who need it.

Chapter five, "Organizing Knowledge and Know-How: Developing Enterprise Systems," recommends the development of an enterprise system, anchored on organizational information and knowledge technologies, as a platform for organizing knowledge, know-how, and data sharing. This chapter not only discusses the benefits and advantages enterprise systems bring to knowledge management, but emphasizes the fact that such implementation should be a result of a business, rather than a technology, decision; otherwise, it may be doomed for failure.

Further, this chapter shows how important it is for know-how to lead to action, to how-to. It is here that the majority of organizations fail, even after spending thousands of dollars with excellent and competent consultants telling them what needs to be done, as most often they fail to execute. It is here, between know-how and how-to, that the knowledge gap of so many organizations exists!

Chapter six, "Fulfilling the Vision: From Know-How to How-to," demonstrates, through techniques, business processes, and case studies, how to effectively cross the chasm from know-how to how-to and effectively execute. Business execution is at the heart of any successful organization and the ultimate goal of any KM initiative should be to improve it.

In the process of bridging the knowledge gap, CKOs and knowledge managers must also rely on collaboration at all levels. Creating a collaborative enterprise is the next challenge. This chapter provides you with an overview of the strategic application of KM through innovation, leadership, senior staff partnership and support, and readiness to deal with human and business changes at all times, with the attitude to quickly adapt.

Chapter seven, "Chief Enchanter Officer and Chief Knock Out: Business in Wonderland?" focuses on a new paradigm borrowed from David A. Heenan and Warren Bennis on the power of co-leadership.[2] This chapter emphasizes the fact that building a great organization requires more than a visionary CEO. It also requires an exceptional co-leader, and it shows how CKOs are the right candidates for that position. For every Ben there should be a Jerry; for every Gates there should be a Balmer; for every McNeely there should be a Joy; for every Holmes there should be a Watson. Shrewd leaders know they need co-leaders, mostly to fill in the gaps left by their weaknesses.

Furthermore, CKOs must be ready to bridge another gap very present in most organizations: that between IT groups, CTOs and CIOs, and upper management and the board. So dysfunctional is the situation that no wonder the knowledge gap is so wide. According to a poll of 555 directors and senior IT staff on CIO.com in May of 2001, about 62 percent of them had no understanding of the value of information technology. Boards, in particular, still mostly consist of a slew of outsiders and a few key inside executives.[3] CIOs, and CKOs for that matter, are rarely among the chosen, despite the fact that on average, boards spend about 160 to 200 hours per year steering their target company's strategy. CKOs and CIOs alike must do all they can to bring IT to the board's agenda. Thus, a tight relationship between CEOs and CKOs is paramount.

Chapter eight, "Helping to Move the Cheese: Closing the Circle of Innovation," provides information on how to deal with changes and use them for business advantage. In a business world characterized by constant change, knowledge officers must be prepared to deal with changes and take advantage of them to promote innovation instead of despair.

This chapter also discusses the concept of "pushing" when business forces or new trends "pull." It provides practical examples on leveraging knowledge, about the competition, about the market, about untapped new trends, for competitive advantage instead of "exit strategies."

---

2. From their book, *Co-Leaders: The Power of Great Partnerships*, New York, John Wiley & Son, 1999.
3. According to veteran board member Norma Pace in an interview to CIO.com, which was also the former senior vice-president of the American Paper Institute who has served companies such as Chase Manhattan Bank, 3M, Sperrys, Sears Roebuck and Hasbro.

Chapter nine, "So you Want to Become a CKO?" is designed as a professional guide to enhance your chances for a successful career. The current wave of globalization in business has pushed the corporate world past the point where CKOs can simply carve KM activities into processes and modules. Today, CKOs should also aim to partner with business management at the highest level, and, in light of a globalized economy, they should also understand the global strategies of the organization and be able to partner with business at the regional level to consummate those strategies.

In order to be successful CKOs must also have a greater alignment with CEOs and the board, in part due to the fact that CKOs should no longer be introverted technologists and information systems whizzes who shun the input of their more schmoozy counterparts. CKOs today must not only be involved with KM projects, but also have a true interest in business processes and goals, as well as experience with non-techie assignments, such as consulting, strategic planning, product development, marketing, and customer service. By doing so, CKOs will be better prepared to identify arising new trends, which are prone to disrupt knowledge flow and create the gaps. Such phenomena are not necessarily bad; on the contrary, they are necessary so that the organization can take advantage of new opportunities and enter new markets.

Chapter ten, "The Need for Gaps: Trusting the Corporate Instinct," increases this healthy tension created by previous chapters. Paradoxically, if there was a need to create knowledge gaps so an organization could develop disruptive knowledge and promote innovations for competitive advantage, once an organization becomes more of an instinctive one, there is an even greater need for new knowledge gaps. The reason is that these new and more frequent knowledge gaps help to validate the corporate instinct. This chapter helps upper management to assist their corporations to live and operate by their wits.

Chapter eleven, "The Science of Bridging the Gap: The Leader's Dilemma," is a segue way from chapter ten. Once knowledge officers are able to create a disruptive knowledge that promotes innovation and prepare the organization to deal with it, the next step is to bridge that gap. As this chapter shows, this task invariably generates a dilemma for the leader. This is because once strategy simulations are successfully done, the experience of introducing a new knowledge gap becomes much simpler for the organization, easier to be recreated by groups and subgroups within the organization through brainstorms, as a means to innovation or generation of new ideas. The science of bridging the knowledge gap becomes, therefore, more intensified.

Such strategy simulations, at the healm of KM, should be seen as the business equivalent of practice sessions for sports teams or rehearsals for music, dance, or drama companies. They are not necessary when people are doing the same work year in, year out. However, assuming CKOs do their job well and the organization becomes more comfortable with disruptive knowledge, we then move into a world in which organizational change is both common, radical, and integrated with very high levels of performance. At this point, KM tools are likely to become very critical, as the organization enters a level of instinctive knowledge generation, not so much structured as it was at first. The phenomenon is very similar to creative writing, and CKOs must be prepared to handle it – otherwise, the risk of chaos is great!

Chapter twelve, "Knowledge Management in Government." Knowledge management initiatives are on the upswing as managers at all government levels face mounting pressure to work smarter and faster while wrestling with the demands of electronic government and a shrinking work force. Practices developed when governmental agencies had more workers, and fewer and far less demanding constituents do not cut it in today's fast-paced environment, where nearly every worker has access to rapid-fire e-mail, the work force is more transient, and the inflow of information is almost uncontrolled. The Internet revolution has brought with it the mandate of speed, service, and global competitiveness. Government agencies at national, state, and local levels are rising to the challenge by leveraging knowledge management techniques and modern thinking.

In summary, this book is about managing knowledge with clout. It is not new that, and most CKOs already know it, knowledge officers need to target the bottom line, and in a very positive way. But now comes the hard part: to learn how they can build better relationships to boost their influence and support for new projects. They must think out of the box of traditional knowledge management best practices so that their projects can succeed and effectively impact the organization, its people, its business, and, ultimately, the bottom line. This is what this book is all about.

CHAPTER 1

Knowledge Officers' Challenges in the Fast-Paced Global Economy

Every executive in corporate America knows that having a service culture is critical to their success.

As corporations migrate to a knowledge-centric position, planning, leadership, and board and executive management support become crucial. However, most often knowledge management (KM) is not easily plugged into a return on investment (ROI) equation. In addition, over the past couple of years of the twenty-first century, characterized by an economic downturn not seen since the information-driven economy emerged in the early 1990s, it has become clear that knowledge officers' performances should no longer be measured by results alone, but also by their goals.

Until recently, the business-critical value of knowledge management investment was all but assumed, and experts on the subject all realized that their assumptions were wrong. Many predicted, and are still predicting, that knowledge management and its derived career paths are doomed to extinction. In fact, during the spring of 2001, *CIO Magazine* commented that knowledge management systems did not work, in particular due to the fact that no one in the organization would use or support such systems, beginning with upper management. And they were right!

The theory that a knowledge management system was only as good as its information technology has been nearly unquestionable. But I believe the thinking behind this theory is murky. You see, just like the first generation of management information systems (MIS) professionals grew up from accounting and financial departments, as those professionals attempted to enhance their accounting and financial practices, so the first breed of knowledge officers grew up from information technology, information systems, and information management. Thus, the first generation of knowledge management professionals and practices has been heavily focused on systems and technology, which is precisely why most knowledge management problems occur.

As companies focused on building knowledge database repositories and data-mining techniques, the majority of them ignored their people and their cultural issues. In addition, I believe the massive investments in knowledge management projects in the 1990s were thought to underlie the historical globalization, merger and acquisition (M&A) activities across the globe that characterized the decade. Technology became one of the most active M&A sectors during the late 1990s, as Figure 1.1 shows.[1] Consequently, the need for information sharing among disparate systems and knowledge-based systems was too great, even though the objective evidence for such a claim is controversial at best. Nevertheless, knowledge management has had a free ride for at least the last three or four years.

Figure 1.1 – Technology became the most active M&A sector during the late 1990s

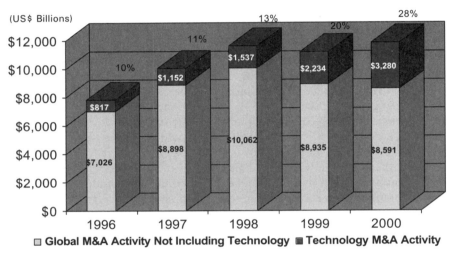

Source: SDC. Note, the percent value represents the technology M&A activity in comparison to the total M&A activity.

THE ERA OF KNOWLEDGE MANAGEMENT ACCOUNTABILITY

Well, the ride is over. The era of knowledge management accountability has come, and corporate knowledge management systems will be judged on the basis of their ability to deliver quantifiable competitive advantage, capable of making your business smarter, faster, and more profitable. In the process, the need to sell the knowledge management concept to employees should not be underestimated. In a fast-paced global economy, CKOs should strive to promote an environment where individuals' knowledge is valued and rewarded, establishing a culture that recognizes tacit knowledge and encourages everyone to share it. How we go about it is the challenge.

---

1.   According to SG Cowen.

The old practice of employees being asked to surrender their knowledge and experience, the very traits that make them valuable as individuals, must change. Knowledge cannot be captured; if it is, it dies. Thus, motivating employees to contribute to knowledge management activities through the implementation of incentive programs is frequently ineffective. Often, employees tend to participate in such programs solely to earn incentives, without regard to the quality or relevance of the information they contribute.

The main challenge here is that KM is overwhelmingly a cultural undertaking. Before setting the course for a KM project and deciding on KM technologies, you will have to know what kinds of knowledge your organization's employees need to share and what techniques and practices should be implemented to get them to share. Thus, you will need a knowledge strategy. A knowledge strategy should reflect and serve as business goals and attributes. A dispersed, global organization, for example, is probably not well served by a highly centralized knowledge strategy.

To be successful, knowledge officers must be able to implement a very transparent knowledge management activity, one that is focused on simplicity, common sense, and at no time imposed. Whatever is imposed will always be opposed, which immediately compromises the value and integrity of the knowledge being gathered or shared. Ideally, participation in knowledge management efforts should be desired by every employee, it should come from within, and its participation should be its own reward. After all, the goal of such initiatives should be to make life easier for employees, therefore positively affecting the bottom line. Otherwise, the effort has failed.

Unfortunately, to date, the majority of KM projects have not achieved the level of success expected. The lack of transparent integration between IT KM tools and the users often have them thinking CKOs and KM managers do not know what they are doing. Thus, today's CKOs must be able to successfully leverage the promise of KM, its peril, and, in many instances, eye-popping costs in infrastructure, deployment, implementation, and use of the system.

No doubt KM can revolutionize corporations' capital knowledge and sharing. But it will not be easy, and is not likely to be cheap, as the challenges are many, and breaking down users' resistance is one of the major challenges CKOs face. You do not get moving just by buying and installing one of the many KM applications already available on the market. My advice is for you to spend quality time planning your KM strategy, and be forewarned that the initiative may be expensive, not only in terms of capital investments, but also in terms of human resource and organizational investments. With that in mind, you will be able to plan better. You should begin with the challenges discussed here. Then, you should focus on the many strategies outlined throughout this book, which affect not only IT support, but also cultural and business issues, and, ultimately, the role of the CKO as catalyst and flagship of the whole process.

DEFINING SUCCESS IN KNOWLEDGE MANAGEMENT
IMPLEMENTATIONS: VISION IN ACTION

The ultimate goal of a CKO should be to bridge the gap between a corporation's know-how and its how-to. Even if a KM implementation is successful from the technical, usability, knowledge aggregation, and retrieval perspectives, empowering the organization to transform its know-how into how-to is still virtually an utopist task. But I believe that the definition of success equals vision in action. Seeking business success, several companies undertake tremendous reengineering cycles and hire expensive consultants to tell them what, very often, they already know, and have known for years, after reports and more reports generated by a number of management and business consulting firms.

You might have a clear vision of your KM project goals, but if you do not have a clear action plan in place, one that can be measured using reliable metrics, you just will not succeed. By the same token, you may have a clear action plan, one that very likely has been outlined, developed and recommended in-house, or by outside consultants, but if you do not have a clear vision of where you are going and of the results you want to achieve, you just will not get there either.

Do not underestimate the complexity of KM implementations. If you look at enterprise resource planning (ERP) and customer relationship management (CRM) solutions you can have some idea. Very few ERP implementations have been fully successful; most of them are still under the implementation phase, being clogged up with CRM solutions, or already undergoing some level of business process rethinking. The same goes for CRM. According to Meta Group's March 2000 survey, between 55 and 75 percent of CRM projects do not meet their objectives. Further, according to Insight Technology Group, more than 25 percent of 226 CRM users surveyed do not think the implementation will add any significant improvement in company's operations, and only 50 percent think there will be some sort of improvement. Now, CRM success results are much more tangible to measure than KM ones!

What those surveys underline is an increasing skepticism about intelligent systems, which CKOs must be able to avoid, if not eliminate. Getting 100 percent satisfaction in KM implementations is not only very expensive, but almost impossible. It is not enough to install a KM system. You need to convince your people to use it, starting with upper management.

In addition, immediate results are near nonexistent, until users are able to feed the system with all their best practices, explicit knowledge, and whatever knowledge they believe can earn them the announced motivational perk. Of course, you can always mention the success of the KM system used by UK Prime Minister Tony Blair through its massive party victory.[2] But that system

---

2. The party relied on RetrievalWare search and retrieval software from the Viennese company Convera (www.convera.com).

had a very specific and narrow goal of attack and rapid rebuttal of the opposite party, which makes it very unique. Today's CKO's challenges are much broader in scope, as well as influential. The following are the most important ones.

THE CHALLENGE OF MANAGING INFORMATION OVERFLOW

According to the Meta Group, in 1998 an average company was managing 100 gigabytes (GB) of information, with volume forecast to increase to 2500GB in 2001. Such data shows an exponential growth that is not expected to slow down over the coming decades. Figure 1.2 provides a sample of the repositories of corporate knowledge, according to The Delphi Group.

Figure 1.2 – Repositories of corporate knowledge

- ◪ Paper Documentation   ◪ Electronic Documentation
- ◪ Electronic Knowledgebase   ◪ Employees' Brains

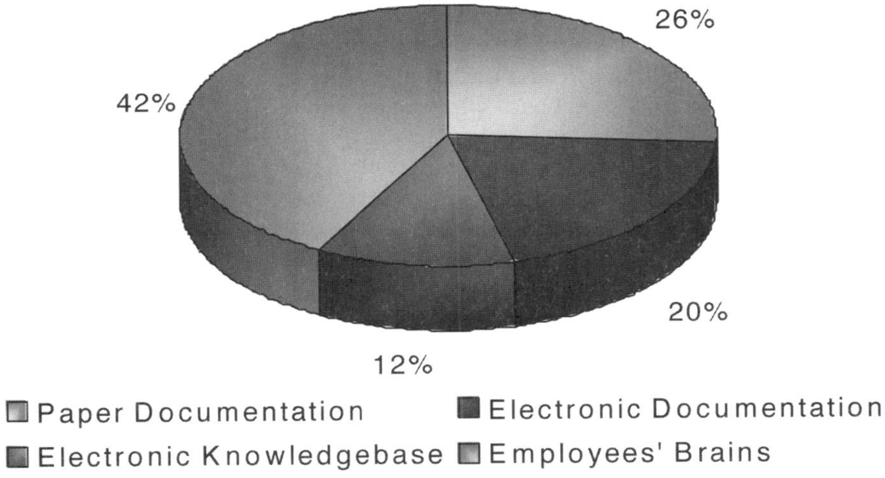

Source: The Delphi Group

According to Maureen Grey, Gartner Group analyst, by 2004, enterprise mailbox volume is expected to increase 40 percent per year. E-mail users at the enterprise are spending an average of 1.5 hours each day on mailbox management tasks, and by 2002 they will be spending an average of 3.5 hours per day maintaining their mailboxes, which will prompt about 60 percent of enterprises to augment their messaging applications with a mechanism to manage must-keep e-mail.

Moving forward in the twenty-first century, CKOs will have to work very closely with CIOs and CTOs to devise a strategy to manage the overflow of data flooding their organizations. CKOs will have to find innovative ways to manage such huge volumes of information being automated and delivered by publish/subscribe technologies. By investing now in information and knowledge management technologies, CKOs will be able to stay ahead of the curve. This situation is so challenging that delaying such information/ knowledge management initiative by a year or two may cause the organization to lose all ability to effectively amass its data, much less provide intelligent, convenient access to it. According to the Seybold Group, those wanting to manage and control the huge amounts of information contained in their unstructured text documents need content management solutions "with an explicit focus on security, access control and an expansive taxonomy of terms that are oriented around a problem-solving focus."[3]

Cleaning Up the Act

Of course, e-mail control and message management are not typically, if ever, the responsibility of CKOs, nor are the tasks of cleaning up and maintaining the current archive of documents. However, managing unnecessary documents, even though it does not increase the value of the documents or the efficiency of the organization, is a vital part of managing knowledge in the organization. That is when CKOs play a major role in interactively working with information systems and technology professionals.

Organizations should implement at least three records management practices, and CKOs should be responsible for understanding them, and developing and implementing them with the support of information systems and technology (IS&T) groups. These record management practices consist of:

- Defining policies, criteria, and timeframes for retention of information based on the regulatory requirements, mission critical status, or operational nature of the information, and/or any other relevant criteria.

- Establishing ownership for business data records – whose responsibility is it for defining the policies around retention and use of the data?

- Implementing these policies across the organization for both paper and digital files, so in partnership with CTO/CIOs you can consider the technology alternatives for managing unstructured text documents.

- Managing documented and undocumented intellectual assets, which include identifying unique technology and processes, and securing patents and copyrights wherever appropriate.

---

3. In "Strategic Directions: Knowledge Management and e-Learning" *CIO Magazine* supplement, 2001, p. 34.

Defining Broader Content Management

According to Cyveillance, as of mid-year 2000, the total number of pages on the Internet topped 2.1 billion; by the end of 2001 the company predicted there would be more than 4 billion pages. Considering that the average web page is 10KB in size, contains 23 internal links, 5.6 external links, and 14.4 images, and adding in the terabytes of unstructured documents in corporate file systems and databases, we can easily understand why organizations need text-mining technologies so badly, which has ratchet up automated analysis and classification of natural language communications.

One of the CKO's challenges here is that people will search for what they know is in a document collection, but they generally will not or simply cannot specify a query for what they do not know is in a document collection. The art of effective text mining is to use computation power to suggest relationships that may well lead to new knowledge discovery on the part of the user.

According to Gartner Research Director Alexander Linden, there are four kinds of text-mining applications:

1. Fact extraction: also known as information tagging, it seeks to derive certain facts from text to improve categorization, retrieval, and clustering. IBM's Intelligent Miner for text does fact extraction.

2. Semantic nets: these are link analyses that measure the occurrence of key phrases in a document to aid navigation.

3. Text categorization: uses statistical correlations to construct rules for placing documents into predefined categories.

4. Topic-based: a clustering of documents via linguistic and mathematical measures of content similarity without using predefined categories. The result is generally a taxonomy or a visual map which delivers a quick overview of large amounts of data.

Text-mining capabilities can be put to work in knowledge management applications, such as skills profiling, to automatically push and/or pull information based on interest profiles and generate overviews of in-house documents for research or reviews. These tools, as well as those that analyze data and information to help human beings acquire knowledge, are now much more accessible to a larger swath of employees, thanks to graphical user interfaces (GUIs), Web-enabled applications, and simplified languages that make possible data analysis from desktop computers.

Knowledge management professionals can take advantage of powerful analytic capabilities when business intelligence (BI) systems, which include query and reporting tools, data mining and online analytical processing (OLAP), are linked to customer and trading partner information sources. These tools enable KM to automate analytic processes to spot patterns on which are based predictions and suggestions that aid sales and efficiency initiatives.

Companies such as PeopleSoft and SAP are capitalizing on this challenge. PeopleSoft's Business Analytics offers a variety of domain-specific business analytics, including workforce, customer relationship management, financial, and supply chain. Its Profitability Management for Financial Services combines a number of industry-specific engines to create an integrated suite of analytics for banks and other lending institutions. Analytical applications within MySAP Business Intelligence also integrate business processes. Its business-area-based applications include customer relationship analytics, enterprise analytics, supply chain analytics, and marketplace analytics.

By tagging digital content with common descriptive mechanisms for data representations and exchange, the activities and transactions of multiple processing technologies – workflow, integration software and middleware, business applications – can be unified and coordinated.

THE CHALLENGE OF A TECHNOLOGY-DRIVEN KNOWLEDGE MANAGEMENT

A mistake several organizations are making with KM initiatives is to think of KM as a technology-based concept. There are no all-inclusive KM solutions and any software or system vendor touting such a concept is either deceived or grossly misinformed. To implement solely technology-based systems such as electronic messaging, Web portals, centralized databases, or any other collaborative tool and think you have implemented a KM program is not only naïve, but also a waste of time and money.

Of course, technology is a major KM enabler, but it is not the end, and not even the starting point of a KM implementation. A sound KM program should always start with two indispensable and cheap tools: pencil and paper. The CKO's challenge here is to plan, plan, and plan. Knowledge management decisions must be based on strategies defined by the acronym W3H (who, what, why, and how), or the people, the knowledge, the business objectives, and the technology, respectively. The technology should only come later.

Another challenge that tends to be technology driven is knowledge flow, which is often a stumbling block in KM programs. The big mistake CKOs make is to look at technology as the main solution to support the flow of knowledge. Knowledge flow is a much more complex issue, which involves the process of creation and dissemination of new knowledge, as well as human motivation, personal and social construction of knowledge, and virtualization of organizations and communities. I believe knowledge flow is only sustained by the human desire to make sense, common sense that is, of issues that transcend the everyday business scope, but it is very much present in every moment of a professional's life, no matter what their trade.

Everyday, as we assimilate, store, and disseminate knowledge, organized or not, we are trying to make sense of issues that relate to our interests, passions, lives, work, and even family. No technology system can capture such unstructured and tacit knowledge, and trying to do so, instead of supporting its flow, stops it. The situation becomes even more complex when we consider the cultural aspects so present in multinational organizations, or those that have gone through a merge with foreign companies.

Common sense should also apply to business processes. Most of our business reasoning and purposes are built around a process of justification for what we would like to do in order to satisfy a business requirement (or is it in order to satisfy ourselves?). In this process, CKOs should be aware of tacit knowledge present by virtue of previous experiences in every employee, as well as their studies, thinking, and cultural background, while they attempt to verbalize it in the form of their responses. Technology alone will not help you in this process.

THE CHALLENGE OF DEFINING SPECIFIC KNOWLEDGE MANAGEMENT GOALS

Since the late 1990s KM has been emerging as a preeminent articulation of post-modern, post-industrial innovational management theory, increasingly adopted by corporations and governments. However, defining specific KM goals has never been harder.

While hyper proponents of KM see it as the ultimate new-age management construction, so vital that yesterday is too late to start a program, and so intangible that no one can agree on what it is, a 1999 Information Week survey of 200 IT executives tells otherwise. As the survey identified, there are major challenges to be undertaken so that KM practices can be taken up, including the difficulty of classifying knowledge and data, the behavior modification required of employees, and, most of all, the buy-in of corporate management. Nonetheless, 94 percent of the surveyed executives endorsed the strategic importance of KM. So, why is there so little successful KM implementation?

First, there has always been confusion about the term "knowledge management," which has been used in information systems, strategy meetings, and many other business disciplines without any consistency. Often you find the term used on trade magazines, by technologists, financial analysts, and even sociologists, all in their own context. Unfortunately, there is no clear agreement over what KM is, which makes the definition of specific KM goals even more difficult.

Second, companies diligently need to be on the lookout for information overload, as quantity rarely equals quality. Thus, another challenge faced by CKOs is to identify and disseminate knowledge pearls from an ocean of information.

Therefore, a KM program should always be in tune with business goals, and no matter what KM goals are, there must be an underlying business reason to do so, otherwise KM is a futile venture. To gauge the degree of alignment of a KM program with business goals, the following are some pointers:

- Does your KM program address the strategic notion of organizational survival and competence within a fundamentally changing and unpredictable organizational environment?

- Does your KM go beyond the traditional information management needs?

- Does KM take into consideration the human-centric notion of knowledge in relationship to the professional activity context of the organization, as well as the lack of it, which will define levels of performance?

- Does it provide for incorporation of the creative capabilities of people needed for innovative breakthroughs with the optimization-based, efficiency-enhancement capabilities of advanced information technology?

When defining specific KM goals, CKOs must keep in mind that such programs are not static, as the value of knowledge can grind down over time. To prevent knowledge from getting stale too fast, KM program contents should be periodically updated, amended, and even discarded when necessary. Chapter eight, "Helping to Move the Cheese: Closing the Circle of Innovation", provides information on how to go about revising KM goals, in particular by always promoting innovation within the organization.

Innovation will address the relevance of knowledge as prone to changes at any given time, often as a result or catalyst of employee skills set changes. Therefore, there is no endpoint to a KM program. Like product development, marketing, and R&D, KM is a constantly evolving business practice.

THE CHALLENGE OF INTRAPRENEURSHIP

One of the major challenges CKOs are facing in this fast-paced, Internet-based, global economy is the redefinition of the employment contracts in the US and other worldwide organizations. This is because, in such environments, the knowledge value chain in the organizational business process becomes increasingly relevant, forcing employees of knowledge-based organizations to act as knowledge intrapreneurs.[4]

In order to compete in time, intrapreneurship is a must, as the nature of these organizations and work roles is necessarily changing. In such an

---

4. Such concept is actually not new, as Dr. Yogesh Malhotra, the founding chairman and chief knowledge architect of the BRINT Institute, had pointed it out back in 1998 on a knowledge management discussion forum at Brint (www.brint.com).

environment, emerging work roles must rely on and exploit an informated[5] environment by making the information base of the organization available to members at all levels, assuring that each has the knowledge, skills, and authority (yes, authority!) to engage with the information productively. An efficient operation in the informated workplace requires a more equitable distribution of knowledge and authority. It requires that new work roles of every employee call them to become an extension of their managers, as well as an intrapreneur in the organizational knowledge-creation process.

The knowledge intrapreneurs should be expected to contribute to the organizational knowledge-creation processes based on developing knowledge relationships and knowledge exchanges within and outside the formal boundaries of the organization. As a result, a new and emerging virtual community of practice and virtual events within and outside the organization will take place, at global levels, harbingering this vision.

THE CHALLENGE OF DELIVERING TANGIBLE BENEFITS WITH KNOWLEDGE MANAGEMENT

In today's event and information-driven economy, companies are discovering that most opportunities and, ultimately, value are derived from intellectual rather than physical assets. To get the most value from a company's intellectual assets, KM professionals are striving to share knowledge throughout the organization, its partners, supply chain and distribution channels, serving as a foundation for collaboration.

Yet to have KM programs delivering better collaboration is not an end in itself and does not necessarily provide tangible benefits to the organization. In fact, it may even increase the level of complexity of the information systems already in place, impairing knowledge sharing and causing a burst of information overflow, often out of context. And without an overarching business context, KM is meaningless at best and harmful at worst. Thus, the new breed of CKOs must follow the words of the strategist Gary Hamel: "wealth creators change the rules."[6] The new breed of CKOs are to become rule makers, and, in the process, they must break a few KM rules as well, beginning with the notion that knowledge is power, advocated by Sir Francis.

There is so much information out there, being delivered to us physically and electronically, that what you know is only power if you know how to use it to help you and your organization to juggle the things that need to be accomplished on a day-to-day basis. This kind of power is not derived from the amount of knowledge you can absorb, capture, catalog, share, or transfer to your organization, but on how quickly you and your KM team can create

---

5. As termed by Dr. Malhotra.
6. G. Hamel, *Leading the Revolution*, Boston, Harvard Business School, 2002.

meaning to information on a continuous, real-time basis. This is not an easy task, as it very often involves figuring out which new factoids, bits, and bytes are critical and valid, from all the gazillions of information swirling around KM databases and systems. And this does not include the tacit level of KM, which by nature, is near to impossible to capture and share.

Making sense of information is a very important process in KM, not only because it can be a catalyst in bridging the gap between know-how and how-to, but because it provides the only way I trust of allowing KM to be successfully measured: by directly impacting the bottom line, and in a positive way, by generating savings, if not competitive advantage. Of course, there are other measurable benefits KM can provide but those are typically more difficult to quantify.

For instance, leveraging customer information inside the organization to create value is a very important task, which directly affects the bottom line of any customer-driven company. Donald Peterson, former CEO and Chairman of Ford Motor Co., comments that "if we aren't driven by our customers, our automobiles won't be driven by them either."[7] Thus, efficiently serving customers is becoming increasingly important in today's event-driven competitive economy. After all, a 5 percent increase in customer retention can generate between 25 and 85 percent increase in profitability. The focus of late 1980s and early 1990s reengineering efforts, centered on productivity improvements and lower product and process costs, are no longer enough to guarantee increasing profits and business sustainability. To remain competitive, companies must generate value for their customers through service that addresses the customer's unique requirements.

The effort is worth it. KPMG Consulting's *Knowledge Management Research Report 2000*, in which 423 organizations were queried, notes that 71 percent of those surveyed said they had achieved better decision making thanks to their KM efforts, 68 percent said they had achieved faster response to key business issues, and 64 percent said they had delivered better customer service. Fewer of those with a knowledge management program complained about reinventing the wheel, more can access customer profile data faster, and more can access an accepted business process methodology faster.

In addition, to deliver tangible results, an effective KM program should help an organization to:

• foster innovation by inspiring the free flow of ideas

• improve customer service by streamlining response time

• improve employee retention rates by recognizing the value of employees' knowledge and rewarding them for it

---

7. P. Peterson, Interview in *KM Review*, (http://www.km-review.com/know_articles/ 01.htm).

- increase revenues by getting products and services to market faster

- streamline operations and reduce costs by eliminating redundant or unnecessary processes.

In the words of Kathy Harris, vice president and research area director at Gartner, "KM benefits are best achieved when [it] is linked to a specific business initiative that clearly provides specific benefits or value to the business."[8] Knowledge is the link, the terrain, that your company (and your competition!) relies on to build a successful business. It is the battlefield where the net economy is taking place. As contenders of this digital Darwinism, corporations must take advantage of the terrain, their capital knowledge, to advance.

To be successful in managing this knowledge, or terrain, you must control scattering terrain, generated by economic shifts, new trends, M&A activity, and so on, not by fighting it, but by embracing it! Sun Tzu's ideas about types of terrain, in The Art of War, define this principle very well. This is what he says about controlling terrain:

> Control easy terrain by not stopping
> Control disputed terrain by not attacking
> Control open terrain by staying with the enemy's force
> Control intersecting terrain by uniting with your allies
> Control dangerous terrain by plundering
> Control bad terrain by keeping on the move
> Control confined terrain by using surprise
> Control deadly terrain by fighting.[9]

Therefore, a creative approach to KM can result in improved efficiency, higher productivity, and increased revenues in practically any business function. Lessons learned can save you a lot of money and time! In addition, documenting best practices, success stories, and lessons learned is an important component of the KM strategy.

THE CHALLENGE OF LEADING A KNOWLEDGE MANAGEMENT PROGRAM

Historically, KM has been characterized as the process through which organizations generate value from their intellectual and knowledge-based assets. Typically, generating value from such assets involves sharing them among

---

8. K. Harris, "Transforming the Way Organizations Work" in *Strategic Directions: Knowledge Management and e-Learning*, *CIO Magazine* Supplement, New York, CMP, 2001.
9. S. Tzu, *The Art of War*, Oxford, Oxford University, 1984 (make sure to replace the word "terrain" with "knowledge" and you should have a powerful strategy for KM).

employees, departments, and even with other companies in an effort to devise best practices. But as discussed earlier, that definition says nothing about technology, as while KM is often facilitated by IT, technology by itself is not KM.

Therefore, if we agree that KM is a business practice, and not a technology-based concept, KM programs should not be lead by the chief information officer (CIO), but by the CKO. Of course, CIOs might be the most indicated professional if the KM implementation is contained within the IT department, with very specific deliverables and expectations. Nonetheless, although it may appear to be obvious that KM programs should be lead by CKOs, many companies have dedicated KM staff headed by CIOs, CTOs, and other high-profile executives. In chapter two, "The New Breed of CKOs", you will find a discussion on the rationale why CKOs are the most indicated professionals to head KM programs and what their attributes must be in order for them to become successful in such a role. The danger of using CIOs and CTOs to lead KM projects is that typically these professionals tend to approach KM programs from the technology point of view, relying on IT. But such reliance to promote corporate competitive advantage no longer provides guaranteed successful results, as the business world has become so volatile that the same information in a certain time and context can be totally irrelevant, if not incorrect, in another time and context. Thus, one of the main challenges in leading KM programs concerns the value of the information being gathered or shared, as not all information is valuable. It is your responsibility, as CKO, to determine what information qualifies as intellectual and knowledge-based assets.

Intellectual and knowledge-based assets tend to be either explicit or tacit. These categories can include assets such as patents, trademarks, business plans, marketing research, and customer lists. Explicit knowledge, the type that can be documented, archived, and codified, although laborious and heavily dependent on IT, is generally manageable. But a much harder concept to grasp is the tacit knowledge, the know-how contained in people's heads. The challenge inherent with tacit knowledge is figuring out how to recognize, generate, share, and manage it. While IT in the form of e-mail, groupware, instant messaging, and related technologies can help facilitate the dissemination of tacit knowledge, identifying tacit knowledge in the first place is very often a major challenge.

I believe the hardest work any CKO faces nowadays, characterized by such information overflow, is figuring out what to do in a world of infinite choices. In addition, as you lead a KM program, it is very important that you are able to bridge the gap between know-how and how-to.

Although we are still in the first chapter, and this book aims to precisely show ways of bridging the chasm between know-how and how-to, keep in mind from the start that the new breed of CKOs should not be so concerned about putting together a KM program that is able to capture all the knowledge there is in an organization, nor should they be consumed in implementing reliable and effective knowledge-sharing systems. These tasks, when the time comes, can be handled by KM managers and supported by CIOs, CTOs, and IT. Knowledge management and knowledge sharing can only be successful if CKOs are able to make the complex clear, which always enables people to work smarter. After all, it is much easier to figure out what is important and ignore what is not.

In addition, CKOs must be able to bring every department and every individual on board with the KM program. The CEO, as well as other high-level staff and decision-makers, must be sold out on the program. Make sure to have a list of very tangible and quantifiable benefits and results KM will bring. If possible, try to map out the increase in revenues the company can expect from improved KM and sharing across the organization. Then you should get ready to persuade the rest of the organization.

An alternative is to outsource the task. Hiring a consulting firm to spend time educating, setting expectations, and listening to concerns expressed by employees before the KM system goes live is advisable. By explaining how the new KM system would make their jobs less complex, simpler, you increase the chances of support from the company as a whole, which will be vital for the success of your project.

Once you have convinced employees that KM is good for business, and for them, it is time to retrain them. KM systems change the way people work. Unless you educate them about such impact and how to use and take advantage of the new system, your project may go awry and people will not use it. Best practices indicate that for every dollar spent on KM systems you will have to spend at least another dollar and a half on awareness and training programs.

Be prepared to find resistance, as people tend to be very uneasy about sharing their knowledge and best practices with others for fear of becoming dispensable, or a commodity inside the organization.

THE CHALLENGE OF MANAGING KNOWLEDGE

Knowledge management above all is a business strategy, and as such it has the potential to fundamentally change the behavior of any organization. KM is so fundamental that it requires calibrated strategies and tactics in every core business function. Thus, one of the main challenges in managing knowledge is to gain full support from the executive staff. If the CEO and the executive management team are not supportive of the KM strategy, rest assured there is no chance KM can play a major role in transforming your organization.

However, many corporations are not yet clear about the need to manage knowledge. In 2000, the Conference Board surveyed 158 companies on the subject and found that 80 percent had launched some kind of KM activity, but only 15 percent had specific, stated KM objectives and goals.

As organizations begin to rely more on KM programs, KM professionals must realize that mere data cannot hope to provide all levels of information today's organizations require. Any fundamental change within the organization requires the generation and effective deployment of a culture that shares and uses knowledge. Knowledge such as how to penetrate and dominate global and new markets, enhancement of employee recruitment and retention, better and more rapid development of products and services must be cataloged, aggregated, and managed.

In times of financial contention, as experienced in early 2000, all business initiatives that are not long established are in danger, in particular KM. Morgan Stanley Dean Witter conducted a survey with CIOs during spring of 2001 and found that 33 percent of them had been directed to slow down or reduce IT spending. Furthermore, when asked from where these cuts would come from, respondents pointed to document management and employee portal projects within the five most likely projects, among 33 others.

Knowledge management initiatives should not have been among these cuts, as any process that can extract, catalog, save, and manage knowledge, and make it available to other employees can ease the impact of downsizing and contraction on a company. After all, in any downsizing, the professionals that stay are very likely those that know where to find the information necessary to conduct the business, and have hands-on execution. Knowledge management can be vital, particularly at such hard times, in promoting effective collaborative environments, which allow knowledge sharing among employees throughout the organization, enabling them to tap into more skills and expertise than they would have been able to in isolated project environments.

Therefore, to be effective, especially in challenging times, the management of knowledge must encompass a structured system, with processes and technologies that inspire people to share what they know and use what they learn. This process should involve:

- aiding and abetting collaboration, knowledge sharing, and continual learning

- capturing the patterns recognized in human experience and insight (knowledge), and making them available to and reusable by others

- improving decision-making processes and quality

- making it easy to find and reuse this knowledge, either as explicit knowledge that has been recorded in physical form or timely access to a human expert's tacit, intuitive knowledge.

MEASURING RESULTS

At the core of the success of any KM initiative is a premise that I believe every professional serious about his career should have. Instead of buying into the concept that you, a professional, or a business, should know what you know and then profit from it, everyday you should strive in obsoleting what you know before others obsolete it and profit by creating the challenges and opportunities others have not even thought about.

Such a premise may go against leading business strategist authors and consultants out there, but I know for a fact that it works and you only need to ask any successful foreign immigrant in this country to confirm it. When I arrived in this country, in 1986, I strived to obsolete myself as a burger maker at Burger King. With the grace of the Almighty, working at the core of the city of Boston, on Summer Street, I tried hard to obsolete myself, and I figured out a way to make twelve burgers in less than one minute. By doing so, I obsoleted my peers' way of making burgers, and in the process I set a new standard for making burgers, got a medal and diploma from Burger King University, and advanced myself to kitchen manager, all in less than three months on the job, and barely speaking English.

Another example is Ram Charan,[10] who, from his childhood in India where he worked in his family's shoe shop, was able to break the rules by obsoleting himself and innovating, and continued to do so all through Harvard Business School, as he reversed the rules of business and instituted the universal laws of business success, all based on common sense.

To remain competitive in the twenty-first century, corporations must employ all the knowledge they can muster. By not sharing this knowledge with other corporations, such companies retain a unique advantage. However, unshared knowledge does not equal success if this knowledge is not shared within the organization and effectively quantified. Beware that intellectual property rights cannot do much to protect corporate knowledge. Only learning, which creates new knowledge, provides the primary competitive advantage, and radically impacts the organization.

As you think about how to measure the success of your KM implementation, consider the following indicators and then plan and execute a clear strategy to address the problems at their source:

- What knowledge aspects do you need to manage in your organization? Concentrate on real business needs, reduction of asset intensity and improvement of revenue collection.

- What are the high-transaction and short-cycle processes you must concentrate on? Some key processes you should concentrate on include accounts payable, customer service, and inside sales, where the impact of your efforts will quickly be exposed.

---

10. R. Charan, *Boards at Work*, New York, Jossey-Bass, 1998; *Every Business is a Growth Business*, New York, Times Books, 2000 (Ram Charan is an adviser on corporate governance, CEO succession, and strategy implementation; he was named as Best Teacher by Northwestern's Kellogg School and as a top-rated executive educator by *Business Week*).

- How important is it for you to include a review of your current business practices? Watch for operations in which an ability to capture and reuse knowledge will improve efficiency, lower costs, and boost profits.

- Are there any knowledge gaps, and, if so, do you know why? Make sure to identify any knowledge gaps and their origins, and try to determine if they are related to systems (IT), processes (management), or people (organization). Figure 1.3 depicts the relationships between information systems components. Knowledge gaps tend to be present in the unstructured nature of important decisions and the diversity of managerial roles, and are often the cause of complexity in decision making.

Figure 1.3 – Process flow of information system models

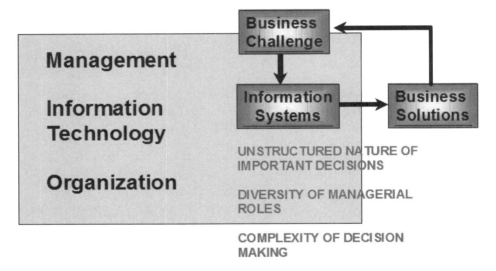

- Is your KM implementation working accordingly? In such a cognitive model, knowledge exists in context, making it difficult to measure success or failure, as results are not tangible, but indirect. Therefore, you will be able to identify the results by measuring the impact of new tools and practices on your business, benchmarking its performance both before and after it has been implemented.

- How can you consistently improve knowledge sharing? Whether intended or not, most organizations reward those who hoard knowledge. Every knowledge-based organization has resident experts who revel in the status their knowledge brings them. Unfortunately, knowledge hoarding leads to reinventing the wheel. In addition, it often causes ill-informed decisions to be made and the incurrence of unnecessary costs and revenue loss. Thus, make sure to implement incentives that encourage employees to share knowledge and discourage hoarding. Figure 1.4 provides an outline of a typical knowledge-based organization. The challenge is to transform tacit knowledge into explicit knowledge, to make the transition from know-how to how-to.

Figure 1.4 – Knowledge-base view of firm

KNOWLEDGE:

> ➤ Central productive/strategic asset
> ➤ Tacit (know-how) and explicit (codified/how-to)
> ➤ Includes information, social relations, skills, etc.
> ➤ Change based on new information
> ➤ Value created by integrating specialized

Knowledge management should be able to provide everyone within the organization with tools that enable them to obsolete themselves daily. Knowledge management tools should also empower workers to renew themselves daily. Measuring results is key in this process, as productive knowledge work should be very tangible, all about how each other's time and attention is used; as you try, the people in the organization try to get their work done. Keep in mind that when it comes to KM, your worst challenge is day-to-day confusion or lack of clear-cut result areas. Thus, to survive and succeed, KM initiatives should bring about very tangible results, which should at least include:

- reduction of product development times – through KM programs, Roche products are sent to FDA approval six months faster

- creation of more opportunities for innovation – KM enabled Dow Chemical to save $40 million a year through reuse of patents

- improvement of customer relationships – Ford Motor Co. saved more than $600 million over three years

- ability to make decisions faster and closer to the point of action – Royal/ Dutch Shell's deployment of a best-practice sharing methodology from Ford Motor Co. in two pilot communities of practice realized cost avoidance and saving of more than $5 million in four months.

While many authors, specialized publications, and corporate executives point out the failures of KM, the facts above show that a well-defined KM project can save organizations millions of dollars, dramatically impacting the bottom line. Thus, today's CKOs must be aware of the diversity of perspectives from which one can comprehend the concept of knowledge. In addition, be aware of the problems with the generally known understanding and notion of management (in KM) that have filled many mainstream business texts, with regards to the value of KM, and of CKOs as well for that matter.

The million-dollar question is: is sharing knowledge a cultural change issue? You bet it is! If ignored, the drain on intellectual capital and negative leveraging will continue inside corporations across the industries and throughout the world, as any employee that leaves a company takes what they know with them. In addition, orienting new employees will continue to take longer and longer, which makes quality of services and deliverables uncontrollable. Needless to say, the loss of opportunity to leverage learning and best practices across all parties involved – customers and professionals alike – and processes will be substantial.

ADDRESSING THE CHALLENGES

Coping with the challenges CKOs face in organizations of the twenty-first century is not an easy task. Today's CKOs' roles are still not well defined, many times confused with those of a CTO, with business and information systems skills, or, from a different angle, those of a CIO, with business and information technology expertise. Much of it is because the role of a CKO in today's organizations falls into a demilitarized zone between the organization and information systems, as depicted in Figure 1.5.

Knowledge management is without a doubt an oxymoron, which explains the difficulty reconciling the soft issues around it, such as innovation and creativity, with the hard issues, such as performance benchmarks measurement and assessment. There is a diametrically opposed assumption about the definition and nature between knowledge and management. Although CKOs tend to understand that management and control are not synonymous, this is not the case for CTOs or CIOs, who rely on controlling systems as a way of management.

The gap springs from the fact that the job descriptions of CIOs and CTOs, although a fairly new breed of professionals, have their roots in a contemporary management theory, typical between 1930 and 1962. During this period, driven by social psychologists, organizational behaviorists, and sociologists, the focus of management was to emphasize individual collective behavior. As discussed earlier in this chapter, the great majority of today's CKO's came from that era or were influenced by it. Many of them were former CIOs or CTOs, or adopted that management theory.

Figure 1.5 – KM is the only discipline with a real chance to manage the systems interdependencies between the organization and information systems

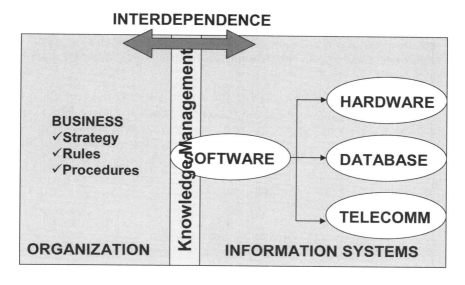

However, today's CKOs must fundament themselves in a post-modern theory of management, which began to gain ground after 1965. Actually, today's CKOs must transcend this post-modern management model, to one that takes into consideration the fast changing business landscape, the roaming nature of professionals. I would call this new management theory a post-Internet one.

As we watch this ever-increasing hype about IT, the gap between knowledge and technology tools on how to solve a business challenge and the actual implementation of these solutions widens. The problem is that new information technologies, such as data mining, intranets and extranets, video-conferencing, publish/subscribe information channels, and web casting, that technology vendors and consultants are offering today are just panaceas for the business challenges of this knowledge era.

As a result of this super information overflow, KM initiatives are often disappointing, as there is a lack of user uptake and a failure to integrate KM into everyday working practices. However, such an outcome can be avoided, and this is what this whole book is all about. For now, just keep in mind these best business practices:

- Make sure to fasten your KM efforts to high-priority business objectives. Just as you would not fish on a pond with a bazooka, do not invest in KM just for KM's sake. To be successful, knowledge and learning goals must be articulated at the same level as an organization's business objectives. This is the only way learning and knowledge sharing can truly become culturally embedded in the organization.

- If you want KM to succeed, you must integrate your people with the organization's business process and the technology you will be using – KM should always be a work-in-progress, never a finite project. Its neverending, integrated process should always be the implementation of a competitive strategy that appreciates that learning and sharing knowledge are equally important.

- When considering starting a KM implementation, the best tools I recommend are actually the cheapest in the whole process: pencil and paper. Make sure to have a knowledge strategy aligned with your organization's business strategy long before considering any technology tool. And make sure the strategy defines all key KM processes:
  a. creation of new knowledge
  b. identification of knowledge
  c. capturing of knowledge
  d. knowledge mapping
  e. knowledge sharing, application, and reuse
  f. protection and security of knowledge assets.

The next chapter, "The New Breed of CKOs", shows you what kind of attributes knowledge management professionals, in particular CKOs, must have in order to succeed at the challenges imposed by today's Internet/global economy business environment.

CHAPTER 2

The New Breed of Chief Knowledge Officers

The CKO – vision, strategy, ambassadorial skills, and a certain je ne sais quoi![1]

At the time of writing, the economy in the US is in a downturn. Some analysts would say the country is in a recession; others would disagree. Either way, the slowing economy, which transcends across the American borders and extends throughout the whole world, is dealing a new blow to CKO-led KM project teams.

These teams are aiming to help organizations harness the intellectual property and best business practices within the organization and among its staff to cut costs and change the way companies use information. From the way companies relate to customers to the way they handle suppliers across the globe, KM is becoming vital to every organization.

In the process, CKOs are being forced to reevaluate their roles and become change agents inside the organization. This new breed of CKOs is also rewriting corporate culture, one KM program at a time. Along with CIOs, these direct descendents of Y2K crisis management teams are more highly disciplined and interdisciplinary than past KM teams.

Today's CKOs, and KM professionals for that matter, are required to change their business structure and the way their KM implementations are managed to enable their projects to remain under budget, meet deadlines, and, most importantly, pay off. Focusing on knowledge sharing, Internet-based applications, and virtual access to data, CKOs are emerging as a driving force in the collaborative implementation of KM. However, given the high risk for KM implementation failures, the new breed of CKOs required to lead such teams must have a multitude of skills, including business, technology, team-building, project management, communication skills, and leadership in order to be successful.

In the words of Rebecca Barclay, this new breed of CKOs must possess "vision, strategy, ambassadorial skills, and a certain *je ne sais quoi*."[2] This is

---

1. R.O. Barclay, Managing Editor, *KM Briefs* and *KM Metazine*.
2. Ibid.

true especially when we consider the traditional methods of calculating return on investment (ROI), which are often ill-suited to measuring the strategic impact of KM applications and initiatives, in particular those applied to customer-facing systems such as customer relationship management (CRM). That is because KM can have a profound strategic impact on a company, far beyond improving processes and productivity. KM can fundamentally change the way a company views its business, its products, and even its business opportunities.

Therefore, the need for a new breed of CKOs that must redefine the roles of the CKO and become more business focused is evident. In addition to possessing business acumen, this new breed of CKOs must be able to approach KM return on investment with a new view towards establishing both an initial justification for projects, and a very clear baseline for ongoing management decisions and incentives. The main goal should be to increase knowledge sharing with very specific deliverables including, but not limited to:

- improving employee satisfaction, which should lead to an enhanced customer service

- increasing individual and program effectiveness, productivity, and responsiveness

- promoting innovation as the outcome of sharing of knowledge and best practices

- making knowledge and tools needed to do the work available for sharing via the internet

- increasing the opportunity for communication and collaboration throughout the organization.

FOCUS ON INNOVATION

Every employee, every professional within an organization is a personal store of knowledge with experiences, training, and informal networks of friends and business acquaintances whom others seek out when they want to solve a problem or to explore an opportunity. Notwithstanding the fact that many of us do not think in terms of managing knowledge, we all effectively do. We get things done and succeed by knowing an answer or knowing someone who does. But curiously enough, until a few years ago, nobody really paid attention to this process, and the management of knowledge was perceived as an exclusively personal endeavor. It was only recently that organizations began discovering that managing knowledge creates value, by increasing productivity and fostering innovation.

Knowledge Management as a Catalyst for Innovation

In today's fast-paced economy, knowledge is changing very fast, and in order to remain competitive, organizations and business executives must be able to continuously learn, which in the process promotes innovation, as Figure 2.1 suggests. Several surveys and statistics across the industries support this fact. Innovative companies are consistently the ones experiencing profit growth at four times the rate of non-innovative organizations. Names such as Ariba, CommerceOne, WebMethods, Syncamore, Siebel, VerticalNet, iCloud, and many others are examples of companies that, by investing in innovative technologies and products, experienced tremendous growth results over the past few years.

Figure 2.1 – KM organizations should continuously learn

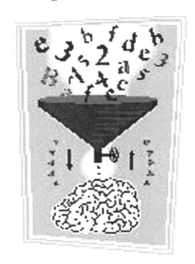

Structured or not, these companies relied on knowledge management as a catalyst for innovation and creativity, providing the means by which innovative ideas could be captured, shared, and leveraged, leading to more new ideas. Call it brainstorming, a brownbag session, or even a strategy meeting, only by readily and seamlessly sharing information rather than hoarding it can innovation be promoted. Only when people work as teams can this flow of information be nurtured to the fullest and be effective. The more diverse their experience, the better the creativity and innovation that ensues.

According to a study conducted by the Massachusetts Institute of Technology, 80 percent of ideas that have led to breakthrough products and services originate from routine discussions. Thus, one of the main goals of

CKOs today should be to invest in promoting the generation and capture of new ideas. Information technology professionals, such as CTOs and CIOS can help with the technology used to capture and share ideas, but CKOs should seriously concentrate on strategies to inspire the flow of new ideas.

This process might involve changes in ambience, and emotional conditions. At MCI Communications, for example, aside from the technology used to manage ideas and new knowledge, the company set up a room that resembled very much a family room, with meeting tables, a fireplace, and 31-inch television monitors. There are also numerous whiteboards and modular furniture that can be configured to any given need. The fact is, for knowledge creation to take place, there must be a shared space that serves as a foundation for it.

This space can be physical (e.g. MCI), virtual (e.g. e-mail, instant message or chat lines), mental (e.g. shared experiences and insights), or a combination of all three. Also, keep in mind that the flow of information or new ideas does not necessarily need to come from within the organization. Daimler-Chrysler, for example, uses KM practices to take advantage of the creativity of their customers and suppliers. Through the Supplier Cost-Reduction Effort (SCORE) program, the company asks suppliers to share their ideas, which in turn helps them get cheaper parts. The goal for each supplier is cost-cutting opportunities that equate to 5 percent of its annual billings to Chrysler. The program has been a great success, with ideas flooding in at a rate of more than 100 a week, with estimated savings of over $2.5 billion to Chrysler.

In promoting programs that foster creativity and innovation inside your organization, keep in mind that only by tolerating risk-taking and rewarding creativity will there be a free flow of information, which is a crucial promoter of innovation and creativity. According to a recent PricewaterhouseCoopers study on innovation and creativity, an essential element of innovation within organizations lies in the effective management process of ideas. Throughout this book you will find techniques to promote such management of ideas and foster innovation.

Ideas Are Only Ideas

Ideas in themselves are not the end, but the starting point. There are situations where ideas should be put into practice, but for the most part they should be considered as raw materials that need to be captured and shared so that new knowledge can be created. CKOs must beware of the fact that not all innovative ideas are right, or ideal, at first. But by capturing these ideas and sharing them with others, they can develop them and perhaps use them as a springboard for new ideas.

Knowledge is the integration of intuition, ideas, skills, experience, and lessons learned, as suggested in Figure 2.2, that has the potential to create value for businesses, their employees, products, and services, as well as customers, and, ultimately, shareholders, by informing decisions and improving

Figure 2.2 – Ideas are only ideas; not the end but the starting point

actions. Ideas, on the other hand, are a by-product of tacit knowledge, which has not much use until it can be turned into an explicit knowledge. It is possible, however, to bridge the gap between know-how and how-to, tacit to explicit, and there are many tools and techniques to facilitate this transfer. Just as with ideas, tacit knowledge has little value in itself. Such knowledge must be transferred, and it is important to create an environment that promotes such transfer.

Improving the Way Tacit Knowledge is Transferred

From biblical times we learn that the best way to transfer tacit knowledge is through face-to-face communication. Between 60 and 95 percent of transferred knowledge, both explicit and tacit, occurs via oral communication.[3] But today's business environment leaves us with relatively little time for face-to-face contact. Thus, another of the CKO's challenges is to facilitate the transfer of tacit knowledge among their employees and knowledge workers.

There are several alternatives worthy of imitation. British Petroleum, for example, developed a Virtual Teams Project that uses a mix of technologies including video conferencing and shared chalkboards to connect teams working at different sites around the globe. The Foxboro Company, in partnership with Boston University, allows employees and affiliates to participate in virtual

---

3. G. Van Krogh, K. Ichijo, and I. Nonaka, *Enabling Knowledge Creation: How to Unlock the Mystery of Tacit Knowledge and Release the Power Innovation*, Oxford University, 2000.

classes delivered via broadband video-conferencing. Another example is PricewaterhouseCoopers, which uses similar resources to harvest teams from the firm's Knowledge Centers on their thoughts, experiences, and war stories. Audio and video recorders are used to ensure all comments are captured.

For a KM program like this, mapping the information flow within the organization is the first step. It is very important that processes, technology, structure, and culture are adapted to reflect a knowledge-sharing environment. These elements are key to ensuring critical information links are maintained, updated, and managed effectively so that the right information not only gets to the right person, but also gets there quicker.

Another problem CKOs must be alert to when using knowledge arises when we attempt to manage it. Knowledge is not data that you can just store and retrieve in a database; it is not information either. More complex than that, knowledge is understanding, and one gains knowledge through experience, reasoning, intuition, and learning. Individuals can only expand their knowledge when others share their own knowledge. Consequently, when one's knowledge is combined with the knowledge of others, there is innovation and new knowledge is created.

Knowledge management, as discussed in chapter one, involves systematic approaches to find, understand, and use knowledge to achieve organizational objectives. Thus, managing knowledge creates value by reducing the time and expense of trial and error, or the reinvention of the wheel. Knowledge management creates value when shared knowledge is put to use and reused. An effective KM program can substantially affect the bottom line of a business by increasing the return on investment (ROI), and many times reducing the total cost of ownership (TCO) on business intelligence.

As we enter a new millennium with the US economy now nursing a hangover having belly-flopped after two years of dotcom-induced indulgence, companies are looking for alternatives to increase revenues and maximize profits. Companies have cut back on advertising, travel, and training budgets, among other things. In the process, mistakenly, many KM programs have been cut back, if not terminated. It is not surprising that in this climate companies are examining every project more closely, but to restrict KM implementations can be a big mistake.

Knowledge management can tremendously increase the ROI by effectively streamlining and sharing intellectual capital within the organization. Yet, many KM managers are scrambling to recalculate the ROI of projects that previously won approval based on the implementation's strategic merit. Chief executive officers and other executives want to see hard numbers to confirm a project's state value.

Such tangible results are very difficult to quantify in KM as not all knowledge takes the form of a best practice. In fact, the most valuable knowledge is the knowledge people have in their minds, known as tacit. This tacit knowledge is also the most difficult to access, because people are often unaware of the knowledge they have or of its value to others. Thus, one of the main goals of KM projects is to attempt to make tacit knowledge explicit, which allows it to be shared and used by others. More than ever before, today's CKOs must be of a different breed, armed with *visionary skills, strategic thinking, ambassadorial skills, and willingness to take high risks.*

FOSTERING ECONOMIC VALUE

Despite the economic downturns, the technology sector is alive, making sure Moore's Law continues to hold and networks continue to proliferate. Along with networks, the amount of data traversing them is also consistently increasing. According to NetSizer, the Internet is expected to grow by 330 per cent in 2002.[4]

This is an information-driven economy, where the ability to manipulate and exploit surging floods of data is fundamental to business success. Many executives will agree with that, but not many know what to do, or have the guts to do it. We need KM professionals with the vision to invest intelligently in the people and the technologies that turn information into profits. A new breed of CKOs must emerge from this slow-growth economic period stronger than their counterparts.

Contrary to best business practices in vogue today, companies must increase spending on KM and business intelligence projects during economic downturns. This is because in tough times companies need even more information than before; otherwise they could not make the swift and accurate decisions so necessary in moments of crisis. Knowledge management professionals become the intelligence "snipers," replacing the "free shooters" that rely on monolithic forms of information farming and retrieval, by identifying targets, focusing on them and acquiring as much intelligence as possible, so that with a single bullet – or course of action – they can hit their targets, once and for all.

Surprisingly, it is estimated that most organizations use only 20 percent of their organizational knowledge. As organizations realize the importance of transferring tacit knowledge, an increasing number of tools and techniques will be developed to facilitate this process, especially for the improvement of customer relationship management (CRM), which is one of the primary objectives of most KM programs. Thus, another attribute of today's effective CKOs is their ability to efficiently use KM to help organizations extend the services they provide to customers by creating value for them.

One of its main challenges is not even lack of information collected. Generally, a lot of information is collected from customers directly, through customer service centers, and indirectly, through marketing surveys. The challenge is that information is collected randomly, where the various groups

---

4. www.netsizer.com.

and departments within the organization have no idea why the information is being collected, or who else in the organization could benefit from it.

For instance, how can KM help business processes benefit from information gathered at the customer service center? Consider a sample of some of the processes in a software development industry:

- design – could develop colors and/or design features that customers want

- marketing and advertising – could identify and promote features customers seem to like the most, or those they are least aware of could be highlighted

- product development – could develop features sought by customers

- production – could concentrate on fixing problems identified by customers

- sales and customer service – sales and customer service staff could be trained to support customers on features they do not understand.

This new breed of CKOs must realize that knowledge is an emergent asset of interpersonal relationships that can only be managed by creating an environment in which open collaboration is the norm, not the exception. Companies that understand this premise will likely increase spending on KM programs to help them increase their peripheral vision and accuracy of strategic and tactical decision making.

Also, realize that KM is not easy to undertake – it can be very complex. Traditional information system professionals, such as CIOs and CTOs, were not inherently prepared to deal with KM. Just as psychiatrists were not prepared to analyze the mind as psychoanalysts were, therefore having the tendency to rely on pharmacology for achieving results, CIOs and CTOs were not inherently prepared to deal with the three fundamental components of KM: people, processes, and technology.

Traditional CIOs have had no direct connection to an organization's business units. However, CIOs are key partners for CKOs, as business demands have been forcing them to evolve into professionals with the ability to work with information, finance, human resources, information technology and systems, and other business units. Nonetheless, although CIOs might very well understand technology and business process, they do not normally understand people.

Furthermore, KM does not focus on people alone, but also on organizational culture, to motivate and foster the sharing and using of knowledge on processes or methods to find, create, capture, and share knowledge, as well as on technology to store and make knowledge accessible. This allows people to work together without necessarily being together, fostering tangible economic values.

That is why today's KM programs need a new breed of CKOs that not only understands technology and information systems, but also understands people.

People are the most important component, because managing knowledge depends upon people's willingness to share and reuse knowledge.

Knowledge Objects and Knowledge Assets

Many of the CKOs today are the CTOs or CIOs of yesterday, some even come from different fields. The great majority of these professionals, however, are aware of the concept that knowledge is an asset. But most "first generation" CKOs had difficulty defining knowledge assets, differentiating them from knowledge objects, and generating an economic value from them. They suddenly found themselves managing KM programs to promote knowledge sharing among organizations and its partners. But most people tend to fear that if they share their knowledge they will lose their importance, their marketability. It is here that most traditional CKOs get stuck. Although they can try to overcome such deep-seated concerns via an incentive for workers to share their knowledge, if they do not have ambassadorial skills, chances are the project will fail. Incentives alone will not be enough.

Instilling Trust in Users

Another area CKOs must pay attention to is trust. If people believe they will benefit from sharing their knowledge, directly or indirectly, as suggested by Figure 2.3, they are more likely to share – and trust plays an important role here. People need to trust that sharing their knowledge will actually empower their work ability, but also trust the knowledge of other people. Whether they will use it or not will depend on their knowledge of and trust in the source of the knowledge. For instance, people are more likely to believe in a new policy for interest rates knowing that it came from Allan Greenspan than from the young economist just hired.

According to Rob Cross and Sam Israelit,[5] people typically will contact someone they know before searching the corporate database or data warehouse. That is why emphasizing the technology for KM solutions can be a mistake: unless people are willing to use it, the most sophisticated solution will not make any difference. Technology is an important enabler to the success of KM, but people make or break it.

CHIEF KNOWLEDGE OFFICERS AS CHANGING AGENTS

Knowledge management is for the most part a product of the incredible changes of the 1990s. Economic globalization expanded, bringing about new

---

5. *Strategic Learning in a Knowledge Economy*, Boston, Butterworth-Heinemann, 2000, p. 74.

Figure 2.3 – People need to see the benefits of sharing their knowledge

opportunities and an aggressive increase in competition. As a result, companies reacted to it by downsizing, merging, acquiring, reengineering, and outsourcing their operations. Benefiting of the latest advances in computer information systems and network technology, businesses were able to streamline their workforces, and boost up productivity and their profits.

Higher profits, low inflation, cheap capital, and new technologies all helped fuel the biggest and hottest bull market the US economy had ever seen. Employment levels were at record highs and skilled workers in high demand. Businesses came to understand that by managing their knowledge they could continue to increase profits without expanding the workforce.

The problem was most of the CTOs and CIOs that preceded this economic boom had never been on the cutting edge of the Internet revolution. Many had never had the chance to lead an ambitious SWAT team of global dimension. Thus, many began failing on their IT and KM implementations. In addition, e-business changed the IT landscape, and the notion of local area networks (LAN), metropolitan area networks (MAN), and wide area networks (WAN) became blurry and better defined not by geographic measures, but by the amount of data they handled and the level of performance they provided. Personal area networks (PAN) and virtual access networks (VAN) surfaced, extending the ability users now have to access and exchange information.

This much-needed new breed of CKOs represents the evolution of the traditional CIO role in many ways. CIOs typically understand how to manage information with IT. CKOs focus not so much on technology as they do on the strategic aspects of knowledge that can be realized through IT, or in identifying and understanding what we know, how and why we know it, and when we know we have acquired it.

The following are new challenges e-business introduced to the IT community, and consequently the way CKOs and knowledge managers implemented their KM programs:

• Borders are disappearing
  – Externalization
  – Regulatory/jurisdictional issues

• Velocity of e-business is increasing
  – Business cycles accelerating
  – Creating new opportunities

• Expectations are rising
  – Increasing customer expectations
  – Integrated/single view
  – Multiple points of customer interaction
  – Privacy, performance, and reliability

It was in the face of those challenges that knowledge management began to attract the attention of the Federal Government, which was also experiencing profound changes during the 1990s. Payrolls were cut by 600,000 positions; the use of information technology was expanded to improve performance, and management reforms were enacted to improve performance and to increase accountability to the American people.

Knowledge management presents to the government today a major challenge. At the beginning of the twenty-first century, the Federal Government faces serious human capital issues as it strives to improve service and be more accountable. It must compete for workers, as its workforce grows older. According to the US Office of Personnel Management, the average age of a federal worker is 46 years.[6] Worse, according to the General Accounting Officer (GAO), approximately 71 percent of federal senior executives will be eligible to retire by 2005.[7] This means that unless the knowledge of those leaving is retained, service to citizens will likely suffer.

What all this data means is that executives will no longer be able to rely on information technologies for taking care of the company's competitive advantage. In addition, organizations will no longer be able to rely on people the way they have been trained in the existing educational, organizational, and business models. In today's global economy, the right answer in one time and context can be wrong in another time and context.

By the same token, best practices may become worst practices unless they are constantly analyzed and revised for their sensibility, which can impair business performance and competence. Thus, the logic of yesterday's success does not necessarily dictate the success of today and certainly will not dictate the logic of success for a brand new tomorrow.

No one can reliably predict the next five years of e-commerce, and trying to collect, filter, and share the tremendous flood of information being generated by knowledge workers, global markets, and the Internet economy as a whole will be a huge challenge for CKOs. Research analysts seem to have lost their beacon already and are having problems predicting even the next twelve months! Forecasts are all over the place: $1.7 trillion in e-commerce in 2005, or $100 billion? Let's face it, no one in 1995 could have ever predicted the business concepts of companies such as Napster, Audiogalaxy, AutoByTel, WebVan, and Peapod, their impact in the society, and the way they purchased and delivered goods. What was AOL in 1995, and who would have predicted it would become the media master company it became?

In order to succeed, CKOs must adjust their vision, humbly grab hold of their *je ne sais quoi*, and react to it by evaluating and reviewing KM practices and strategies, as a catalyst tool to refocus and reanalyze business data. Believe me, this is just the beginning. In the next five years, information will continue to flow at the speed of light, making it harder and harder for CEOs and senior staff to hold their lines in this supercharged economy. Along with tremendous change in the public and private sectors we see an explosive growth of the Internet and the emergence of e-business and e-government. There is so much information available and pushed at us that at times it is very easy to drown in

6. Full-Time Permanents "Profile of Federal Civilian Non-Postal Employees" *US Office of Personnel Management*, 30 September 2000.
7. "Major Management Challenges and Program Risks: A Government Wide Perspective," *General Accounting Officer Report GAO-01-24*, 1 January 2001

an information overflow. Yet, the work is changing at such a fast pace that our need for constant and up-to-date knowledge that enables us to respond to the rapid changes in the workplace continues to widen every day, every minute. Thus, one of the main challenges CKOs face in the twenty-first century is to seek better ways to help professionals to learn and work smarter. Knowledge management is one of the most reliable means to address human capital issues and to take business, and e-business for that matter, to the next level.

Much more is still to come, faster and faster: e-commerce is only 1 to 2 percent of GNP, and yet it has changed the rules of business everywhere. This data alone shows us, CKOs, that we do not need business predictions, but instead skilled analysis of e-commerce experience, and synthesis of the management lessons and proven strategies.

Knowledge management offers a tremendous edge for business advantage, but only if taken seriously and implemented correctly. Enough of fancy data mining, complex business integration, strategy meetings line up, and focusing on technology and systems to promote KM! I always believed the mantra that success is vision in action. CKOs must have a vision for what they need to achieve, without biased influence of technology or past generation information systems models. We must reinvent ourselves and the KM systems we rely on every day, all the time.

A KPMG report released in October 2000,[8] showed that while companies practising KM were better off than those that did not, actual benefits did not live up to the expectations of 137 companies. Unless CKOs and KM professionals decide to bridge the gap between know-how and how-to, for the most part KM will continue to be dismissed as another management fad that does not deliver on its promises. KM does bring a much-needed value to any organization, yet measuring its value is a challenge.

Forecasting an Information Society: Watching for Standards

If you are reading this book, chances are you too are aware of the need for, are concerned about, and are trying to build the infrastructure and apparatus for this knowledge revolution we are now part of. Toffler's third wave[9] has arrived, and in a few years it will look much like the wave in the movie *Deep Impact*.

One area we must focus on is standards, which are very important in attempting to manage KM infoislands, as it is the fast-growing pace of technology and the lack of standards that bring about many implementation problems today. Information systems and technology projects are failing for many reasons, but mainly due to the lack of integration among technologies and among people using these technologies. As changing agents, CKOs are the best breed of professionals capable of giving the industry some idea as to

---

8. *Knowledge Management Magazine*, October 2000, p. 38.
9. A. Toffler, *The Third Wave*, New York, Bantam Books, 1991.

where we, as an information society, are heading, and where we might fit in both as technologists and human beings.

When we look at examples of successful deployment of information systems that integrate users and technology seamlessly, we find that such projects were carried out by a multitude of professionals, interacting with their talents as a symphony would, orchestrating every bit of technology and human interaction. Take the example of the world's largest cement company, Mexico's Cemex, which realized a total of $5.6 billion in revenues in 2000. The company already uses a combination of the Internet, wireless, and GPS systems to get cement to customers faster, decrease order errors, and use fewer trucks to do more work. Such synchronized use of technology, information systems processes, and people was responsible for a worldwide return on assets of 17 percent to Cemex in 2000.

Sorting the Fish, CKOs, and CIOs

There has never been a need to manage intellectual capital, the sum of human, structural, and customer capital, as there is today. Such demand has created opportunities for a new breed of KM executives skilled in leveraging valuable organizational knowledge.

Call them CIOs, CKOs, CLOs (chief learning officers), or anything else you choose, there has been a growing need for a new breed of KM professionals. These new professionals look a lot different from their counterparts, displaying real differences in what they do and why they do it, as well as a subtle hierarchy of value in their work. Nevertheless, by experience I can tell you that, of all executives, CKOs are the ones that can have the greatest impact on the productivity and motivation of people in an organization.

Although CKO job descriptions often lack well-defined benchmarks, they are the ones better positioned to set strategic policy for an organization's acquisition and distribution of knowledge and learning, as increasing people's capacity to take action enables them to respond more effectively and efficiently to their tasks and customers.

The twenty-first century CKO must incorporate many of the skills and abilities of a CIO and couple them with a distinct sense of vision. The difference between a CKO and a CIO is the same as the what and the how of information and knowledge. The CIO is concerned to know-how to gather information, ensure that it is disseminated, and establish benchmarks. The CKO is in charge of how-to transfer knowledge, and is interested in what is important in gathering information, what kind of knowledge is needed to build the company, and ensure a competitive advantage.

There are considerable differences in the roles of CIOs and CKOs, and the more clarified they are, the better these professionals can work as a team, as illustrated in Figure 2.4. CIOs are emphatically technology driven. Thus, it would require a major shift in mindset and priorities for a CIO to design the

Figure 2.4 – Sorting the fish, CKOs, and CIOs

kind of strategic knowledge and learning environment needed in a competitive organization. That is why most CIOs are not prepared to handle design solutions that produce the action essential for success, as they do not have the background and training to do so.

CKOs as Visionaries and Knowledge Bridges

To remain competitive, a business must focus not only on generating profit, but also on educating employees and growing their capabilities to take care of customers' needs. Driving a business from the perspective of knowledge and learning rather than strictly from a financial bottom line will give companies a competitive advantage now and throughout the twenty-first century. CKOs will be key professionals in this process.

Companies are still underestimating the value of CKOs for increasing the competitive advantage of the organization and turning the company into a learning company. Most companies are just starting to realize the value of CKOs. Most of them within the operating groups, which are beginning to rely on them on marketing calls, pre and post-sales meetings, and high-level interaction with customers and potential customers. CKOs add great value in these areas, as typically they are able to bridge the gap between information, knowledge, and a firm's customer base. And, because of their value, they are increasingly being asked to interface with boards of directors as well.

As the speed of business increases, so does the rate of professional turnover inside companies, particularly in the professional service sector. Whenever knowledge walks out the door, or organizations need to start projects from ground zero, the value of CKOs and KM programs becomes very evident. Lost knowledge takes a tactical toll as companies spend money recreating it and bringing people up to speed. By managing organizational knowledge, a CKO changes organizational culture, people become empowered to make decisions, and cycle times are reduced.

If you want to find a suitable CKO, or if you are wondering if you have the talent it takes, be aware that the best CKOs are driven by the challenge of changing how organizations think about knowledge, and about themselves. CKOs are real visionaries, and there is no salary, title, or any other corporate perk that motivates them more than the challenge of finding solutions, and remaking the thought process that drives them.

That is another reason for the lack of success in corporations that develop CKO positions from a CIO perspective, as their background is typically derived from the financial side of the business. In such situations, very little is accomplished, and changed within the company.

What does it take to be a CKO?

The best CKOs are not necessarily experts in human performance and measurement, but they are people-oriented and have a good sense of what is happening in the marketplace in terms of rapidly changing tools and technology. CKOs need basic business acumen, a sense of vision, and an entrepreneurial spirit.

Chapter nine, "So You Want to Become a CKO", focuses solely on the qualities and attributes CKOs should have or develop. Some of these specific qualities that are discussed in more depth in chapter nine include:

- being realistic about the value of knowledge and its application
- being respected within their peer groups
- bringing to the group something that is not always definable
- being capable of conceptualizing valuable and doable situations
- having a reservoir of information that could be useful as a resource
- have a full understanding of the interaction of technology with people
- being perceived as creating value within their organization
- being a thinker who can think through issues.

Companies going through total quality management (TQM) and reengineering projects are lacking an important element of success if CKOs are not part of the strategy. For these projects to be successful, someone in the organization must be responsible for transferring the organization's knowledge so that people can learn and grow from it, becoming more productive in the process. CKOs approach the future by managing knowledge in ways that effectively tie together people, technology, and process, and that provide a competitive edge for business.

A CKO's Job Description

When defining a job description for CKOs, there are several overall responsibilities that must be incorporated. CKOs must be able to oversee knowledge management programs and their integration. Many times, such a role reports to the CIO, but it is becoming strategically valuable to have CKOs reporting to CEOs. More specifically, CKOs should be responsible for managing and overseeing knowledge management and technology resources in a manner consistent with the company's mission and program objectives.

A CKOs primary goal should be to ensure the management of knowledge and information assets enterprise-wide in order to improve decision-making processes. By knowledge management I mean all actions should ensure collection, storage, distribution, integration, and application of knowledge within an organization.

If this is the company's first foray in becoming a knowledge-based organization, the CKO must effectively manage its intellectual capital (knowledge), and information and records assets. In this process, it is very important that CKOs ensure timely and accurate information to the company's staff and the public, which invariably will require designing and implementing knowledge management architecture to support multiple roles and missions.

Another of a CKO's roles is to ensure effective knowledge collection and transfer of corporate knowledge and information assets to achieve gains in human performance and competitiveness. This is not an easy task and CKOs must promote effective strategies to ensure dissemination of information and knowledge sharing. Alternative vehicles for disseminating knowledge include electronic filing and electronic issuance, making information readily available at the source, avoiding hardcopy reports and forms, and the establishment of standards for industry. This typically includes the responsibility for overseeing the overall planning, direction, and timely execution of knowledge management programs.

Furthermore, the CKO's role should also include the acquisition of appropriate information and technology resources to enhance the ability of the workforce to gather knowledge-based information to perform missions more efficiently and effectively. Such a role may be better executed in partnership with CTOs, CIOs, and other IT groups.

The CKO's function should be viewed as crucial to the success of business and marketing strategies. Information collection, analysis, monitoring, and knowledge management are essential to the integration of business strategies, marketing planning, and future directions of the company. Thus, the CKO should feel comfortable developing opportunities to share knowledge with other groups within the organization, as well as partners, members of the supply chain, and the distribution channels of the company. Examples such as Daimler-Chrysler, British Petroleum, and Cemex, mentioned earlier in this chapter, are good paradigms for a baseline. Other important qualities CKOs should posses include the ability to manage knowledge, corporate strategies, technology for leveraging intellectual capital, and know-how to achieve gains in human performance and competitiveness. Also, CKOs should have the ability to formulate and implement knowledge management policy initiatives, and to direct an organization in the accomplishment of short-term and long-term objectives.

OVERCOMING ORGANIZATIONAL BEHAVIORAL CHANGES

One of the main challenges KM faces today is with regard to organizational and behavioral changes, as suggested in Figure 2.5. These are the most difficult tasks when implementing anything, in particular KM. Implementing technology, buying software is the least complex variable of the equation. Thus, today's CKOs must be aware of these challenges.

Figure 2.5 – Overcoming organizational behavioral changes

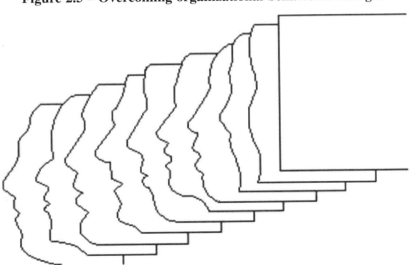

In the past, behavioral changes were not taken so much into consideration. Decisions were made from the top down and all the organizations underneath just adapted, losing their professional individuality and becoming squared and aligned with their organizations, as Figure 2.5 suggests. As Hately and Schmidt put it, peacocks are transformed into penguins.[10] Today, organizations are much more decentralized, and the global economy and shorter business cycles allow for options people did not have before. No longer are professionals looking at positions within their companies as permanent. Typically, professionals move around within two to three years. Whatever can be done to minimize turnovers becomes very important, as well as capturing the knowledge of those leaving before they do so.

The Power of Mentoring

A good strategy to promote desired organization behavior is mentoring. Not only is it a good channel for knowledge transfer, but it is also an effective way of developing loyalty and accountability among professionals, in particular among those being mentored and the ones that mentor them, as Figure 2.6 suggests. I often use mentoring strategies to get those being mentored, let's call them disciples, in line and unified with a particular goal at hand, and to give them vision. The dynamics invariably work because they feel ownership for the project, an integral part of it. Instead of considering themselves a hired hand (compensated by salaries), mentoring, or discipleship, gives them the vision they need to achieve success.

Over the years, I have seen mentoring evolve from an experimental technique, to a management strategy, to a full-blown cult. Seasoned professionals offer guidance to aspiring entrepreneurs; wise alumni take uncertain young graduates under their wings; those who have kicked drugs help addicts who want to quit; cancer survivors give hope to the newly stricken.

Mentorship can be an effective strategy that today's CKOs can use. However, if you are going to play the role, you need to understand what your disciples require, and how to practice the fine art of encouragement. If you can always be an encouragement to your organization, and teach them to do the same, I guarantee you will have a tight team, brought together not for salary, titles, or corporate perks, but for a vision, a dream, and the feeling of purpose and self-worth. A small team like this can win big battles!

Now, be careful not to turn mentoring into a commodity, and do not let anyone else do it either. The danger in mentoring as a KM strategy is that those being mentored tend to believe they should have a mentor who saves them, guides them, and watches out for them for the rest of their careers. In other words, make sure they do not check off. As mentors, CKOs may play

---

10. B.J. Hately and W. Schmidt, *Peacock in the Land of Penguins*, San Francisco, Berrett-Koehler, 2001.

Figure 2.6 – The power of mentoring

many roles, from being an active guide and occasional counselor, to a constructive critic. The more hats you can wear, and wear well, the better, though it is rare to find one person who can do all of the above.

Mentoring 101

When mentoring groups or even individuals, there are many techniques to aid you in the process. You should first ask the person or group you are going to mentor to take a good look at themselves. There needs to be an assessment of what they are after, followed by a realistic evaluation of what kind of mentor they need – you may not be it! In bridging the knowledge gap in an organization, for example, one mentor is not enough, and you should tap into as many resources as you can, which might include the IT organization, the CIO, the CTO and their group, and very likely the CEO.

Today's CKO should evangelize the practice of building mentoring programs into their organization's human resource departments, their own KM group, or even make mentoring a formal responsibility of managers, as suggested in Figure 2.7. Make sure that mentors and mentees do have a set time together when participants discuss expectations, and map out how and when to fulfill them. Keep in mind that contact between mentor and mentee is

Figure 2.7 – Mentoring 101

sometimes as informal as a weekly telephone check-in or occasional excursions out of the workplace, where both parties feel free to let down their hair. At the other extreme are programs with written contracts, structured activities such as "shadowing" (where the mentee follows the mentor around for a prescribed period), and formal evaluation of the mentoring relationship by a third party.

Some people are hesitant to approach a mentor for fear of being a drain on their time and energy. However, the high degree of satisfaction in helping someone develop and the pleasure of being exposed to new ideas are always rewarding and responsible for keeping such programs flowing. For their part, mentees learn new skills, new competencies, and the complex politics of an organization. And the company gains by boosting motivation and advancement, which leads to greater employee retention. Thus, mentoring is a win-win situation.

HELPING IMPROVE KNOWLEDGE MANAGEMENT RESULTS

Corporations have been struggling to find beneficial ways to effectively capture and commoditize knowledge. Partly, it has been because such efforts cost a lot, and the payback has not always been obvious or quickly forthcoming; but it has also been because too many knowledge management (KM) initiatives have stood alone, facing off against thoroughly resistant corporate cultures.

This is yet another challenge for this new breed of CKOs: to introduce momentum on effective knowledge management strategies and solutions. KM results will effectively impact organizations only if it tangibly delivers:

- Knowledge and skill sets, which must be explicitly included in an extended enterprise's supply chain and distribution channel, made available at the right time and in appropriate quantities for workers and their tasks, so that usefulness and value can be maximized.

- Usable and reusable knowledge, which must be available for the right people at the right time, otherwise the enterprise will lose marketplace momentum.

- A new kind of knowledge, as nearly everyone in the enterprise must acquire a new kind of knowledge, such as information about customers and the value chain that feeds them.

As KM results become more tangible, quantifiable, and measurable, I strongly believe companies will be pulled towards knowledge management. About two years ago, I was invited to join a technology startup. Today as I look back, I have a lot of respect for the company's management and its investors for their forethought in bringing a CKO as employee number eighteen in the company.

To date, in less than thirteen months, this company, Virtual Access Networks, entered the market, developed a terrific product, made its debut at Comdex Fall 2000 in Las Vegas, and was awarded the best enterprise product at the show. Even more amazing, during these thirteen months that preceded the launch of the product and award, the company changed its original name, changed the market focus and product, as well as its core technologies and key personnel. Needless to say, its original business plan and company mission was also changed and realigned. Yet, the company was able to get its act together, grow to 75 people, and deliver a state-of-the-art product.

Teamwork was top priority. Mentorship happened weekly during what we called *Jedi* meetings. Our goal was to have a product and a company ready to be out of stealth mode and launched in thirteen months, from scratch. As Jedis (inspired by Star Wars!), everyone was a team player. The organization in these meetings was flat, so there was no difference between upper and middle managers, and everyone felt responsible for their successes and failures.

Best Practices Recommendations

In becoming one of the new breed of CKOs for the twenty-first century, there are several areas you will need to focus on. Chapter nine deals with personal and professional attributes you must cultivate and acquire. The following are other business, logistic, and strategic issues you should be aware of.

Business Needs Must be Isolated

You must have a clear business goal in mind before attempting to implement any knowledge management program. Whatever you do with KM, you must affect the bottom line. Thus, you must identify the ability to capture and reuse knowledge in such a way that it makes it profitable. Invariably you will need to do an evaluation based on how your company operates its current business and also on your existing technology infrastructure.

You must nail down what your business drivers or goals are, otherwise, there is little chance you are going to get there with whatever decision you end up making. For instance, consulting firms, with 45,000 consultants traveling around the globe doing similar tasks and similar projects, but in completely different regional or technical silos, might want to make better use of that information across boundaries. In this context, to attempt to bridge the gap between know-how and how-to, you might ask yourself what kind of information you must provide to your clients. Do you provide information to managers of project teams? In what sense do you want to bring these people together in real-time? In an offline mode? Only after you have worked out these issues do you begin to go out and seek tools.

Business Impact Must be Measured

The main goal of KM is to bridge the gap between know-how and how-to, or what Pfeffer & Sutton calls "the knowing-doing gap."[11] Ultimately, it is to make business more valuable, and you need to find ways to ensure this happens! For instance, can your KM implementation reduce your product development cycle by 30 percent? Can it reduce the amount of time it takes to get technical approvals (i.e. government, standard committees, etc.) of your product? If you want upper management support for KM and you really want to impact the bottom line of the business, you must have very measurable results that show the value of your KM initiative.

Johnson & Johnson, the pharmaceutical giant, decided to analyze its FDA product application process in an effort to learn why the company was not getting new products to market faster than the competition. What it found out was that the company would submit an application to the FDA, which would review it, and bounce it back with questions. The submission team would then research the questions and resubmit the application.

How can KM help here? Stop for a moment and think about it. What if all questions the committee raised on similar J&J products that had already won approval were captured, so they could have access to the answers given before? J&J started keeping a repository of previous applications, which now enables

---

11. J. Pfeffer, and R. Sutton, *The Knowing-Doing Gap*, Boston, Harvard Business School Press, 1999.

them, before any submission, to dig out the files, look at previous rejection questions, and make sure the new submissions have a provision for them. Such KM strategy dramatically reduced the amount of time J&J applications take to get through the FDA process. As for the bottom line, by releasing a product a month earlier, the company was able to realize $30 million on one product alone. This is a very tangible result – no executive team would argue.

Being part of this next breed of CKOs can be a double-edged sword. Chances are, in most companies, you will be very successful and popular only by hoarding what you know. After all, you become the resident expert on a subject and enjoy the status it brings. However, beware that hoarding knowledge leads to duplication of work and turf wars. It becomes your responsibility (remember the mentorship?) to teach new, collaborative behaviors. This is not a popular task, and it can meet with a lot of resistance. But you will soon find out that is where rewards come in. Thus, always keep in mind incentives for sharing. If you do not have them, knowledge management technologies will never create them.

Take the example of the PR agency Hill & Knowlton, which recently implemented a company-wide intranet where its professionals could access staff bios, work on group profiling, client information, industry news, and even e-mail exchanges relevant to issues they were working on. The big challenge was getting people to share their knowledge on the intranet. That is when incentives came in. Ted Graham, their Worldwide Director of Knowledge Management Systems, created a best-seller list of the most frequently accessed contributions. Being on the list gave employees recognition, and, in the process, knowledge sharing became part of Hill & Knowlton employee performance reviews.

But at Hill & Knowlton, the incentive does not stop there. Every time an employee opens a document or contributes information, there is a chance of collecting credits, which can be redeemed for books, CDs, and even Caribbean vacations. This stimulates knowledge seeking and gets employees to explore the intranet beyond their own client accounts. It is all part of changing a company's culture. And if you do not change the culture, you will never manage the knowledge, and KM will be truly a bust.

Strategic Orientation

Strategic orientation is very important if you want KM to succeed. It all starts with communication, which is the organization's lifeblood, in enabling and energizing employees to carry out its strategic intent. To effectively help any organization with KM you will need the capability to rapidly identify, send, receive, and understand strategic information that is credible, sensible, and relevant.

However, in today's dynamic organizations, you will need to do more than successfully execute a strategy, or bring about operational or cultural change. You will need a broad awareness, understanding, and acceptance of strategic intent by all people in the organization, as a foundation to their commitment. Therefore, decisions on strategy and policy must take into account the imperative and the challenge of communication, and the tools and talent of the communication function must be oriented to the organization's strategic priorities.

Prime for Integrity

All communications should be credible. To be credible, they need to have integrity, and that only a constant and complete consistency between communication and conduct can deliver. Thus, make sure to build credibility by integrating an organization's formal, semi-formal, and informal voices. The rhetoric by which an organization manages its affairs and presents itself to others is manifestly important, but its impact as communication is never equal to or greater than that of the organization's decisions and actions. So, always do what you say you will do, for through such decisions and actions, an organization continually tests and defines itself.

Only through mutual dignity and respect will communication thrive. Organizations that are blessed with such relationships will, over time, develop greater internal commitment and thus outperform and surpass organizations that are not, as an organization's success ultimately depends on the fully aligned, discretionary, principled, and inspired effort of its people. Communication based on mutual dignity and respect is the foundation of such effort, and therefore to the success of the organization.

Get Strategic Information Flowing

The flow of strategic information enriches and empowers an organization, as it must nurture and sustain the systematic flow of credible, sensible, timely, and relevant information so as to bring all their resources to bear on the execution of their strategic intent. That requires the full commitment of leadership, the application of appropriate technology, and the broad participation and support of employees.

Leadership's support of upward flow of information is critical. Leadership must be receptive to upward thrusts, especially of negative information, as it is a reflection of the trust it holds in people. The flow of strategic information through an organization is a barometer of its ability to compete, regardless of the kind of information flowing.

All Messages Should be Clear and Powerful

Unless your communication is clear, you might as well not communicate, otherwise you may end up confusing people, leading them to complacency, or generating false expectations, even chaos, which could be very detrimental to

KM implementations and communications as a whole. Thus, when communicating, make sure to do so with simplicity and complexity, with an economy of words, but a wealth of meaning. The language should be the one of ordinary people, used in everyday conversation, free of jargon and technicalities.

Communicating through parables is often very powerful, as it usually addresses the concerns and needs of listeners, and naturally takes the form of a conversation more than a lecture or announcement. In addition, make sure to communicate clearly and powerfully through messages that are coherent, consistent, and complete. Make sure to acknowledge their own limits, explain their rationale, and speak to whatever questions they have raised.

External Perspective

Strategy is the means by which an organization copes with its external environment, its customers, competitors, and suppliers, as well as the communities and governments where it operates. Thus, whatever strategy you may devise should take into consideration internal communication systems, which require an external perspective and orientation.

Therefore, when implementing a strategy, you must understand not only the strategy itself, but also the reasons for it and the measures of its success. Only a communication system anchored in the company's external environment can provide that information in a compelling way and place it in a tenable context. The external orientation may include the arenas of public policy and philanthropy; in its totality, information with an external bearing must be balanced, strategic, and truthful.

The Power of Listening

Listening involves hearing, sensing, interpreting, evaluating, and responding. Good listening is an essential part of being a good leader, and the cornerstone of this new breed of CKOs. You cannot be a good CKO unless you are a good listener. You as a CKO must be very aware of the feedback you are receiving from the people around you. If you are not a good listener, your future as a CKO will be short.

Good listening includes a package of skills, which require a knowledge of technique and practice very similar to good writing or good speaking. In fact, poor listening skills are more common than poor speaking skills. I am sure that on many occasions you have seen two or more people talking to each other at the same time.

In improving your listening skills, be aware that there is shallow listening and deep listening. Shallow or superficial listening is all too common in business settings and many other settings. Most of us have learned how to give the appearance of listening to our supervisors, the public speaker, and the chair of the meeting while not really listening. Even less obvious is when the message

Figure 2.8 – The power of listening

received is different from the one sent. We did not really understand what the message was. We listened, but we did not get the intended message. Such failed communications are the consequences of poor speaking, poor listening, and/or poor understanding.

Listening skills can always be improved, as suggested by Figure 2.8. Perfection in listening, just as in other communications skills, does not exist. There are several good books and many articles on good listening. There are three basic listening modes: combative, attentive, and reflective. Most of us would describe our listening as attentive, that we are interested in the other person's point of view. I have had many departmental managers come up to me in a combative mode when discussing potential impacts of KM in their departments or groups. They clearly did not want to hear my explanations, but wanted to promote theirs. All too seldom do we take the reflective mode in which we take an active roll in the communications process. We are not just passive vessels into which information is poured, but we think critically about the topics, the messages we receive.

The following attributes of good listening are suggestive of the skills needed for a new breed of CKOs. There is some overlap between the various attributes, but each suggests something different.

- Attention: attention may be defined as the visual portion of concentration on the speaker. Through eye contact and other body language, we communicate to the speaker that we are paying close attention to their messages. All the time we are reading the verbal and nonverbal cues from the speaker, the speaker is reading ours. What messages are we sending out? If we lean forward a little and focus our eyes on the person, the message is we are paying close attention.

- Concentration: good listening is normally hard work. At every moment we are receiving literally millions of sensory messages. Nerve endings on our bottom are telling us the chair is hard; others are saying our clothes are binding; nerve ending in our nose are picking up the smells of cooking French fries; our ears are hearing the buzzing of the computer fan, street sounds, music in the background, and dozens of other sounds; our emotions are reminding us of that fight we had with our mate last night; and thousands more signals are knocking at the doors of our senses. Focus your attention on the words, ideas, and feelings related to the subject. Concentrate on the main ideas or points. Do not let examples or fringe comments distract you.

- Do not interject: there is a great temptation at many times for the listener to jump in and say in essence: "Isn't this really what you meant to say?" This carries the message: "I can say it better than you can," which stifles any further messages from the speaker. Often, this process may degenerate into a game of one-upmanship in which each person tries to out-do the other and very little communication occurs.

- Empathy, not sympathy: empathy is the action of understanding, being aware of, being sensitive to, and vicariously experiencing the feelings, thoughts, and experiences of another. Sympathy is having common feelings. In other words, as a good listener you need to be able to understand the other person, you do not have to become like them. Try to put yourself in the speaker's position so that you can see what they are trying to get at.

- Eye contact: good eye contact is essential for several reasons. By maintaining eye contact, or by focusing on the face, some of the competing visual inputs are eliminated. You are not as likely to be distracted from the person talking to you. Another reason is that most of us have learned to read lips, often unconsciously, and the lip reading helps us to understand verbal messages. Also, many of the messages are in nonverbal form, and by watching the eyes and face of a person we pick up clues. A squinting of the eyes may indicate close attention. A slight nod indicates understanding or agreement. Most English language messages can have several meanings depending upon voice inflection, voice modulation, facial expression, etc.

- Leave the channel open: a good listener always leaves open the possibility of additional messages. A brief question or a nod will often encourage additional communications

- Objective: we should be open to the message the other person is sending. It is very difficult to be completely open because each of us is strongly biased by the weight of our past experiences. We give meaning to the messages based upon what we have been taught the words and symbols mean by our parents, our peers, and our teachers. Talk to someone from a different culture and watch how they give meaning to words. Another listening challenge is to listen openly and objectively to a person with very different political or religious beliefs. Can you do that? You have a tremendous talent if you can, but relatively few people can listen to, understand, and appreciate messages that are very different from their own. If you cannot, it is time to start, because as a leader you will need to understand a wide range of opinions often on controversial subjects.

- Receptive body language: certain body postures and movements are culturally interpreted with specific meanings. The crossing of arms and legs is perceived to mean a closing of the mind and attention. The nodding of the head vertically is interpreted as agreement or assent. Now, be careful, as nonverbal clues such as these vary from culture to culture just as the spoken language does. If seated, the leaning forward with the upper body communicates attention. Standing or seated, the maintenance of an appropriate distance is important. Too close and we appear to be pushy or aggressive and too far and we are seen as cold.

- Restating the message: restating the message as part of the feedback can enhance the effectiveness of good communications. A comment such as: "I want to make sure that I have fully understood your message..." and then paraphrase the message in your own words. If the communication is not clear, such a feedback will allow for immediate clarification. It is important that you state the message as clearly and objectively as possible.

- Strategic pauses: pauses can be used very effectively in listening. For example, a pause at certain points in the feedback can be used to signal that you are carefully considering the message, that you are "thinking" about what was just said.

- Understanding of communication symbols: a good command of the spoken language is essential in good listening. Meaning must be inputed to the words. For all common words in the English language there are numerous meanings. The three-letter word, "run" has more than one hundred different uses. You as the listener must concentrate on the context of the usage in order to correctly understand the message. The spoken portion of the language is only a fraction of the message. Voice inflection, body language, and other symbols send messages also. Thus, a considerable knowledge of nonverbal language is important in good listening.

- You cannot listen while you are talking: this is very obvious, but very frequently overlooked or ignored. An important question is why are you talking: to gain attention to yourself?

In summary, good listening is more than polite silence and attention when others speak, and it is altogether different from manipulative tactics masquerading as skill. It is rather a high virtue, a value, a reflection of the bedrock belief that learning what other people have on their minds is a wise investment of one's time. It requires intellectual humility and the willingness to learn from people at all stations of life. Through visible presence, one not only learns by listening, but also establishes a welcoming rapport that builds relationships of respect and dignity, conducive to frequent, candid, and rapid communication.

Communication Structure and Process

The structure and process of internal communication should reflect the fact that communication is a means, not an end, to success. The fundamental purpose of workplace communication is to enhance the business performance of the organization. Communication succeeds only to the extent that it enables and energizes employees to align their work with the organization's strategic intent.

A preoccupation with artistry or diction may divert attention away from the business issues at hand. The responsibility and tools for strategic communication should be distributed throughout the organization, so that each employee is an integral part of the process. The communication function should build alliances with the management teams of operating units. Given a choice between centralizing and decentralizing the communication function, the latter affords more regular contact with line managers, which in turn builds mutual understanding between line and staff functions.

Evaluating Your Systems

Measurement is a vital aspect of a high-performance system of strategic workplace communication, but it must be undertaken with care and skill. It is a myth that everything of importance in organizations is measured: integrity, perseverance, teamwork, agility, and other essential attributes of a vital work culture all but defy measurement.

The importance or value of strategic communication is not an appropriate subject for measurement; by definition, it is always and precisely the value of the strategy, the change, or the goal that it supports. Nor are the tactical and mundane aspects of communication a worthwhile focus of measurement. Rather, the measurement of communication must concentrate on its effectiveness with respect to strategic direction, so as to adapt it to changing circumstances, to engage management in the essential tasks of leadership communication, to establish a basis for accountability, and to chart progress.

The best measurement processes address not only formal communication but also semi-formal and informal communication. They focus on outcomes, not outputs or inputs. They measure against a progression of awareness, understanding, acceptance, and commitment, and they reflect the fundamental purpose of communication as a bridge between strategy and its successful execution.

Constant Improvement

More than just another management fad, continuous improvement is a neverending quest for a better way. It is both a personal and professional habit, and an individual and organizational commitment to change, progress, and growth. Without it we become stagnant, and we cease to grow. The philosophy, processes, and tools of the quality literature offer abundant means for improving strategic workplace communication, but they require a genuine receptivity to improvement.

The time and resources devoted to a thoughtful, well-managed program of continuous improvement will return their investment many times over. Research into best practices should be undertaken from time to time with the understanding that each organization is unique and must ultimately find its own path to its own future. Above all, our processes must be driven by the legitimate needs of the customer, whose satisfaction is our reason for being.

In conclusion, becoming a new breed of CKO will take time and effort, and it is an everlasting goal, as we must constantly reinvent ourselves. As changing agents we must be willing to change ourselves as necessary, adapting to the new nuances of the business environment, cultural changes, technology, and the essence of information. We must be able to identify knowledge as the raw material for innovation. We must be able to capture it and establish strategies, systems, and processes to transfer this knowledge before we can turn it into action. Chapter three, "Identifying, Capturing, and Transferring Learning into Action," deals explicitly with that.

CHAPTER 3

Identifying, Capturing, and Transferring Learning into Action

As chameleons, in e-business, companies must adapt and learn to strive in their environment very quickly.

What, you might ask, is the big deal about KM? I would not argue that the movement is getting a bit long in the tooth. The number of knowledge management conferences is down, even though I have been presenting papers on knowledge technologies almost three times a year. I am still waiting for *People* magazine to stop being stubborn and name a KM expert as one of its 25 Most Intriguing People of the year. Even my wife, not known for her high level of interest in business trends, has suggested that I would be wise to move on to other subjects.

It is true that knowledge management is no longer treated as the next big thing. But I hope you don't mind if I disagree. After all, you got to chapter three, and hopefully chapters one and two already convinced you that e-learning alone will not do the trick. Some people thought I was nuts to try to market a new book on knowledge management. I actually had to go abroad, and here you are reading the book. I am glad your forethought brought you here. What KM professionals need to understand is that no movement can remain a media darling forever, but life goes on – hence the need for KM.

Knowledge management may be quiet, but it is not dead. As chapters one and two pointed out, KM is just beginning to penetrate the fabric of many businesses, and statistics alone prove it. The problem is that the early, flashy-but-insubstantial applications, such as best practices and lessons learned, have given way to broadly focused initiatives that are transforming the way organizations work, in particular at the government circles and fortune 100 corporations. Any change takes time, and for the most part, it is never amenable to shallow, sensationalistic journalistic treatment. In fact, only the most profound, gifted analysts and writers can comprehend and express it. But the new breed of CKOs discussed in chapter two also can, and they are the ones holding the KM flag today!

The value of organizational learning should be recognized, as knowledge management can easily be seen as a key corporate asset that must be leveraged and exploited for competitive purpose. In this emerging, globalized, and rapidly changing market, creative ideas and innovative thinking are essential. Many organizations, at least in theory, have been trying to become learning organizations. However, the effort has not been as practical as it should have been, and best practices are not easily found. This chapter attempts to provide you with a roadmap to turn your company into a learning one, with practical examples that you can apply next day. This chapter also helps you, as CKO, to arm yourself with the attributes required to successfully meet and fulfill this challenge. After reading this chapter, I strongly suggest you add another layer of knowledge about learning organizations by reading Bob Garratt's book entitled *The Learning Organization: Developing Democracy at Work*,[1] which will arm you with all the "how-tos" (now that you have the "know-how") of turning an enterprise into a learning one and surviving to talk about it.

BUILDING A LEARNING ORGANIZATION

How do you know if you have a learning organization? What are the clues you should look for? In building and maintaining a learning organization you must look for traits that define the organization, nurture some of them, and eliminate others, so you can bridge the knowledge gap in the organization and allow successful knowledge transfer into action, from know-how to how-to. But what are the traits that should be nurtured, and what about those that should be eliminated? Such a task is near to impossible, unless you have a clear idea of what a learning organization means to your organization. You must have a very well-defined learning agenda.

Having a Defined Learning Agenda

Any learning organization should have a defined learning agenda. Does yours have one? Does your organization have a clear picture of the knowledge requirements it needs to strive and be successful?

- Does your organization know what it needs to know, regardless of the subject, be it competition, market capitalization, technology trends, customer profiling and services, production processes, knowledge collaboration and information gathering, etc.?

- Is your organization pursuing these knowledge goals with multiple approaches? Once your organization is able to identify its needs for knowledge, it must pursue it with several approaches, which should not be reduced to training and education alone. It should include experimental approaches, research studies via analyst firms or in-house resources, simulations, customer surveys, benchmarking when appropriate, etc.

---

1. London, HarperCollinsBusiness, 2000.

Being Open to Dissonant Information

Learning organizations should be open to dissonant information. To bridge the knowledge gap that stops organizations acting on what they know, or need to know, learning organizations must become simultaneously effective and efficient in their actions. However, this requires a higher level of continuous learning between the leaders who drive the organization, including CKOs, CEOs, the staff delivering the organization's products or service, and the customers of this organization. You must look at your organization as a complex adaptive human system, trying to become a generative system, more than just mindless machines or structured systems. A learning organization is one that breathes and lives out of paradox, of dissonant information, so learn not to shoot the messengers who bring bad news or raise paradoxical ideas! Your goal is to help the organization flourish in such an environment, as a child does in its early stages of life. Be prepared to believe in, strive for, and guide your organization when facing paradoxes such as these:

- *You may be losing when wining*. When your product is a success, or your processes are working, the tendency is to let them be, not to fix what is not broken. However, if you look back to all the successful stories, some businesses disappeared, or were replaced because they failed to respond to a new challenge. The American automobile industry went through it with that of Japan. Apple Computers committed the same mistake with their Apple and Macintosh lines of computers. What happened to excellent software applications such as WordPerfect, dBase II, III, and IV, and Lotus SmartSuite? What happened to Netscape, or better yet Mosaic? Organizations, and their products, will die if they cannot keep up with the rate of change in their industry. Trying to play the new game by the old rules is a recipe for disaster. I have seen several organizations not being able to make sense of pseudo-chaotic information and feedback coming in from a tumultuous global market, and trying to react with obsolete tactics, only to waste capital, people, time, and eventually the eagerness to fight on. That is when you must realize that in today's business, learning organizations must compete and cooperate with their competitors. The "either/or" solutions will no longer hold, except for when we either compete successfully or die. I recommend a great book, entitled *Co-opetition*, by Brandenberger and Nalebuff,[2] for an excellent discussion on co-opetition.

- *Choices as chance*. If your company is not adopting generative learning, which is discussed in more detail later on in this chapter, then you are relying on adaptive learning systems. Such systems always show patterns that can never be predicted in advance, regardless of the familiarity you have with the inputs. This is because you are relying on a reactive system. Thus, the

---

2. New York, Doubleday, 1997.

outcomes are the result of mere random choices made by members of the staff or organization. Choice here is synonymous with chance, and chance is the one driving the outcome! How about that for a managerial style? I hope you will find it as disturbing as I did when I finally accepted this paradox!

- *Being reasonable can be limiting.* In today's business front, being rational is not necessarily being business savvy. Actually, most entrepreneurs I know or read about use a great amount of intuition in their everyday business decisions. Leaders with tremendous business acumen often feel the advantages that their structural positioning in the business network offers them, and learn how to exploit the stream of opportunities that their position allows to flow in their direction. A key factor here is that professionals must learn to identify these opportunities, use intuition in association with the structures surrounding the business and themselves. For too many CEOs and other senior staff, relying on intuition and feelings, and trying to fasten these insights to business structures is intimidating, to say the least. Most executives are convergent-thinkers, data-rational, reductionist managers to accept such paradoxical management challenge. That is why every business plan has a provision for an exit strategy, which I call the moment when the ostrich puts its head in the sand, and does not even know from where the kick came. Instead, I advocate a more Hellenic posture to business, armed with a breastplate but totally unprotected back, just in case I feel tempted to turn my back to business challenges.

- *Organizations are not simply structures.* Organizations are much more than simple structures, as they suffer the influence of human process energies, both negative and positive. People are driving the organization; if people are energized, the organization will be energized.

Changing the behavior of such organizations is a very difficult task and many give up in the process. Actually, that is one of the main reasons the big six consulting firms keep on returning to the same organizations, telling them the same things over and over through reports and best practices, which basically challenge their status quo and call for changes in those areas. A true learning organization will not avoid discussing sensitive matters, and will make necessary changes when issues such as dissention of ranks, unhappy customers, preemptive moves by the competition, and disruptive and new technologies arise. Typically, information gathered in these areas is filtered and there is a resistance to deal with it, especially at the senior level, which tends to avoid being confronted with ideas that may affect its status quo or require it to change or leave its comfort zone.

Avoiding Repeated Mistakes: Surviving Business Darwinism

Certainly it would be very hard to find a business professional that would also be an adept to Darwin's theory of the origin of species. But much can be learned from Darwin's theory and strategically applied to learning organizations today. Just as in the theory of evolution, in business, only the fittest survive.

As organizations virtualize themselves to reach across borders, on a global market perspective, the Web has become a business world, in which companies (or species) must constantly adapt to their changing business environment or face extinction. The Web has become a world in which business must continue to grow in a profitable direction, developing new skills and traits, or perish.

For learning organizations, doing business on the web requires companies (or digital life-forms) to instinctively know with whom to cooperate and with whom to compete. All this takes place in an environment where the business conditions (or life) can suddenly and drastically change, for better or for worse. More than ever, mistakes can be deadly. As Darwin commented, surviving in this complex web of relations is a tough task. So it is for a company to survive and conduct business on the web.

Strong market forces in the increasingly competitive web economy are forcing companies to develop new strategies for economic survival. As the web traverses its especially frenetic evolution, it also gives birth to an entirely new breed of start-up companies and enterprises that could not have existed in a traditional economy. Further, these new companies are forcing older corporate models to evolve in new ways, reengineering themselves and producing new business models necessary for their own survival.

E-business is becoming a fierce battlefield, and rivals are clawing their market share by developing new business models and inventing breakthrough business tactics especially suited to their swiftly shifting surroundings. Just like chameleons, in e-business, companies must adapt and learn to strive in their environment very quickly. Thus, learning organizations must learn from their mistakes and past experiences, share the knowledge internally, and ensure that errors are not repeated elsewhere.

It is possible to turn a failure into a success, a weakness into a strength. A productive failure is the one that capitalizes on the lessons learned to lead to insights, understanding, and innovation. The key to preventing repeated mistakes is to accept when one is committed and to learn from it. Learning organizations will draw their strength from their weaknesses, as it is not the success they remember the most, but the mistakes they learned from, which allowed them to achieve success.

The resistance to dealing with the knowledge gap and remaining an adaptive learning organization will be responsible for several business failures. The proof of it is the dotcom phenomenon. This scenario is only going to get worse and companies embracing e-business must realize it. At first the web was an unformed mass of perky expressions and corporate brochures, as early users somewhat feared the technology. But then, fear gave way to experimentation and successful experimentation gave way to confidence. Now, confidence is inspiring users to trust the Web, and do business in it, faithfully. This faith is leading to mass acceptance, generating the biggest marketplace ever known.

This new trend is pushing the world's biggest companies to gaze towards a future in which much, if not most, of their purchasing, invoicing, document exchange, and logistics will be transferred from stand-alone computer networks connected by people, paper, and phone calls to a seamless web that spans the globe and connects more than a billion computing devices.

Therefore, I strongly believe online business-to-business (B2B) will explode at an unprecedented rate, becoming the centerpiece of a mind-boggling multi-trillion-dollar web economy. Worldwide shipment of e-procurement solutions (ePS) software, for example, will grow to almost ten times its present size, from $243 million in 1999 to almost $2.2 billion by the end of 2004, with a cumulative average growth rate (CAGR) of nearly 55 percent.[3]

Organizations that resist such a trend or attempt to adapt to it later on in the game will do so at their peril. By eliminating the tedious paper-based procurement process, buying organizations are saving money previously allocated to the many resources needed to complete these processes. E-procurement solutions reduce costs not only by simplifying order processing, but also by drastically cutting or eliminating maverick spending, and providing access to marketplaces and trading communities that feature supplier products at competitive prices.

Danger Lurks Beneath

Beware that even though the web economy is thriving, adaptive learning organizations engaged in e-business must watch the danger lurking beneath. On the web, everything is possible, so do not be surprised when some of today's most dominant e-business is rendered helpless in the face of rapid, unforeseen change. As dotcoms fight over their share of the Internet market, competition gets more and more barbarous, giving room to rapid consolidations and hostile takeovers. Take the examples of AOL buying Netscape and sprawling companies such as GE/NBC, Disney, and CMGI investing in Snap, Infoseek, and Alta Vista. Another example is Qwest Communications, which, after absorbing US West and recently reaching new heights in valuation and market share, was faced with a takeover by Deutsche Telekom AG, and is now struggling to survive.

I believe these early skirmishes are only the tip of the iceberg of what is to come. There are lots of companies on the Web, but not many businesses. Unless organizations become learning organizations, carefully planning their e-business strategies and monitoring them constantly, they will end up being

---

3. According to the ARC's E-Procurement Solutions (ePS) Worldwide Outlook (1999).

victims of the e-business natural Darwinism. I strongly believe most organizations will resist this concept, as they resist the value of CKOs and knowledge management. Thus, there will be super-consolidations in the e-business horizon, with very few winners. After all, who needs thousands of bookstores, or drugstores on the Web?

Learning organizations should not only be concerned about low prices, but with branding, efficient inventory and distribution systems that enable them to better manage their total cost of ownership (TCO) and substantially increase their return on investment (ROI).

In helping learning organizations to better position, manage, and compete in e-business, integration applications are a must. For instance, take the e-procurement trend. There is no doubt that for B2B applications e-procurement is the killer application for the commercial use of the Internet. Given the number of benefits these applications offer businesses, organizations may not survive if they do not invest in them. E-procurement solutions simplify e-business transactions between companies, making this kind of application crucial to the success of B2B e-business.

As for business-to-consumer (B2C) e-commerce, we have another major challenge for learning organizations. Web sites require excellent sales support to attract the customers and to be successful. Ordinary database and full text queries as well as simple profiles do not provide the expected level of service. Knowledge technologies can fuel intelligent searching, personalized feedback dialogs, and sophisticated knowledge navigation, which provide customers with the kind of help and comfort they look for. The results are higher traffic, turnovers, and increased customer satisfaction.

Therefore e-commerce web sites have to provide easy to use interfaces to attract customers. The number of clicks to place the product in the shopping cart has to be as little as possible, and additional information about related products has to tempt customers to buy more. Both requirements can be partly fulfilled by traditional database applications and search techniques, but knowledge technologies can fuel e-commerce applications. Case studies show that e-commerce sites powered by knowledge technologies can drastically increase the traffic, customer satisfaction, and shop turnover.

Preserving Critical Knowledge

Is your organization prepared to lose a talented professional? What would your organization do if critical skills were to disappear with the departure of a key professional? In other words, is your company prepared to lose critical tacit knowledge?

Explicit knowledge can always be captured by knowledge technology solutions, KM implementations, and knowledge databases, but tacit, unarticulated, and unshared knowledge locked in the head of a single professional can be devastating to a business. Learning organizations can avoid such problems by institutionalizing essential knowledge. That requires senior management to codify it in policies and procedures, retain it in reports, e-mails, and disperse it through brownbags, and other forms of organizational gatherings. To avoid losing valuable knowledge, learning companies turn knowledge into a common property, instead of a providence of individuals or small groups.

Acting on What the Organization Knows

The definition of success is vision in action. Thus, for learning organizations to be successful they must turn their vision into action. Action without vision is like sailing uncharted waters without a compass. By the same token, vision without action is just an idea, a dream. Learning organizations should not just be a repository of knowledge. For that, let the universities and business schools do their job.

Learning organizations make sure to act on what they know by taking advantage of new learnings and by adapting their behaviors accordingly. If organizations do not use the information they have worked so hard to acquire, what good is it? What good is it if an organization realizes an untapped market but fails to take advantage of it?

Therefore, it is very important that a learning organization is aware of what knowledge is, how to identify and capture it, as well as transfer it across the organization, effectively turning it into action. Otherwise, the organization will never grow or succeed.

Figure 3.1 depicts what I call "the knowledge gap tornado", or "knowledge tornado" for short, which establishes the necessary steps learning organizations must go through in order to increase their understanding of business and themselves as organization, their weaknesses and strengths. Failure to overcome a stage, or step, brings the organization back to the previous stage it was in, and eventually back to the eye of the knowledge tornado, characterized by business and strategic chaos. Conversely, as the learning organization learns and advances, it goes through several growing stages and eventually closes the knowledge circle, only to restart it again, with a new learning agenda, but this time with much more business wisdom than before, allowing it to tap into new silos of knowledge that prepare and sustain the organization to the next level of its growth, in an outer circle around the tornado. This process is progressive and endless...

Figure 3.1 – The knowledge tornado

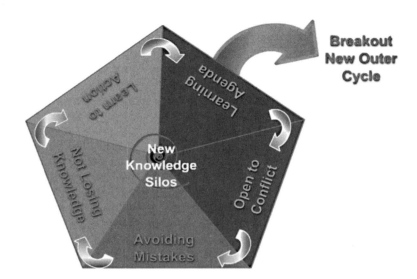

Learning Agenda

As seen in Figure 3.1, the first step in becoming a learning organization is to have a learning agenda. Otherwise, what you have is an adaptive organization, bowing with the wind of business, rolling with the punches of the competition. If your organization has a learning agenda, as discussed earlier in this chapter, then it will be ready to move on to the next stage: being open to conflicts.

Open to Conflicts

At this stage, the learning organization will face a lot of conflicts, as it will be faced with the different and individual agendas of several senior staff members and the organization as a whole. To avoid these conflicts can be fatal for the organization. It can bring the organization back to its first stage, where a learning agenda needs to be redefined or truly established. However, if the organization is open for conflicts, it can then deal with the acceptable differences, goals, and mission statements, and get a unified set of goals for the entire company. Once senior staff and the rest of the organization are unified in an understanding of what they are, where they are, and where they want to go, as well as what it will take to get them there, then the organization is ready to move to the next stage: avoiding mistakes.

Avoiding Mistakes

This is an equally important stage. At this point, learning organizations should have a well-defined learning agenda, which means they should know where they need to go and have a plan to get there. The organization should also have purged the demons afflicting its goals, and resolved any conflicts it had with members of the team and strategies for achieving such goals.

Now, it is time to avoid the mistakes of the past, and learn from current mistakes so as to avoid them in the future. Failure in doing so will inevitably bring the organization back to the previous stage, being open to conflicts. Invariably, this is the cause of recurring mistakes, either because they were not dealt with in the past, or because there was conflict avoidance when dealing with them that prevented the organization from learning. Beware that once an organization steps back into a previous stage, the lack of momentum and increased inertia tends to bring the organization all the way back to the eye of the knowledge gap tornado! Therefore, at this stage, the organization must be very keen to avoid repeated mistakes, and concentrate on getting ready, shielded from potential loss of knowledge, in case of losing a key professional or group.

Preventing the Loss of Knowledge

At this stage, the learning organization has shifted from an adaptive learning to a generative learning mode. It is now thinking proactively, instead of reactively. The goal here is to proactively shield itself from loss of knowledge, which would bring the organization back to a repeated mistake, a previous stage. At this point an organization should not only be ready to prevent the loss of knowledge but also to turn learning into action.

Turning Learning into Action

This is the final stage of the knowledge tornado before the organization restarts the process, now at the outer ring of the tornado. If successful, the learning organization will be able not only to turn learning into action, which will tangibly and measurably impact the organization and the business bottom line, but also to receive a sort of reward, by acquiring a new silos of knowledge developed during its growth and transformation into a learning organization.

This silos of knowledge is very important in fueling the next cycle of growth of the company, making it knowledgeably stronger, more competitive, and united on all fronts. At this stage the company breaks free from the stronger centrifugal forces of the tornado, as it distances itself from the eye. In addition, the company has business and learning momentum in its favor.

As with all the other stages, if the learning organization is not able to turn learning into action, chances are it is lacking knowledge somewhere, or it has lost knowledge in the process, either through the departure of a key professional, where knowledge had not been institutionalized or by a failure in the institutionalization of knowledge within the organization.

IDENTIFYING KNOWLEDGE

Let's take as an example the World Bank Group, which has been dispensing loans to developing countries for more than 50 years. In 1996, the then president of the bank, James Wolfensohn, announced that the bank would strive to become a knowledge bank. Since then, a variety of initiatives have appeared that have penetrated almost every corner of the organization, including the IT-like usual knowledge repositories and benchmarking efforts with other companies and consulting.

What this bank has that few other organizations can boast is integration with the organization's basic mission and processes, they have been able to identify, capture, and transfer learning into action. And the evidence of it was expressed in the bank's new, modified mission statement: "To help people help themselves and their environment by providing resources, sharing knowledge, building capacity and forging partnerships in the public and private sectors."[4] The bank was so serious about KM that its strategic plan included a section on knowledge management that defined the concept and how it would be applied within the organization. Last I checked, by end of fiscal 2000, the bank had spent almost $45 million, which translates to about 5 percent of operational expenditures, on KM.

One of the tactics used by the bank to promote the identification, capturing, and transferring of learning into action included an expectation that every staff member would devote two weeks of their time a year to knowledge creation, sharing, and learning. With that, the bank created communities of practice, which they called thematic groups, with a goal to create and share knowledge in key content domains. The bank, at the time of these writings, has now more than 100 such groups and almost half of the bank's employees are active members of at least one group. And the bank efforts are producing results.

For instance, one of the groups is using KM-based approaches to circulate ideas around the bank in handling problems related to slums in developing nations. In this case, they developed a CD-based electronic tool kit for those who need help in designing and implementing large-scale urban infrastructure projects. They also developed an approach to tacit knowledge download, or capturing of knowledge, to help new staff members learn from experienced ones.

Staples, in Framingham, Mass, has invested in KM in the hopes of

---

4. www.worldbank.org.

encouraging their technical support employees spread in nine different locations to share their technical know-how and best practices. Marcia Mitchell, Staples' senior IS project manager, says that the project has resulted in shorter training sessions for Staples' employees, and faster response times from support personnel to customers.

Other companies, however, such as Cooper Tire & Rubber Co., have not figured out how to make KM work for them. The fact that a KM system is successful in one organization does not guarantee its success in another. For instance, some companies cannot afford KM systems that require additional effort on the users' part. Actually, most of them need KM systems that will sift through the types of documentation and tools that are already in use and then present the information gleaned in an organized and accessible manner.

Gathering Knowledge

One of the major mistakes KM professionals make is relying on technology to deliver KM successfully. Technology, in particular KM software, should never dictate a KM strategy, nor hold back its implementation. As discussed in earlier chapters, technology is only part of the KM riddle. Just as using Microsoft Word does not make its user a better writer, buying IT implementations does not necessarily guarantee an organization's ability to identify, capture, and transfer knowledge, in particular, into action.

Harder than dealing with the technology is getting people to accept and effectively utilize KM, as most often it will require changing their work habits and attitudes, which typically is not an easy task, as employees are never excited about sharing all they struggled to learn. That is why one of the biggest challenges to successfully implementing KM is to appropriately address the cultural change issues. The hype behind knowledge management may wax and wane, but the business transformations under way in many private and public companies are true indications of the long-term value of knowledge and its management.

CAPTURING LEARNING

Learning will always occur inside organizations, but sometimes it occurs in an unstructured fashion, more as a result of benign neglect than deliberate and active support. This is so because CKOs and KM professionals want to invest in learning, but do not want to invest in nonproductive time. Unfortunately, organizational learning is still being viewed more as an academic, training, even philosophical, and, therefore, inefficient practice, than as a strategy that can directly affect businesses' bottom line.

At the heart of organizational learning you should be able to find a series of processes that can be designed to capture, deploy, and lead. In other words, organizational learning encompasses a process of detection and correction of errors, as organizations learn through individuals, acting as agents, but prone to mistakes. The massive transformation in our business world is impacting every organization in the globe, requiring them to renew and grow, and learning strategies might be the only alternative to sustain such a level of transformation (innovation) and growth.

Learning in Action

While learning need not be conscious or intentional, it does not necessarily increase the learner's effectiveness. In addition, if the process of learning cannot be measured, for example by promoting observable changes in behavior throughout the organization, such effort would have failed. This is actually the typical situation organizations find themselves in: they are able to acquire the necessary know-how (the acquisition of knowledge) but have trouble mastering "how-to" deploy, distribute, and implement the measures that will promote changed behavior within the organization.

Therefore, KM professionals, in particular CKOs, should keep in mind that for learning organizations to succeed, four constructs must be integrally linked in the learning process of an organization: the acquisition of knowledge, the distribution of information, information interpretation, and organizational memory. In theory, the defining property of organization learning is the combination of same stimulus and different responses. However, it is quite rare to find such a scenario in organizations, which makes me believe that either organizations do not learn in a consistent way, or that organizations learn but in nontraditional ways. Some may argue that organizations are not built to learn, but if you agree that organizations are not the buildings and the processes they sustain, but the people, the professionals, that are part of it, then organizational learning involves a different kind of learning than has been described in most literature available.

Disruptive Technologies: Technological Proficiency or Learning Failure?

Consider the example of the impact of disruptive technologies in business. People familiar with the history of how disruptive technologies encourage start-up companies to replace large, established firms and technologies are not surprised by the Linux phenomenon. After all, a disruptive technology can crack any established technology by replacing the existing network of products with a new and larger network. The large one consumes the smaller one operating in the same space because the value of the network increases exponentially as its size increases. This is especially true if current customers are the primary source of information.

But a disruptive technology does not initially operate in the same space as the established technology. It starts by finding a new market that has needs the old technology cannot satisfy. The Internet, for example, did not initially compete with such traditional media as magazines, television, and movies. Suddenly, you have the phenomena of America Online taking over Time Warner. As the industry shifts to an electronic medium, virtually all of the leading traditional printed news companies that do not shift along to an e-format will eventually be displaced, much like a digital Darwinism phenomenon. Thus, as part of the learning-into-action process, suppliers must understand the disruptive technology trend and strategically position themselves to take advantage of the emerging technology or risk being surprised and sidelined.

Each time they fail to shift to the Internet, to e-formats, or to the next technology after that, often due to their current customers being used to and happy with the current format, their chances of failure increase. The reason for it is that the gap between their current customers accommodated with the current product and the new customers demanding a new version of it, an electronic one, puts a major strain on the business bottom line. The problem is that a disruptive technology does not initially compete directly with the existing technology, even without taking the network effects into consideration; the only successful way to market the new technology is to carve out a niche by leveraging the new technology's distinctive advantages.

For instance, Microsoft is being challenged by a disruptive technology, the Open Source development model. Instead of relying on a team of highly trained professionals, the Open Source model relies on a loose association of hobbyists organized through the Internet. Often, this software development model tends to beat the old way of writing software because of the stronger synergy created by a much larger development team, motivated not by tangible rewards, but a sense of accomplishment and virtual community. While traditional software development is motivated by the sale value of that software, Open Source development is motivated by the software's usefulness.

The Linux user-base surpassed the ten million mark two years ago, and it is growing at about 212 percent annually. Assuming it slows down to a 100 percent annual growth, it will surpass the Windows installed base in about three years. At that point, the network effects will favor Linux and hinder Windows.

The scenario above illustrates the difficulties of effective implementation and, by implication, the power and potential of improved organizational learning, which is essential to achieving desired results. Quite often, the necessary knowledge does not exist, and so must be created from scratch, as in the case of disruptive technologies. At other times, it already exists and has to be transferred elsewhere in the organization. But the challenge here is not to look at learning only for learning's sake, but to get the job done.

Peter Senge, in his book *The Fifth Discipline*,[5] describes the learning

---

5. New York, Currency/Doubleday, 1994, p. 124.

organization as a "group of people continually enhancing their capacity to create what they want to create." If his premise is true, it is also true that the "rate at which organizations learn may become the only sustainable source of competitive advantage."[6] This is not just a westerner's view of learning organizations: Jkujiro Nonaka, the Japanese scholar, describes learning organizations in a very similar way. Although these definitions provide great know-how into the problem of leaning inside organizations, they do not provide a means to effectively deploy this know-how, they do not show how-to implement action, how-to turn learning into action, as they lack a tangible and actionable framework.

Adaptive Learning vs Generative Learning

When it comes to learning, a characteristic of corporate business operations is always based upon coping with challenges that arise every day, and adapting to them as required. Such an adaptive learning trend is actually a beginning, but as Senge points out in *The Fifth Discipline*, this increasing adaptiveness is only the first stage. There is a tremendous need for companies to focus on generative learning, also known as double-loop learning.

Adaptive learning organizations only focus on solving current problems without examining the appropriateness of actual learning behaviors. They focus on incremental improvements, often based on the past track record of success. Thus, in such a learning environment the fundamental assumptions underlying the existing ways of working are never questioned. The essential difference is between being adaptive and having adaptability.

Conversely, instead of reacting and adapting to new situations and challenges, generative learning adopts a more proactive approach, as it emphasizes continuous experimentation and feedback, always examining the way organizations define and solve problems. Thus, I believe, a very innovative role of CKOs today is to promote generative learning within the organization. CKOs are the right professional for the job because generative learning is all about creating alternatives, creating new paradigms. It requires a systemic thinking that encompasses business process, human behavior in organizations, cultural stereotypes, keen vision, and, above all, strategic thinking. Further, CKOs must ensure the sharing of visions and remember that success is the equivalent of vision in action. A vision without action is the same as never waking up from a dream. By the same token, action without vision is the same as sailing without a compass, without a destination.

Generative learning, aside from a shared vision, also requires a great amount of personal mastery. It goes on to include not only proficiency in its business trade, but also team learning and creative tension, which is a very hard environment to be created in and to stay in, as this situation is reflected between

---

6. P. Senge, *The Fifth Discipline*, New York, Currency/Doubleday, 1994, p. 178.

the vision and the current reality. Generative learning, unlike adaptive, pushes the envelop on the way Japanese companies typically attempt to accomplish the same thing with strategic and interpretive equivocality, as it requires new ways of looking at the world and reacting to it, not by adapting, but by interacting with it. That is the double loop.

To survive and be successful in the twenty-first century, organizations must continuously adapt to the ever-changing business environments and trends, operating themselves as prototypes, or morphs organizations, maintaining themselves in a constant state of frequent, almost continuous change in structures, processes, domains, goals, etc. Operating in such a mode, obsoleting itself continuously, is not only very efficacious for the company, but, I believe, it is a requirement in order for it to survive in this global, fast-changing, and unpredictable business environment. As organizations remain in an ongoing state of experimentation, chances are they will inevitably learn about a variety of design features and remain flexible, ready to morph again as new business and requirements dictate.

The CKO's Role in a Learning Organization

CKOs should, by trade, be professionals skilled in the art of designing, teaching, and stewarding. They should be able to take advantage of KM practices and implementations for building shared vision and challenging prevailing mental models. They should be responsible for building organizations where people are continually expanding their inner and outer capabilities to shape their future, and the organizations with which they are affiliated. CKOs should be the leaders responsible for learning inside the organization.

Unlike CEOs and other executive roles, CKOs' key roles should not be getting the right strategy, but fostering strategic thinking to help the executive staff and the organization as a whole to define strategies. The concept of planning, in this context, is then correlated to the concept of learning, instead of preparing or arranging.

Shell Oil provides us with a good example of it when the company was faced with dramatic changes and unpredictability in the world oil markets. The company's executive staff realized there had been a shift in their basic roles. They no longer saw their roles as producing a documented view of the future business environment five or ten years ahead. They realized their real target was now the mental model of their decision makers. Thus, they had to reconceptualize their basic roles as fostering learning rather than devising plans and engaging managers in ferreting out the implications of possible scenarios. This strategy conditioned managers to be mentally prepared for the uncertainties in the task environment. This was the way Shell was able to institutionalize its learning process.

CKOs should be aware of the fact that the key ingredient of a learning organization is how they process their managerial experiences. Learning organizations and their managers learn from their experiences rather than being bound by their past experiences. In generative learning organizations, their ability, as well as that of their manager, is not measured by what they know, as that is the product of learning, but rather by how they learn. Through management and KM practices, CKOs must encourage, recognize, and reward openness, systemic thinking, creativity, a sense of efficacy, and empathy.

The Role of CTOs and IS in Learning Organizations

Information systems (IS) have an important and active role in learning organizations, as depicted in Figure 3.2; so do CTOs in managing such processes. IS serve at least four main processes within the organization, including knowledge acquisition, information interpretation, information distribution, and information memory.

Figure 3.2 – Types of information systems and their role in the organization

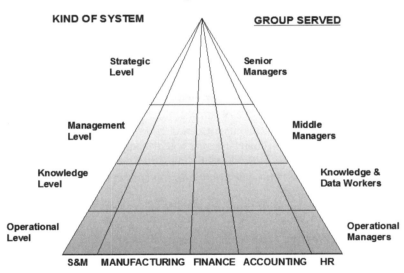

For instance, CTOs can use IS in knowledge acquisition through market research and competitive intelligence systems. Scenario planning tools, another area for planning and execution, can be used for generating forecasts and statistics analysis. In addition, the use of groupware tools, the Internet, intranets and extranets, e-mail, and bulletin boards systems (BBS) can facilitate the processes of information distribution and information interpretation. The archives of these communications can provide the elements of the organizational memory, which needs to be continuously updated and refreshed through data mining activities. Figure 3.3 lists major types of IS in place today.

Figure 3.3 – Major types of IS systems

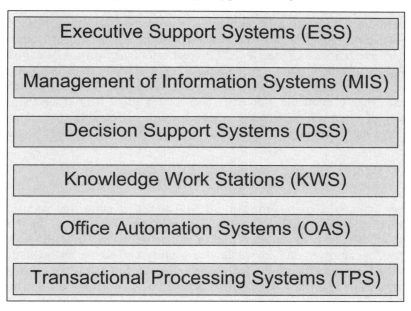

Despite the many applications of IS and information technology (IT) in cataloging, distributing, and storing knowledge, management of information systems (MIS) tends to reinforce the prevailing and rigid structures of information systems and technologies (IS&T). The heavy focus on technology, quality control, and audits is adequate for single-loop learning, or adaptive learning, but not for generative learning. MIS's overarching command-and-control structures are, in my view, one of the causes for the gaps of knowledge within organizations.

Existing IS focus on the convergence of interpretation and are not geared for multiple interpretations. Such characteristics of Lockean and Leibnitzian systems, prevalent in most MIS organizations, are limiting factors in generative learning, and CTOs must be careful not to perpetuate such models. Conversely, Kantian inquirer offers complementary interpretations, while Hegelian inquirer offers a contradictory one. The dialectic of convergent and divergent inquiry facilitates the surfacing of hidden assumptions, essential for generative learning. Thus, CTOs must work closely with CKOs and KM professionals, to implement inquiry systems such as Kantian and Hegelian, to facilitate multiple interpretations, and the discarding of outdated and misleading knowledge.

CTOs must be watchful of implementation gaps of MIS, especially when the technology is used to dealing with the more complex and ill-structured problems faced by the organization. The large amount of learning done in any organization is single loop, mostly because the underlying program is never questioned, as it is designed to identify and correct errors so that the job gets done and actions can remain within current policy guidelines.

Therefore, to orchestrate the promotion of generative learning, CTOs must view MIS as a part of a more general problem of organizational learning. Unless organizations can identify and correct errors they cannot be called a learning organizations. Such a requirement is more complex than it appears to be, as it implies that learning also requires the organization to have a capacity to know when it is unable to identify and correct errors. Unfortunately, the majority of organizations tend to create systems of learning that restrain generative learning inquiries, which makes it very difficult for IS to be effective.

TRANSFERRING KNOWLEDGE

Another major challenge surrounding CKOs today is motivating people to contribute and share their knowledge, as, be it for lack of time to write something that can help someone else, or simply uneasiness in sharing what they know, employees and other knowledge professionals are not willing to spend the time (and their knowledge). To tell them that knowledge sharing improves learning, which has a direct impact on the business bottom line, does not always have a high rate of success. However, examples of successful learning organizations such as IBM and Johnson & Johnson show that knowledge sharing pays off.

In the twenty-first century, more than ever before, an organization's success will be measured by its level of adaptability and flexibility, not the usual short-term profitability and productivity indicators. These indicators are nothing more than a current snapshot of the company's success at that particular time, not the strength of their management and their ability to remain successful in the long run. The many dotcom examples can attest to that. Companies such as Copper Mountain, CMGI, WebVan, and many others were able to provide stellar financial results during the late 1990s, but once the dotcom bubble burst, so did their profitability and productivity indicators.

Improving Collaboration

It is true that new ideas are essential if learning is to take place. But the fact that your organization generates an abundance of new ideas and these ideas are being turned into knowledge does not mean you have turned your organization into a learning one. In fact, raw and unfiltered information is often of limited value. CKOs and KM professionals must be skilled in giving meaning to the data they have collected, and must make sure this information is shared across the organization. Unless raw knowledge is interpreted, the information generated from it will remain unutilized. In addition, to improve knowledge interpretation and sharing, organizations must get better at collaboration. CKOs must simplify the process of sharing knowledge. If the value proposition of doing this is not made clear, it will not get done.

KM strategies allow for collection, management, and dissemination of best practices. But KM also enables a focus on data warehousing and/or data mining to anticipate new customer trends. Further, KM can be a successful tool for enterprise document management. Of course, there is only a small sample of options, but KM should be seen as a powerful tool in promoting collaboration and ultimately knowledge sharing inside and outside the organization.

The choice of technology you make in promoting collaboration, and therefore learning, will depend on the business processes and requirements that are the targets of your KM implementation. Learning does not occur for its own sake; it attends to the design and pursuit of very clearly defined needs. Technology will enable it, but will not deliver it. Enterprise portals, for example, have been the chosen delivery framework for knowledge management actions. But beware that without concomitant changes in the way people work inside the organization and the way they carry out their jobs, improvements in collaboration are resumed only to a possibility, not necessarily reality. Learning, and collaboration for that matter, require action.

In "Simplicity, Speed and Self-Confidence: An Interview with Jack Welch",[7] Ram Charan discusses GE's problem-solving process modeled after a New England town meeting. "Work-Out," as Welch called this process, had two main practical goals: one was intellectual; the other was practical. The practical goal was to get rid of bad habits accumulated since the establishment of GE. The intellectual goal aimed to redefine the relationship between supervisors and subordinates by putting these leaders in front of their own people several times a year to let them learn what and how their people think about the business, themselves, and their leaders.

Work-Out is a great example of an organization in action. You see creation and interpretation processes at work here. You also see an opportunity for retention of knowledge and change in behavior, with great chances for meaningful results. Notice that technology here is not much emphasized.

Another example, one relying more on technology tools, is Proctor & Gamble, which is using what they call the Plumtree Corporate Portal, to bring together content from one million web-pages and thousands of Lotus Notes databases in an enterprise-wide knowledge base. The strategy is creating one view of a business with hundreds of organizational units worldwide. Not only the portal is organizing access to documents in an enterprise-wide Web directory, but it is also integrating information and services from other systems.

---

7. *Harvard Business Review*, October 1989.

Knowledge management portals can also be used as an effective strategy to deliver customizable, multidimensional interface to enable searchable access to data and applications. These portals can include not only content management tools, such as search and retrieval, access to electronic news and information, as well as repository for documents, websites, and databases, but also collaboration and group productivity tools.

Several vendors such as IBM and Microsoft have knowledge portal product offerings. Lotus' Discovery Server is an example, offering a knowledge portal that enables the management of personal and community information and activity, as well as tools for user profiling and expertise location, and content tracking and analysis.

P2P Collaboration

A novel way to promote collaboration and manage knowledge is through the use of peer-to-peer collaboration technologies. Some Internet collaboration infrastructure based on P2P architecture enables the connection of organizations' internal people with business partners, independent contractors and customers, supply chain and distribution channels, regardless of their function or geographic location. Such capabilities give businesses the means to design and assemble virtual service communities.

Independent software vendors (ISV), such as Novient's services, provide applications that enable the optimization of organizations' service processes by matching available people and skills to project requirements, and automating the service delivery process. All activities in the organization, especially knowledge capture and dissemination, must be optimized both technologically and organizationally. That is because if faster time-to-market is to be a realistic proposition for competitive businesses, then new knowledge of market conditions, customer needs, and internal capabilities and capacities must be generated in real time.

The Use of Push Technologies for Capturing and Collaboration

In this globalized market, business professionals are becoming more and more roaming. It is very common to find business professionals carrying their favorite digital device, varying from low-end personal digital assistants (PDAs), such as Palm's 100m or Handspring's Visor models, or more sophisticated smart handheld devices (SHD), such as iPaq running Microsoft's PocketPC and small footprint versions of Office suite. Now, imagine if these professional users, aside from their personal information manager (PIM) tasks and e-mail, could have virtual access to customer relationship management (CRM) and enterprise resource planning (ERP) applications.

Today, the first wave of universal access is present as a form of digital sludge where data flows from one carefully approved device to another through ironclad intermediaries who are programming like crazy to keep up with differing platforms and devices. In parallel, the tools for harmony are also being developed. Platform-independent languages like XML are crying for the attention of digital craftsman to form clever utilities that mitigate or solve the growing access complexity problem.

Out of the scramble for dominance of the access market, Web-enabled technologies are emerging. Such technologies are device and platform-neutral. They ride on top of all data systems instead of between them; a topware, rather than a middleware concept. The notion of digital gatekeepers with proprietary translators is doomed to obsolesce, because these new technologies rely on open architecture, available to everyone. These technologies enable rather than compete and thus change the way the entire world looks at the access and distribution of data, and knowledge for that matter. iCloud[8] has one of the best technologies I know that delivers its promise, a product called FASTCloud.

iCloud technology offers solutions to an ever-increasing urgent and global business need: it encompasses open and pervasive technologies that enable business processes and data to speak to one another across multi-platform networking settings and heterogeneous platforms, integrating a variety of individual systems into a seamless whole. FASTCloud directly addresses, and solves, today's daunting corporate challenge of integrating, exchanging, and redirecting data between disparate legacy systems, a hodgepodge of hardware, operating systems, and networking technology, topped with proprietary packaged applications, and much more.

Instead of a "topware" solution, much emphasized by enterprise application integration (EAI) proponents, iCloud's technology introduces the notion of topware, acting as a virtual conveyer over the multitude of disparate systems, making possible the movement and exchange of data. iCloud's technology is a knowledge technology that can dramatically transform tomorrow's IT architecture into today's telecom model: easy to use data and content services that are always available anywhere, on wired and wireless platforms.

As corporate dependence on knowledge technologies continues to grow more complex and far reaching, the need for a method for integrating, exchanging, and redirecting data among disparate applications into a unified set of business processes has emerged as a major priority. Generations of information technology have created a large number of islands of data and valuable contents.

Now, business requirements, characterized by alliances and partnerships, corporate acquisitions and global presence, are demanding that seamless bridges be built to join these infoislands. In addition, there is today an urgent demand for ways to be found to bind these information repositories into a single, unified platform. The development of virtual accessible networks, which allows many

---

8. www.icloudinc.com

of the stovepipe repositories of information that exist today to share both processes and data, finally provides a solution for this demand.

Powerful, Elegant Data Extraction

iCloud's technologies propose a very different method of data extraction, interoperation, and exchange than that using traditional middleware, synchronization, or even publish/subscribe methods. FASTCloud provides a set of integration-level application semantics, known as Virtual Agent for Parsing of Objects and Records (VAPOR), which as a core technology allows for a series of connectivity ports (known as FASTCloud) to a multitude of applications. Put another way, FASTCloud creates a common way for data to be extracted, exchanged, and directed cross platform and among disparate devices, wired or wireless.

More importantly, unlike middleware and EAI halfway solutions, this technology approaches this challenging enterprise problem in a distinct way. Specifically designed based on FASTCloud, iCloud's Remote Agent for Intelligent Normlization of Bytes Over Wireless (RAINBOW) provides data portability to a variety of heterogeneous devices such as cellular phones (WAP/ I-mode), PDAs (HDML), PDF files, etc. Figure 3.4 depicts how iCloud's technology extracts, normalizes/transcodes, and delivers information, allowing for a true knowledge-sharing environment with a great potential to fill in the gaps between infoislands if deployed correctly.

Figure 3.4 – Using iCloud technology to bridge the knowledge-sharing gap between infoislands of informatiom

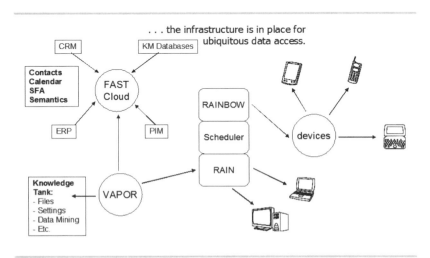

iCloud's technology can be tremendously helpful in the capture, normalization, and transformation, as well as distribution of knowledge, because it delivers on Barnes-Lee's notion of Semantic Web. Capturing collective intellectual capital and making it available throughout the organization and among all partners, no matter where or when it is needed, is a vital asset for any KM initiative, which makes it a strategic imperative. New ideas must be distributed rapidly throughout the organization, from professional to professional, group by group.

Knowledge itself cannot be managed. But knowledge which is captured and turned into an asset (tangible or intangible) is indeed a commodity that one can count on, literally, to improve the performance of the company and help generate profits.

Push technologies, in which information retrieval is initiated by a sending system rather than the individual receiving the information, can transform a portal into a kind of corporate cockpit that instantly notifies managers when key performance indicators stray outside acceptable boundaries.

CHAPTER 4

Learning Organizations: Striving by Transferring Knowledge

Knowledge transferring will only be successful when you are able to fully and effectively engage all of your people, with a technological system and within cultural surroundings where they can all be comfortable practicing it.

The transfer of knowledge within a learning organization is a complex task. However, taken seriously and with the support of senior management it can be accomplished. Not that I have met any learning organization in its full sense; I haven't, and I don't think I ever will. But generative learning conditions are to be cultivated, even though you may never be able to become a truly learning organization. Achieving such a level is like achieving the full sense of personal humility, or even Zen. As soon as you believe and affirm you have reached it, you have just missed it.

Nonetheless, organizational learning is very important, in particular in the twenty-first century's globalized, fast-paced, and multicultural business settings. CKOs, executive staff, and knowledge professionals must be aware that if organizations are not able to cope with the rapidly changing business environment, which also encompasses technology and human behavior within the organization, they will die. I strongly believe that organizational learning will become as important to corporations as vitamins and minerals are to the human body, without which the whole system gradually breaks down and becomes ill, and, if not replenished, it eventually succumbs.

Senior executives, and ultimately the board of directors, are the ones in charge of ensuring the organizations' regular intake of learning (vitamins and minerals). Executives, in particular those with knowledge and information expertise, such as CKOs and CIOs, should then be responsible for designing, installing, and maintaining the systems, including information systems and technology (IS&T), with the support and expertise of CTOs. The major challenge here is how this executive team will ensure the adequate amount of learning necessary for the organization to flourish. This is mainly because many executives do not even realize there is a challenge to begin with.

The fact that, as discussed in earlier chapters, a large percentage of US government workers will be retiring in the next few years and no knowledge transfer strategy is in place yet (even though the US government is aware of it, earnestly working towards it, and appointed its first CKO in the spring of 2001),[1] or that the tragedy at the World Trade Center in New York (11 September 2001) unveiled a reactive step-up in airports and airlines security policy and procedures that were long due for review, or even the fade of successful business icons that suddenly disappeared, such as Digital Equipment Corporation (DEC), Data General, and more recently Hewlett-Packard's merge with Compaq, are examples of the lack of interactive loops of what Bob Garratt[2] called policy (customer focused), strategic (director/senior staff focused), and operational (staff focused) learning.

According to Garratt, these loops of learning (and transferring of learning) allow the critical review of all levels of the organization. Such continuous learning enables the organization to sense and respond to the changes in its external and internal environments to ensure the survival and development of the energy niches that support it. This is a very holistic approach, much like nurturing a living organism, as most of the learning and transferring of it inside the organization is personal, private, very often uncodified, hidden, and, most of all, a defensive way of coping with the effects of a seemingly nonlearning employer.

TRANSFERRING KNOWLEDGE

Why is knowledge transferring so important? Back in 1498, Wang Yang-Ming was already saying that "knowledge is the beginning of practice; doing is the completion of knowing."[3] The former Chairman of SAS Airlines, Jan Carlson believes that an individual without information cannot take responsibility; an individual who is given information cannot help but take responsibility. The same is true for CKOs and their responsibility in bridging the knowledge gap inside the organization. A key strategy in this process is the effective transferring of knowledge.

To bridge this knowledge gap, CKOs must realize that the utmost knowledge base in any organization does not reside in computer databases, but in the heads of the individuals inside the organization. The majority of professionals inside knowledge-based organizations worldwide have college degrees. Many of them hold postgraduate degrees and a large amount of know-how based on previous experiences and specializations. The challenge is, how do you get each one of these professionals to share what they know, not compulsorily, but freely and openly with everyone else in the organization? In addition, how do

1. *Knowledge Management Magazine*, June 2001.
2. B. Garratt, *The Learning Organization: Developing Democracy at Work*, London, HarperCollinsBusiness, 2000.
3. W. Yang-Ming, *The Philosophy of Wang*, trans. Frederick Goodrich Henke, The Open Court Publishing Co., 1916, *passim*.

you get them to accept responsibility for their actions? Where should your focus and line of action be? In my experience, they have to cover a multitude of areas, including:

• identifying target individuals

• knowing the barriers in the organization

• having a code of ethics

• fostering culture change

• promoting innovation by thinking out of the box.

Identifying Target Individuals

For any successful knowledge transfer activity, it is important for you to identify the individuals from whom you need capital knowledge transferred. Unfortunately, I find that the more important the transfer of knowledge, the more difficult it is to identify and locate the relevant professionals, never mind get them sharing what they know. Take for instance the global consulting companies. To locate their professionals can be hard at times. If you were to calculate the amount of professional consultants between offices across the country and the globe at any point in time, you might find that 86 percent of them (excluding administrative personnel) are outside the office and many times outside the country.

In an organization where the office is not the place where business is conducted, knowledge transfer can be a very hard job to accomplish. The same is true for any other organization, maybe not at such high levels as the professional consulting industry. For instance, if I am in my office for 40 hours a week, then my time in the office is less than 25 percent of my available time. If I consider the times I am working from home or a hotel room, then the percentage falls even further. Among the big six consulting firms, you may find that their consultants are in the office less than 14 percent of their available time.

Therefore, knowing where your people are and how they will contribute to the transfer of knowledge is very important, and must be taken into consideration before you establish a collaboration strategy.

Knowing the Barriers in the Organization

What are the barriers you are likely to face in attempting knowledge transfer implementation? These barriers are real, and they exist in every organization. An example is the structural barriers of hierarchical organizations, such as departments, groups, and divisions, etc. Different operating companies in different countries, language, and cultural barriers are often present as well.

There are many more barriers and you must take the time to identify them and have a strategy to overcome each one of them prior to any knowledge transferring initiative.

In order for any knowledge transfer initiative to be successful, you must not focus your efforts on a department or an operating company, but on the total company, across all of these barriers. To do this you will have to focus on increasing the ability of the individual in communicating his thoughts to others in the organization, as it would be the collective result of a lot of individual actions that would be necessary to produce a result for the company. The question is how do you increase the power of these individuals to sharing their thoughts to others in the organization?

There are many areas you should concentrate on in attempting to become a learning organization and striving to transfer knowledge at the same time. The main areas of attack should include:

- increasing the power of individuals in sharing their thoughts

- overcoming the organization's barriers.

Increasing the Power of Individuals in Sharing Their Thoughts

Typically, most organizations gather information on the front line, and then pass it to someone next to them up the line. The process then continues further up the line, with each individual adding some perspective to make it better. Finally it reaches some guru who gives the information the benefit of his infinite wisdom, typically an executive, an officer within the organization, and then the information starts coming back down the line, or is stored into the knowledge base, the memory, of the company. Curious enough, in many cases the originator of the information will not recognize the information when it gets back to them, and worse, the information will not communicate what they had intended. If there was a system in place that could let the individual with the need for knowledge talk directly with the individual or group that have the latest and best knowledge, then this whole confusion could be eliminated.

For knowledge transfer to be effective, it is essential for individuals seeking the knowledge to be able to clearly communicate what they need so that the individual providing the information will be able to provide a rapid response to them. You can do this by radically changing the span of communication of the individual from his immediate work group to the entire company and beyond to anybody on any network that they need to go to for information. The greatest database in the organization is housed in its people's minds, and that is where the power of the organization actually resides. These individual knowledge bases are continually changing and adapting to the real world in front of them.

It is the role of CKOs and KM professionals to make sure to connect these individual knowledge bases together, bridging the knowledge gap, so that they can do whatever they do best in the shortest possible time, and without the risk of knowledge loss. I strongly believe that the greater the span of communication and collaboration that you give to individuals, the greater the span of influences they will have. The greater the span of influence, the more powerful the individuals will be. If the span of communication is limited to a small horizon such as a work group on a local area network (LAN), then the influence that the individuals can bring to bear will be minimal, the change will be minimal, and the benefits to the organization will also be minimal.

As you expand the ability of the individual members of the organization, you expand the ability of the organization itself. As you change the span of influence of the individual, you change the power of the individual and you change the power of the organization as well. Buckman Laboratories, for example, were very successful in this strategy, by increasing the span of communication of their individual associates from their immediate workgroup to the global world of the company and to anywhere else they need to go for information. They gave their people access to the world, both inside and outside of the company.

It is this change in the span of communication of the individual that provides the basis of the cultural change that organizations are experiencing worldwide. At Buckman, all those individuals that have something intelligent to say now have a forum in which to say it. Management can no longer hold them back. These people became obvious and respected in the organization based on what they could contribute to others, not on how well they could please some boss. Furthermore, those that will not or cannot contribute also become obvious and can be intelligently eliminated from the organization.

Therefore, if you want your organization to become a learning organization and increase its power in the marketplace, increase the span of communication, collaboration, and knowledge transfer of the individual associates of the organization. Allow them to talk to whomever they need to for information. This is how you can improve the speed of response to the customer towards instantaneity.

Overcoming Organizations' Barriers

Organizations' barriers are the major factor responsible for the knowledge gap within corporations. The collection of minds that exists within organizations across company, geographic, cultural, and language barriers is great. It is necessary to effectively transfer knowledge across time and space to meet the needs of the learning organization and, ultimately, their customers.

Ideally, the knowledge transfer between the organization and its customers, as well as among themselves, should happen instantly. But this is not an easy task, and one near to impossible to fulfill, unless in very specific environments. But if you can reduce the transferring time, the feedback, from weeks and days to a few hours, or no more than a day or so, then you would have achieved a major milestone in knowledge transferring. The speed of response is a very important and measurable aspect of a successful knowledge transfer, in particular at the furthermost reaches of the corporation. This is because fast response time can drastically eliminate distance.

When you provide a feedback to another member of your organization or a customer in a timely fashion, the distance between you and your office or your company and the customer becomes irrelevant. That is why many help-desk systems as well as customer support services outsourced overseas, mainly in India, are being so successful (many are not, but for other reasons, such as inability to absorb local neologisms and cultural nuances!). The customer in the US does not really care if the solution to the problem is coming from the next town over or from overseas. All the customer cares about is that the knowledge required is transferred in a timely fashion.

Having a Code of Ethics

A code of ethics is the glue that holds a learning organization, any organization for that matter, together. It provides the basis for the respect and trust that are necessary in a knowledge-sharing environment. These fundamental beliefs are crucial for communication and collaboration across the many barriers to knowledge transfer that exist in any organization. A sound (and realistic!) code of ethics should be seen as an integral part of the effort to achieve and maintain knowledge sharing in a learning organization.

Taking Buckman Laboratories again as an example, a clear code of ethics was key in their knowledge sharing implementation, because they were separated by many miles, diversity of cultures, and languages, which required a clear understanding of the basic principles by which they would operate. Some of these basic principles may include, but should not be limited to:

- A forward-looking attitude about the future of the organization should be constantly nurtured, so that generative learning, instead of adaptive, can take place, allowing individuals inside the organization to proactively control their destiny instead of letting events overtake them.

- All decisions should be made according to what is right for the good of the whole company rather than what is expedient in a given situation.

- Customers, and their total satisfaction, should be the only reason for the existence of any learning organization. To serve them properly, the organization must supply products and services which provide economic benefit over and above their cost.

- Each individual's contributions and accomplishments should be recognized and rewarded.

- Learning organizations are made up of individuals, each of whom has different capabilities and potentials that are necessary to the success of the company.

- People's individuality should be acknowledged by treating each other with dignity and respect, striving to maintain continuous and positive communications among everyone within the organization.

- The highest ethics must be used to guide the organizations' business dealings, to ensure that every individual within the organization is always proud to be a part of the company.

- The only way to provide high quality products and services to customers is to be driven by a total customer satisfaction motto – and not fear of being let go, or personal gain – in everything the company does.

- The organization's standards should always be upheld by the individuals and by the corporation as a whole, so that people may be respected as individuals as well as an organization.

- The responsibilities of corporate and individual citizenship should always be discharged in order to earn and maintain the respect of the community.

- There should be a policy of providing work for all individuals, no matter what the prevailing business conditions may be.

Fostering Culture Change

The board of directors and executive staff are responsible for the climate they create in the organization. Such a climate has a major impact on the organizations' ability to share knowledge across time and space. Over the years I have seen this as the most difficult aspect of knowledge transfer to achieve. By default, people have always taught themselves to collect knowledge over the years as a way to achieve power, or as a way of professional self-preservation, to say the least. What is taught in colleges and universities is that knowledge should be acquired and used, but we never learned how to share it.

If businesses are to be successful in this knowledge economy of the twenty-first century, we must reverse that tendency. In this new economy, the most powerful individuals will not be those building their own infoislands, but those who are willing to become a source of knowledge to their peers and the organization as a whole by proactively sharing what they have. Continuity and trust, so necessary to accomplishing proactive knowledge transferring within the company, must be promoted. Further, this same climate of continuity and trust should be fostered with customers.

Aside from collaboration within the many groups of a learning organization, knowledge transferring also promotes the building of relationships of continuity and trust with customers. This fringe benefit of knowledge transferring is only possible if built by the individuals of the organization. Thus, those with account responsibility, for example, are automatically involved with the customer by the nature of their position. Software engineers and product developers, as well as applications experts and industry specialists should also be involved in this process, provided they are effectively engaged in the front line. This is true for everyone in the organization. Actually, the number of people in the organization involved in relationships with customers can effectively determine the momentum of the whole organization not only in how efficiently it is becoming a learning organization, but also in how proficiently it is exercising the transfer of knowledge.

Another important aspect to consider is with regard to the quality of the people that you, as a learning organization, can bring to this relationship with partners, supply chains, and distribution channels, which will determine the level at which your organization can operate in this relationship. The higher the quality of the individuals engaged in this knowledge transfer, the higher the quality of the knowledge that can be brought to bear on any problem that your customers and co-workers bring to you. But do not underestimate other levels of the organization, as every individual independent of their role can effectively contribute to this KM initiative.

At Buckman, their goal was to have 80 percent of their organization effectively engaged on the front line by the end of 2000. Such a level of knowledge sharing/transferring assumes different shapes according to the organization in which it is implemented. It may translate, as in Buckman's case, into how they get as many people as possible creating and transferring as much knowledge as possible in the best way in order to have a positive impact on the customer. Some organizations may focus on making sure that there is a high level of interaction between the organization's people and paying customers for a measurable frequency and duration. For others, it might be to ensure that the majority of their people actively use their electronic forums, web portals, and e-mail, or even to ensure that they get their accounting right, which may include profit recovery activities, so that their groups measure up to this new corporate goal.

My advice is, no matter what the nuances, idiosyncrasies, and specifics of any given learning organization, the goal of knowledge transferring strategies is to bring the full weight of the knowledge that exists in the hardware, software, and people, in a relevant and useful manner, to bear upon the requirements of the customer. I believe that any learning organization, especially those that realize they must adopt a generative learning attitude as opposed to an adaptive one, are doing a lot of these things already. But if they can get all of their people exercising knowledge transfer at all times, a tremendous power can be unleashed. The goal here is not to go after definitions, numbers, procedures, or any other quantifiable business goals. It should be about involvement, commitment, creativity, passion, and, ultimately, the freedom to do everything the organization can, and to use all of the knowledge it has, to make sure that they have done their best to satisfy their customers – inside and outside the organization – in every way.

Knowledge transferring will only be successful when you are able to fully and effectively engage all of your people with a technological system and within cultural surroundings where they can all be comfortable practicing it. Only then will you have sufficiently addressed the collaboration and knowledge transferring issues of your organization.

Promoting Innovation by Thinking Out of the Box

By nature, CKOs are (should be!) professionals capable of influencing others. As discussed in chapters three and nine, the multi-disciplinary background CKOs must have greatly enhances their span of influence over diverse groups inside the organization and out. Hence the importance of CKOs today in being instrumental in bridging knowledge gaps inside the organization, as these professionals have been able to achieve faster growth of the talented people in the company by promoting new ideas, innovation of thinking, and, ultimately, helping learning organizations to think out of the box. Such professionals are able to influence others across time and space with a resultant increase in morale.

Chief knowledge officers are not the only ones responsible for fostering innovation. Many other professionals within the organization also contribute, beginning with the board, executive staff, and technologists. The fact is, everyone in a learning organization should be able to promote innovation. The important thing to realize is that to achieve these benefits everyone in the organization must accept the fact that radical and rapid change will be part of the learning organization's life. Consider these best practice facts:

- No matter whom or where people are in the world, everyone should be able to contribute to solutions of any problem in the organization, regardless of its nature or where it occurs. The challenge is to structure the organization to recognize this fact. Another challenge is to structure this new learning organization around the flow of knowledge, rather than geography.

- Today's offices are too redundant to the functioning of a learning organization. You must, therefore, make sure to build communities of people that trust each other so that they can function effectively without an office. This means to enable people to be effective even while roaming, at a hotel room, at home, at the airport, at a satellite office. In other words, you must be able to move the office to where the people are, anywhere and anytime. Done? Now it is time to move the entire organization to wherever it is needed at any point in time. This without affecting the knowledge flow.

- In this new knowledge economy, where customers are much more aware of sales processes, speed in responding to them is vital if you want to remain competitive in the marketplace. Thus, here you have another challenge: to make sure the farthest groups and individuals within your organization have the same speed of response as everyone else.

- Make sure everyone is engaged with customers, or potential customers. Otherwise, why have them around?

- Every individual's ability to acquire and use knowledge is very important to any learning organization. Therefore, the quality of the people that you hire is critical to the future of this new learning organization. What is in the collection of minds of the organization's associates determines how well the organization will function. In this process, watch for reactions coming from the human resources group. You may find your organization will need to hire teachers or coaches.

- If everybody is critically important to the organization's ability to close the gap between the know-how of the organization and the how-to serve the customer, then what needs to happen so that the minds of your associates can be expanded, so that they can be the best that they can be? Ask yourself how you can deliver learning anytime, anywhere. You may rely on programs such as The Learning Space, developed by The Lotus Institute as an application under Lotus Notes and the Global Campus initiative of IBM.

To reap the benefits of knowledge transfer, you should invest in it like any other investment that will change the organization. It requires active entrepreneurial support from the board and executive staff down to junior associates. Knowledge transfer, as well as knowledge management as a whole, resides in culture change. And if you want to change the culture of an organization, the leader of that organization must lead it. This means the CEO needs to hold the flag, by adopting the changes, by using the latest hardware and software for communications, and by being open and accepting changes.

Remember, everybody in the organization is watching. If the head of the organization does not walk the walk, then the rest of the organization will not see it as important and will not adopt the changes either. Make sure that whatever statement of direction you have is backed up with actions, otherwise nothing will happen in the organization.

Therefore, keep in mind that knowledge transfer is more than collaboration with industry on specific products or technologies with commercial potential. It is a long-term process that establishes symbiotic ties between industrial and academic researchers. Transfer of knowledge can be further achieved through education, outreach, publications, workshops, and an array of other means.

Important vehicles for knowledge transfer are workshops and symposia that highlight research achievements to a targeted audience from industry, academia, and government, and that allow group discussion on topics with broad impact and long-term importance. Through these meetings, center researchers disseminate information to a large audience and build research collaborations. They also introduce new technologies and provide hands-on training in new methodologies.

KM STRATEGIES TO FOSTER KNOWLEDGE TRANSFER

As discussed in chapter three, learning must be turned into action in order to be effective. A learning organization is a breathing organism, and if it is not flourishing, it is dying. Thus, knowledge performance is achieved by valuing and using the knowledge of the organization on the job, turning learning into action. You might be in for a surprise here, but do the people of the organization know how to create value and make money for the company? If so, do they know what kind of knowledge they need to do this?

Just as in any professional sports team, players (employees) have their strengths and their weaknesses. They perform better in one position rather than others. As part of becoming a learning organization, you might have to deal with miscast positions, as well as not-so-fit players. The way employees deal with knowledge and the positions they hold can mean the difference between your organization's success and its failure. Thus, be prepared to conduct some knowledge performance targets to match your employees' strengths with the right roles within the organization.

Building a KM strategy is often the best starting point when attempting to implement a knowledge transfer strategy. The implementation will require you to know and understand what knowledge and systems the organization needs to enhance for its competitive advantage. There are six key components of KM you must address:

- KM Applications
- Intuitive Content management
- KM Culture
- KM-based Governance

KM Applications

There are several KM and knowledge technologies you should consider in fostering knowledge transfer within learning organizations and across KM communities. The UK's Knowledge Media Institute at the Open University in Milton Keynes is a good place to start in searching for a variety of KM application strategies and tools. Nonetheless, I would like to bring to your attention one of the latest methodologies in developing collaborative modeling, organizational memory, computer supported argumentation, and meeting facilitation, known as the Compendium methodology, which also includes a suite of tools.

The last I heard about Compendium in the US was at the Knowledge Technologies 2001 conference in March of 2001,[4] in Austin TX, where I was

---

4. For more information about these events, check www.KnowledgeTechnologies.net.

presenting a paper on using the power of dynamic transcoding proxies (DTP)[5] for effective knowledge sharing. However, the methodology is a result of over a decade of research and development, in particular in the UK, offering innovative strategies for tackling several of the key challenges in managing knowledge and its applications, including:

- the improvement of communication between disparate communities tackling ill-structured problems

- real-time capture and integration of hybrid material, including both predictable/formal and unexpected/informal, into a reusable group memory

- transforming the resulting resource into the right representational formats for different stakeholders.

An Overview of Compendium

Compendium was first developed back in 1993 to aid cross-functional business process redesign (BPR) teams, and has been applied in several projects in both industry and academic settings.[6] As defined by Sierhuis and Selvin,[7] Compendium was originated as an attempt to solve the challenge of creating shared understanding between team members during meetings and brainstorm sessions in war rooms, typically those teams working over weeks or months on the design of business processes,[8] keeping track a plethora of ideas, issues, and conceptual interrelationships. Compendium allowed them to keep track of it all without the need to sift through piles of easel sheets, surfacing and tracking design rationale, and staying on track and updated on projects' overall structures and goals.

Compendium is particularly effective in face-to-face meetings, which are potentially the most pervasive knowledge-based activities in the workplace, but also one of the hardest to do well in the light of KM and knowledge transfer. Under the Compendium perspective, such meetings and brainstorm sessions can:

- turn into untapped knowledge-intensive events, instead of being typically unfocused, as they can be improved with facilitated application tools that help participants express and visualize views in a shared, common display

---

5. Technology developed by Virtual Access Networks (www.thevan.com).
6. For more information, I suggest you to visit www.kmi.open.ac.uk/sbs/csca/cscl99.
7. M. Sierhuis and S. Selvin, "A Framework for Object Oriented Performance Analysis." *White Paper*, Florida State University, 2002.
8. M. Sierhuis and S. Selvin, "Towards a Framework for Collaborative Modeling and Simulation" Workshop on Strategies for Collaborative Modeling and Simulation, CSCW'96: ACM Conference on Computer-Supported Cooperative Work, Boston-MA, USA, 1996.

- become more tightly woven into the fabric of work, as they are preceded and followed by much more communication and the generation of associated artifacts.

Intertwining the process and products of meetings into this broader web of activity should be a priority for any learning organization wanting to effectively improve the knowledge transferring process.

Researchers have found that a combination of facilitation with visual hypertext tools can improve potentially unproductive or explosive meetings between multiple stakeholders with competing priorities. This is made possible by the capturing of diverse perspectives, which can also be structured and integrated in such a way that all participants collectively have ownership of these perspectives, as a trace of their discussions. Such an approach enables a structured group memory which shows where the same concepts have been discussed in different contexts, and why decisions were made, and allows related concepts to be harvested from multiple meetings in the form of conversational maps.

In addition, these conversational maps, designed to support the granular representation of concepts such as hypertext database objects, can be spatially organized, recombined, and reused in multiple contexts, and can be integrated with pre- and post-meeting activities and documents. Development efforts are under way to convert material in conventional applications, such as written documents, e-mails, and spreadsheets, into concept maps, so that their contents can be analyzed in new ways, and integrated with other maps.

Compendium is an excellent tool for enabling groups to collectively elicit, organize, and validate information required by a particular community for a particular purpose, by integrating it with pre- and post-meeting processes and artifacts, through the generation of maps that can be transformed into other document formats, enabling asynchronous discussions around the contents of maps, and other forms of computation and analysis. I believe that the domain independence of Compendium's mapping technique for meetings, combined with its interoperability with domain-specific applications, provide a powerful technique for knowledge construction and negotiation.

Compendium is represented by a series of techniques revolving around a graphical hypermedia system for the development and application of question-oriented templates, which serve as semiformal ontologies to structure the subject matter of a particular project, as shown in Figure 4.1. It also comprises a set of metadata codes that can be assigned to any concept in a database, as depicted in Figure 4.2. The approach in itself enables the ability to move between formal and prescribed representations and informal, *ad hoc* communication, incorporating both in the same view if that is helpful to the participants. In addition, hypertext nodes and links can be added either in accordance with templates or in an opportunistic fashion.

Figure 4.1 – Compendium question template representing the concerns of a particular stakeholder group

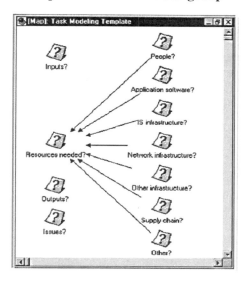

Figure 4.2 – Optional metadata codes added of a node assist subsequent harvesting and analysis of elements

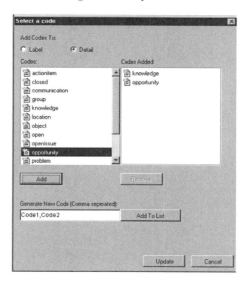

Compendium's domain-modeling simulation can be very useful in knowledge transfer projects, as it enables the development of a conceptual model first. Compendium is specifically good at allowing designers, knowledge engineers, and domain experts to collaborate on the development of a conceptual model of the system. Indeed, the beauty of a conceptual model in Compendium is the lack of syntactic and semantic complexity that comes with other conceptual modeling languages (such as semantic networks). In other words, answering questions in a natural language is easier than having to understand what the arrows and boxes mean in most other languages.

Intuitive Content Management

There are several content management techniques available in the IT and data mining industries, most of them well publicized. I believe, however, that when it comes to knowledge management, in particular the transfer and sharing of knowledge, there is a need for a more content, and context, sensitive approach. In addition, as organizations and the organizations' memory morphs into a more virtualized and borderless entity, the web, and a browser, are playing a major role in enabling virtual access to large amounts of information, residing in not only one, but several silos across the network, be it an intranet or an extranet.

Therefore, it is essential for knowledge managers to become more familiar with and to better understand Tim Berners-Lee's semantic web vision, which is to make web content practically processible by any computer and other wired and wireless devices, be it a thin or a thick client. I predict that in the coming years, not far from today, semantic web will tremendously impact knowledge transfer among organizations by making the web more effective for its users, and by turning a browser into a simple, but powerful tool for knowledge gathering, processing, and sharing.

The level of knowledge transfer effectiveness will be achieved through the automation or the enabling of data mining and KM functions that are currently difficult to perform, such as locating, collating, and cross-relating content, and drawing conclusions from information found in two or more separate sources. This will be a very important step, because typically, software developers tend to get so enthusiastic about the systems they are creating that they stray away from a focus on the user's requirements. Such a limitation, or lack of usability features, becomes very obvious in web-based applications, as this environment is very unforgiving when the user is ignored. It is indubitable that if you create a site that is hard to use, nobody will use it – period.

Information mobility technologies such as iCloud[9] are delivering to this vision of a web environment that machines can understand to make data

---

9. For more information on the company's products and technologies for data extraction, normalization, and redirection, check their website at www.icloudinc.com

integration easier. If we agree that the end purpose of semantic web is to make the user's life and cross application and platforms easier, then there are a variety of uses for such technology, most of them directly correlated to the user's frustrations in trying to accomplish very simple tasks. The synchronization of personal digital assistants (PDAs) such as Palm's, Handsprings, and iPaq's with a web page, the ability to have some kind of universal view over your e-mail, documents, and web-browsing history are some of the problems currently unsolved because of the fragmentation of data due to custom and proprietary data formats. Providing an integration of these is an obvious use case, and a very important one in knowledge transfer activities.

Meeting some obvious use cases, as well as customer relationship management (CRM) and enterprise resource planning (ERP) information integration and mobility, has a degree of serendipity in the Semantic Web and iCloud's work. What drives the company's technology for information mobility and Semantic Web, which is part of their core competencies, is a vision that expresses the desire to get all these sources of information available out there in hundreds of infoislands tied together. Once this has been accomplished, then exciting things can happen. The folks at iCloud know that building the Semantic Web is a research and development project, not a manufacturing process. So, I am sure there will be some dead ends, and some discoveries of exciting and unforeseen proportions. It is important for KM professionals to be aware of this, plan for it, and capitalize on the portion of the technology already available. For instance, the company has a product that already enables users to virtually, and wirelessly, access data on CRM applications, such as Siebel, Goldmine, and Act!, from any device, anywhere, as well as combining and integrating data among those applications and others.

I feel privileged and fundamentally excited to be one of the architects of these technologies at iCloud, and therefore understanding the technology and being one of the earliest beneficiaries of features such as being able to recover and integrate my data from disparate sources and proprietary formats. The technology, which is codenamed FASTCloud, addresses and solves my constraints on time to deal with several applications, the difficulty of finding information, and the redundancy of having my data scattered across multiple devices.

The World Wide Web Consortium (W3C) has put forward a very clear architecture for the Semantic Web (SW), which was described by Tim Berners-Lee at XML 2000 in Washington. This architecture is cleanly layered, starting with the foundation of URIs and Unicode. On top of that sits syntactic interoperability in the form of XML, which in turn underlies what I would define as the data interoperability layer, the resource description framework (RDF) and the RDF schemas. These layers sum up most of the SW that is presently available in implementation form. And without looking further up the SW stack, an extraordinary amount of utility can and has been obtained from just those layers, including digital signatures, which are right up the side of the stack, emphasizing their widespread utility. Also, at each stage there is an allowance for contents from a layer to be labeled with an assured provenance.

On top of RDF lie ontologies, which allow the further description of objects and their interrelations, past the basic class-property descriptions enabled by RDF Schema. The W3C in conjunction with DARPA and the European Union is pursuing the development of languages in this area right now.

The vision for Semantic Web is that once all these layers are in place, we will have a system in which we can trust that the data we are seeing, the deductions we are making, and the claims we are receiving have some value. That is the main goal I see with Semantic Web, one that I share with the folks at iCloud, to aggregate knowledge and create new knowledge, in a trusted fashion, accessible, and shared over the web.

Now, as long as we do not restrict Semantic Web technologies to just those explicit layers in Berners-Lee's idealized diagram, then very real integration projects can take place. For instance, despite the fact that many would say there is no compatibility between Sun Microsystems's J2EE and Microsoft .Net, which potentially could be a major producer of infoislands, with XML and Semantic Web, the two are very compatible. Of course, there are obviously differences between the two and what *is* on the web, HTML, should not even be mentioned. The beauty of XML is that it is in the perfect place to act as a bridge between those technologies and any disparate system. The key here is to focus on XHTML, instead of HTML, as it can be semantically decorated by means of things such as the class attribute, and XSLT can be used to extract RDFs. Likewise, there are other semantic applications, such as Topic Maps, that are pure XML applications. XML provides the bridge to all these technologies and schemas.

KM Culture

When it comes to developing KM strategies to foster knowledge transfer, Microsoft is a great example. The company puts a great emphasis on its human resource capabilities, which systematically acquire and develop the best possible knowledge workers for their given positions. Microsoft's Project Skill Planning "und" Development program, known as SPUD, focuses on human resource development, definitions, ratings, and linkages.

One of Microsoft's competitive advantages since its establishment in 1975 has been the quality of its people. Microsoft has always gone to amazing lengths to hire people with strong intellects and capabilities. As we read *Microsoft Secrets: How the World's Most Powerful Software Company Creates Technology, Shapes Markets, and Manages People*,[10] one of Microsoft's key

---

10. R.W. Selby, *Microsoft Secrets: How the World's Most Powerful Software Company Creates technology, Shapes Markets, and Manages People*, Louisville, Touchstone, 1998.

strategies is to "Find smart people who know the technology and the business."

Openness to change and the ability to foster cultural changes are important for any potential candidate to be part of the Microsoft team. The company is always seeking high levels of competence as one of the main attributes, because of the fast-changing nature of the industry in which it competes. For instance, back in 1995, Gates and other Microsoft executives concluded that they had to embrace the Internet and incorporate it into virtually all products and services. As a result, software developers and marketers needed to be able to acquire new skills quickly. There was no other option. Now, only five years later, its entire organization realizes that Web services and XML will be the basis of business transactions, office applications, and information exchange. Microsoft is responding with the .Net platform, which is requiring the whole organization to acquire new skills – and fast. The development of XML-based technologies to promote Web services, such as SOAP, UDDI, WSDL, and so on, has required its personnel to reinvent themselves and be successful. Talk about radical cultural (and skill sets) change!

The SPUD initiative is being managed by the "Learning and Communication Resources" group within Microsoft IT, which also has responsibility for training and education for IT personnel. The goal is to use the competency model to transfer and build knowledge, not merely to test it. When Microsoft IT employees have a better idea of what competencies are required of them, they will be better consumers of educational offerings within and outside Microsoft. The project is also expected to lead to better matching of employees to jobs and work teams. Eventually the project may be extended throughout Microsoft and into other companies.

There were five major components to the SPUD project:

1. development of a structure of competency types and levels

2. defining the competencies required for particular jobs

3. rating the performance of individual employees in particular jobs based on the competencies

4. implementing the knowledge competencies in an online system

5. linkage of the competency model to learning offerings.

Developing the Competency Structure

As soon as the SPUD project started Microsoft had already defined certain competencies they were looking for, but at that time, they were largely restricted to entry-level skills. The Northwest Center was also studying entry-level skills for software developers, such as requirements definition for a new system. These base-level competencies became known as foundation knowledge in the four-type model used in the SPUD project, as shown in Figure 4.3.

Figure 4.3 – Microsoft's basic level of competence as defined in the types of competencies under its SPUD program

As depicted in Figure 4.3, above the foundation skills level there are local or unique competencies. These are advanced skills that apply to a particular job type. A systems analyst, for instance, might need a fault diagnosis competency for local area networks.

The next level of competency is global, and would be present in all employees within a particular function or organization. Every worker in the controller organization, for instance, would be competent in financial analysis; every IT employee would be competent in technology architectures and systems analysis.

The highest level in the competency structure is universal competencies, which would apply to all employees within a company. Such competencies might be knowledge of the overall business a company is in, the products it sells, and the drivers of the industry. A course for all employees sought to provide general knowledge of the software industry and Microsoft's strategies.

Within each of the four foundation competencies there are two different types. Explicit competencies involved knowledge of and experience with specific tools or methods, such as Excel or SQL 7.0. Requirements definition competency, for example, is an implicit competence. Implicit competencies involve more abstract thinking and reasoning skills. At Microsoft, the implicit competencies are expected to remain quite stable over time, although with .Net, few are being added. Explicit competencies, of course, change frequently with rapid changes in fortunes of particular languages and tools. Within all four-competency types, there are 137 implicit competencies and 200 explicit ones.

Within each type of competency there are also four defined skill levels. A worker might have, or a job might require, any of the levels below:

• Basic

- Working

- Leadership

- Expert

Each skill level for each competency is described in three or four bullet points that make the level clear and measurable. The goal of the skill descriptions is to avoid ambiguity in rating jobs and employees.

The pilot for the SPUD project had gone well. Implementation was proceeding across geography and function, starting with the operations function, then the applications function, and all jobs in Europe. One issue to be determined was how the competency model might spread to product-oriented software developers within Microsoft. Many of the same competencies were obviously relevant in the product domain.

KM-Based Governance

Information and communication technologies (ICT) have been infiltrating all facets of human existence in the last few years, leading to changes in the way people interact with society and the way societies themselves evolve around individuals in their evolution process. All global societies are increasingly transforming into knowledge societies and their members into knowledge networkers, who are more informed of the events happening locally and globally. For instance, during the tragic terrorist attack on NY's World Trade Center, in September 2001, many high school students were gathering information over the Internet, AOL's Instant Messenger, and pushed news technology and reporting to the rest of their schools. I was stranded in London, UK, unable to fly to the US. But despite the breakdown in phone communications, I was able to contact my teen via e-mail and he was already well informed about what had happened only a few hours past. This while, many of these events had not even been made official by the government authorities.

Such actions are based on the strong foundation of knowledge, not only technological, but universal, objective, timely, and triangulated from various sources. People are becoming more aware of their rights and opportunities that lie ahead of them, and are developing capabilities to make informed choices in all areas that influence them, including the sphere of governance.

We live today in a wired (and wireless!), interconnected world, and members of these knowledge societies have increased freedom, flexibility, and opportunities to decide how they would like to be governed and by whom. The consequence of it is that it is not the leaders who govern people but it is the people who let the leaders govern them, and this premise is becoming increasingly true inside business organizations as well.

The use of information and communication technology (ICT) has been consistently widening in recent years and is leading to distributed knowledge and power structures across the globe. Such KM practices are having a major impact in the political scenes, by helping to reshape democracy and the way citizens interact with the government.

Pro-active knowledge societies are forcing governments to constantly improvise and revamp their information services, to bring in greater efficiency, accountability, and transparency in their functioning. An important tool in developing learning organizations is to explore innovative e-governance models based on the application of KM principles and information and communication technology (ICT).

Access to information plays a critical role in the setting up of KM-based governance and control mechanisms. Such a process can be founded on the extraction and accumulation of information, and using it to create hierarchical structures on which power gets unequally distributed. The skew in the distribution of the power is proportional to the critical information residing at each hierarchical level. Some facts pertinent to information and governance you should be aware of include, but are not limited to:

• Access to information and knowledge forms the basis of decision-making and concerted action.

• Circumscription of information and knowledge with a few levels opens up avenues for its manipulation for exploitative purposes.

• Judicious and well-informed decision making is dependent on the quality and timeliness of information.

Chapter twelve is a special chapter on KM and e-government.

DEVELOPING KNOWLEDGE SHARING PROFICIENCIES

For a learning organization to foster knowledge sharing it must become proficient in collaboration. To do that the organization must be able to shift from a culture where hoarding knowledge is power, to one where sharing knowledge is power. This is not an easy task, as individuals are the ones holding the knowledge, and most often they feel very insecure about sharing knowledge, becoming obsolete for the organization and losing value, which then generates the fear of being let go.

Therefore, the main challenge here for KM professionals is to get people to share what they know. Sharing is the basis of collaboration among people and any learning organization. Curiously, people across the organization often do not know what it means to share and use knowledge. CKOs and KM professionals must educate and empower the organization to understand such a collaboration concept, and get them going. Therefore, it becomes imperative that a dedicated team is created, with special skill sets, to act as knowledge brokers inside the organization.

The following strategies of collaboration offer different benefits to a learning organization. These models require special measures of organizational support, and the more models an organization adopts, the greater the chances of becoming a successful learning organization.

- Meeting and working the network of collaboration. This collaboration strategy usually commences with a face-to-face meeting, a strategy or brainstorm meeting, a business or social gathering, or even a telephone call or e-mail exchange. Two people meet, identify some synergies, identify value in each other, and then resolve to keep in touch. Although collaboration at this stage does not yet exist, it has a lot of potential. If the strategy is successful, over time these two people will trade stories and backgrounds, compare acquaintances, unearth each other's skills, interests, and areas of expertise. Furthermore, they might build trust and rapport, even though they may not even, at that stage, have any interest in helping one another. But they remain open to the possibilities that may arise to possibly working together on a project, or have a chance to share some valuable knowledge.

Such a process is far beyond the organization's control, as at this level, the process is still highly personal and often arises through serendipity (God set the times and the places!). This personal collaboration strategy requires very little technology beyond basic communications, is often unplanned, and little support beyond providing opportunities for exposure to others is necessary. Executive education courses, seminars, symposia, trade associations, service organizations, charities, on-line discussion groups, book signings – indeed, any forum where interesting people congregate – provide rich environments for creating relationships.

- User Groups and Task Forces: a need for collaboration (collaboration here is premeditated, as there was a need to focus on a very particular subject or object). Typically, this type of collaboration assumes the form of user groups, focus groups, task forces, and so on, because a group or individual lacks all the skills or resources necessary to accomplish the desired outcome. For instance, President Reagan appointed a panel to investigate the explosion of the space shuttle Challenger. One panelist, Dr. Richard Feynman, used a cup of ice water and a strip of rubber to demonstrate that the explosion occurred because a rubber O-ring had failed at low temperature. But Feynman only got the idea to consider temperature because Donald Kutyna, an Air Force general on the investigative panel with him, remarked to Feynman that while working on his car, he had wondered about the effects of temperature on rubber.

Just by asking questions you can promote collaboration. Bringing together communities of practice is also a more elaborate way to promote collaboration. This strategy builds on the serendipitous nature of the first (i.e. "I know a guru who can help us with that issue!"). But for active collaboration to start, or for such teams to form, people have to be able to find each other, and the life of these collaborating teams may extend beyond the current need, but it is more likely that they will evolve or dissolve as needs change.

An organization should have a consistent technological infrastructure, compatible messaging system, integrated hardware and software platforms with software version control, and a resolve to stay current with developments in technology. A typical technology package to support active collaboration should include voicemail and e-mail, access to LANs, MANs, and WANs as necessary, and keep an eye on personal area networks (PANs). It should also have an on-line subject matter expert registry, conferencing capabilities, and groupware. More sophisticated systems will add workflow enablement, language translators, knowledge-based systems, and intelligent agents.

Generation of ideas should be fostered in every learning organization. Translating great ideas into new contexts can save the organization time and money, while raising the average level of outcome quality and implementation. Of course, you may decide to modify previous inventions as they change environments, but that is OK. Velcro, for instance, has continually tailored its original product to include new resins with unique properties for specialized applications, inexpensive disposable closures for diapers, and heavy use closures like those on a blood pressure cuff.

The major requirement when transferring knowledge is to have a robust corporate memory, with a KM gathering and collaboration system for users to contribute or review ideas, experiences, and work solutions, as well as to access the contributions, searching broadly across disciplines. Web portals are particularly suited to supporting such contribution and retrieval, and for enabling unexpected connections and discoveries.

CHAPTER 5

Organizing Knowledge and Know-How: Developing Enterprise Systems

Learners, in a world of change, inherit the world, while learned remains beautifully equipped to deal with a world that does not exist.[1]

A lot has been discussed about the limitations of an adaptive learning organization and a generative one. We live in a world of rapid changes, economic and technological as well as cultural and political. In order to remain competitive organizations must be able to transform, both to adapt to the changed business environment as well as to proactively ready themselves for the next wave of changes.

Transformation, in turn, requires excellence in strategy, organization, and systems. When these three components are effectively considered, not only can you reduce the implementation risks associated with any transformation within an organization, but success can readily be achieved. After all, the goal of CKOs and knowledge managers is to make sure every individual in the organization is ready for transformations at any given time.

The ultimate goal of KM is to enable the development of collaborative enterprise systems that allow every individual inside the organization to become learners, as, to quote Hoffman, "learners, in a world of change, inherit the world, [while] learned remains beautifully equipped to deal with a world that does not exist."[2] CKOs can tremendously increase an organization's effectiveness through common knowledge practices. Knowledge is the key differentiator in today's business, and the one responsible for the entire business transformation-taking place. So, you either lead it or follow.

Capitalizing on knowledge is actually not as complex as managing it. When it comes to running a business successfully, the greatest CEOs rely not on complex mathematical formulae, but on common sense – necessary business acumen, as Ram Charan[3] calls it. I believe, as part of this business acumen, CKOs should help CEOs and the executive staff to also understand how to

---

1. W. Hoffman, *Essays on the Economics of Education*, Western Michigan University, 1993, p. 183.
2. Ibid.
3. R. Charan, *What the CEO Wants You to Know: How Your Company Really Works*, New York, Crown, 2001.

build enterprise systems, to deal with its peril, promises, and future. After all, information must be managed.

ORGANIZING KNOWLEDGE AND KNOW-HOW THROUGH BUSINESS THINKING PRACTICES

Organizing knowledge and know-how requires interdisciplinary and multidisciplinary skills. Having a great focused knowledge on a particular segment of the company or industry will not suffice; on the contrary, it will create barriers to the full understanding of business and common sense across the organization. That is why I keep emphasizing the role of CKOs in developing business thinking practices that not only the executive staff can tap into, but the whole organization. Any learning organization must understand the total business cycle every business abides by in order to be able to measure quantifiable business results, as depicted in Figure 5.1

Figure 5.1 – Understanding the main elements of a total business cycle is important in developing business thinking practices

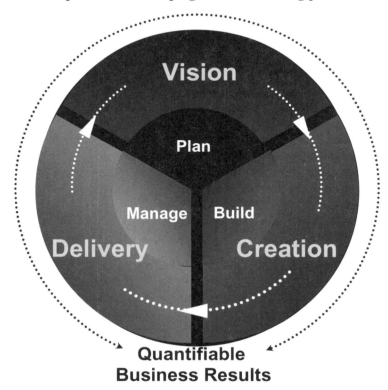

As we learn to view a learning organization as a whole, not broken into departments, functions, or tasks, it will begin to function in a more fluid way. Meetings will be less bureaucratic and more goal oriented. The organization will also be more transparent between distinct groups and the total business cycle phases.

At the Core of Every Business Thinking Practice

At the core of every business thinking practice you will find that the goal is to make a profit. To make money a business needs to generate cash, add that to return on assets (ROA) and to growth. Now, how do you get the whole organization to think that way? By being their best coach.

The difference between an organization and a football team is that the organization has to deal with very tangible milestones (well, the team must score!) and needs to produce quarterly reports. In both instances, to be successful, you still have to develop a knowledge strategy, one that organizes knowledge and know-how, and then enables it to be shared throughout the organization and among its business partners.

To seek competitive advantage you must be convinced that the organization's knowledge needs to be organized and managed more effectively, being readily available to be exploited in the marketplace. Knowledge and know-how, as well as other forms of intellectual capital, are your company's hidden assets. Although they are not visible in quarterly reports and annual report balance sheets, they underline the creation of value and future earnings potential. That is why knowledge-intensive companies such as Microsoft, Roche, and Glaxo Wellcome have market values at least ten times the value of their physical assets.

Thinking Practices Generating Knowledge Advantage

One of the main thinking practices in KM is to realize how organizations can use knowledge to secure a strategic advantage. Basically, it is by generating greater value through knowledge, thus acquiring know-how, in products, people, and processes. For instance:

- People's know-how: Anglian Water, one of the leading providers of water and wastewater services in the UK, has been investing in learning organization programs as one way of nurturing and applying underutilized talent within the company.

- Processes' know-how: Texas Instruments realized that it was typical to often find differences in performance levels of 3:1 or more among different groups performing the same process. They decided to invest in KM applied to its processes to close the knowledge gap, which saved the company the cost of one new semiconductor fabrication plant, or $1 billion dollars in investments, if you prefer.

- Products' know-how: Petrobras, the Brazilian petroleum company, one of the largest in the world, realized that intelligent products could promote premium prices and be more beneficial to users, so they invested in an intelligent oil drill that bends and weaves its way to extract more oil than before from the pockets of oil under oceanic ground formations.

Such examples of strategic advantage developed through knowledge management are only one way that investing in knowledge pays off. Another is through active management of intellectual property (IP), portfolio of patents and licenses, as well as organizing knowledge so you can exploit it internally by generating information and know-how.

Promoting Team Work as a Knowledge Transfer Tool

If we take the example of a cardiac surgery team, we find this is a team that must work together very closely. In an operating room, a patient is rendered functionally dead while a surgical team conducts the surgery. The amount of synchronized knowledge transfer, in real time, and teamwork that goes on is just incredible. Any mistakes can be disastrous.

The most interesting thing is that such teams are not that different from your executive staff or any other cross-functional team so crucial to business success. Learning organizations can learn a lot from such high-risk surgical teams, in particular with regard to executing existing processes efficiently, and, most importantly, to implementing new processes as quickly as possible.

In the process of becoming an effective learning organization you will have to adopt new technologies and very likely new business processes, which is a highly disruptive task. In addition you will have to focus on how your organization's teams learn and why some learn faster than others. To be successful, organizations must capitalize on leaders that actively manage their group's learning efforts. And when implementing new technologies and processes, make sure these innovations are directly targeted at learning, every individual in the team is highly motivated to learn, and upper management is fostering an environment of psychological safety through effective communication and innovation.

Of course, to convince traditional organizations that teams learn more efficiently if they are explicitly managed for learning poses a challenge in many areas of business. One of the main challenges is that the majority of team leaders are chosen not for their management skills, but for their technical expertise. Thus, to be successful, organizations must invest in team leaders that are adept at creating learning environments. Upper management must be able to look beyond technical competencies and work with leaders who can motivate and manage teams of disparate specialists.

Using teamwork as a knowledge transfer tool enables you to tap into not only the explicit knowledge of team members, but also the tacit knowledge.

The goal should be to adopt a new sense-and-respond business model that can help the organization anticipate, adapt, and respond to continually changing business needs. Team members should be able to identify the three main stages of learning and strive to close the circle of learning, as depicted in Figure 5.2. Stages of learning: by identifying, striving, and closing the learning stages, circle members of a learning organization can be better equipped to sense-and-respond to new business needs.

Figure 5.2 – Stages of learning: by identifying, striving, and closing the learning stages circle members of a learning organization can be better equipped to sense-and-respond to new business needs

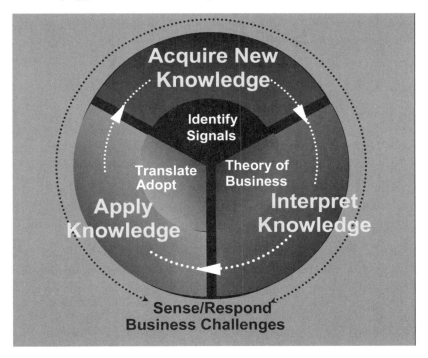

In order for teamwork to be effective, it must be able to generate and share new knowledge. As Figure 5.2 shows, there are three learning stages any individual or team must go through to successfully learn, deploy, and share newly acquired knowledge.

In the first stage, the acquisition of information, the raw materials of learning are gathered. It is very important for those in this stage to know what they want to know, from where, and for what purpose. Otherwise, not only will they end up with an information overflow, but they will also know a lot of irrelevant stuff. As discussed in chapter one, Sir Francis' premise that knowledge is power no longer holds true if knowledge is not followed by action, action that is successful and purposeful.

The second stage, the interpretation of information, requires the development of perspectives, positions, opinions, and elaborated understanding. At this level, materials collected in the first stage are analyzed and reviewed. Here, you must make sure that there is an understanding about what that information means, and the cause-and-effect of the relationships it will produce once applied.

The last stage, the application of information, is when organizations finally decide to engage in tasks, activities, and, very importantly, new behavior. It is here that analyses are translated into action. It is here that the organization must ask itself what new activities are appropriate or necessary, and what behaviors must be modified. David Garvin wrote extensively about the process of turning learning into action in his book *Learning in Action,*[4] which I strongly recommend if you really want to put your learning organization to work.

Adapting to Unpredictable Demands

Organizations will be able to adapt in a systematic way to the unpredictable demands of rapid and relentless changes if they are designed and managed as an adaptive system. However, even though adaptive strategies are very important in the face of change, the ultimate goal of any learning organization is to be able to predict the changes before they occur and position themselves proactively, instead of reactively. The questions knowledge managers and executive staff should be asking at all times are first, how can they integrate the organization as a whole to achieve its business purposes, and second, how can they cope with the rate of change inside and outside the organization, and still be able to create an organization's "central brain" that keeps the rate of change of the organization equal to or greater than the rate of environmental change.

Bill Gates, in his book *Business @ the Speed of Thought,*[5] alludes to the importance of an organization's digital nervous system. Enterprise systems can enormously help organizations to think rationally about developing this much-needed digital nervous system, as they present a new model of corporate computing. Although CKOs may not have the power to implement such systems, which legally comes from above, from the board, the key idea here is to tap continuously into the natural daily learning of every individual in the organization.

---

4. Cambridge, Harvard Business School Press, 2000.
5. New York, Warner Books, Penguin, 1999.

In *Unleashing the Power of Learning*,[6] Browne comments on BP Amoco as one of the most serious implementers of digital nervous systems, because of their focus on continuous learning, across the organization and hierarchically. Notice that enterprise system implementations must take into consideration both micro and macro-political levels. The micro-political level or internal world of the organization deals with the energies and blockages generated by the existing organization's capabilities. The macro-political level, or the world outside the organization, deals with the changes in the political, economic, social, technological, and physical environment trends, in an attempt to increase the organization's effectiveness.

Enterprise systems also allow companies to replace their existing information systems, which are often incompatible with one another, with a single, integrated system. The object is to streamline data flows throughout an organization. Software packages, such as those offered by SAP, IFS, and PeopleSoft, can dramatically improve an organization's efficiency and bottom line. But despite the many advantages these systems provide, you must be careful with the risks they bring, in particular for their ability to tie your hands!

The drawback with such systems is that they tend to impose their own logic on a company's strategy, culture, and organization, typically forcing them to change the way they do business. The great majority of the ERP implementations have not been successfully concluded, yet. Take the example of FoxMeyer Drug, which claims that its system helped drive the company into bankruptcy. I believe that while the ability to turn data into information to solve problems is key for the success of any learning organization, the personal capacity and attitude of individual problem solvers should not be neglected. Bob Garratt discusses this subject in depth in his book *The Twelve Organizational Capabilities*.[7]

Therefore, be it because you need to assess your organization's capabilities or the enterprise system, make sure to assess the pros and cons of implementing the system very carefully, as any new system introduced can produce unintended and highly disruptive results. Many companies incur huge losses more often than they should when entering uncharted waters, such as new alliances and partnerships, new markets, products, or technologies. Often, many of these failures could have been prevented if upper management had approached innovative ventures with the right plan and control tools. Both the board and executive staff should always be ready to fight the techno-babble of functional specialists, and collective critical debate makes it easier to take wise decisions. Discovery-driven planning is also a practical tool to be used at such times, as it acknowledges the difference between planning for a new venture and planning for a more conventional business. Often, the organization may have to evaluate

6. J. Browne, "Unleashing the Power of Learning" *Harvard Business Review*, September/October 1997, pp. 146–8.
7. London, HarperCollinsBusiness, 2000.

the bottom line and work its way up the income statement first, before determining the need for a new venture's profit potential.

To comply with such an action learning process, I believe Figure 5.2 must be modified to provide some "circuit breakers" that would flag learning situations that could lead to pernicious actions for the organization and business as a whole. My model is based on Garvin's model, as he discusses it in *Learning in Action*.[8] However, I borrow from Garratt's concept of an action learning cycle as well, as discussed in *The Learning Organization: Developing Democracy at Work*,[9] only to expand these models to provide validation at every step. Figure 5.3 depicts my view of an action learning cycle for the twenty-first century learning organization, where time is an asset, mistakes are almost unforgivable, and the inability of an organization to adapt to new environments is synonymous with slow death, as organizations must strive to obsolete themselves everyday before the market does it for them.

Figure 5.3 – The action learning cycle for the twenty-first century organizations

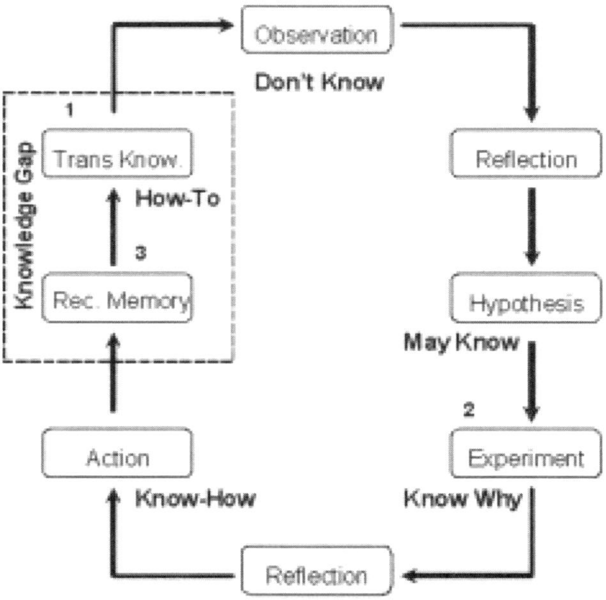

8. Cambridge, Harvard Business School Press, 2000.
9. London, HarperCollinsBusiness, 2000.

As Figure 5.3 shows, the design of an action learning process is based on simplicity. And simplicity should be viewed as understanding the whole. It should generate excitement, should be easy to view, and should be timeless. The role of the CKO is to help organizations to go through change. Once upper management, the executive staff, figures out a strategy, the CKO's job should be to help translate it to the remainder of the organization that has to do the work. Building trust and competence for this to become an organizational way of life is not done quickly, and tends to be complex. It is a good idea to conduct learning process action pilots, followed by public evaluation, so you can build trust. At the same time, through learning, you build values and behaviors that are rewarded, so that they become part of the organization culture.

From this reflective process depicted in Figure 5.3, learning organizations can break away from the action-fixated cycle of nonlearning, which so bedevils many organizations throughout the world. Typically, individuals tend to avoid a reflective approach to their work and end up jumping into inconsequential and fruitless actions because they already have a hard time just figuring out what they are supposed to do. The twenty-first century economy, with its reengineering and total quality management (TQM) strategies, with its leaning approach, has streamlined task work. However, knowledge work has become even more cluttered and confusing than ever before. Thus, making fast and correct choices, while the economy changes before our eyes every second, is now the toughest part of getting any work done.

In Figure 5.3, projects are integrated into an organization-wide, action-learning-based transformation process. This enables learning to be continuously available from each project, and the organization will see more easily the patterns arising from that learning. The main differentiator in the paradigm I propose is that:

1. In the first stage of the learning cycle, the observation stage, individuals should feel comfortable to be in a position of *not knowing*, so they can actually observe new learning patterns. Pride, ego, seniority aspects, and corporate hierarchy should all be left aside.

2. In the second stage, reflection, any new information acquired must pass through a filter of reflection. This is necessary not only to evaluate the relevance of such information, but also to determine how practical, how applicable such information is for the task at hand or future tasks. In the twenty-first century economy, there is no power or sense in becoming an *Encyclopedia Britannica*, as the most important aspect is to be able to turn knowledge into action, to be able to cope with the change of environments, and, ideally, anticipate changes to come.

3. In the third stage, hypothesis, individuals should be able to reach a point where they have acquired enough information to formulate a hypothesis. They should be able to have an idea of what they learned, of what they

now *may know*. When testing a hypothesis, keep it deductive, rather than inductive, disciplined, rather than playful, targeted, rather than open-ended. The goal here should be to prove, to prepare material for validation during the next stage, experimentation. As pointed out by Lawler,[10] managers tend to fail here because they believe they are failing to mesh with the realities of life in their organizations. This is very important so they can go to the experimental stage with a clear focus of what needs to be tested, what needs to be validated. The question is, what do they think they know? What do they think they are learning?

4. In the fourth stage, experimentation, the goal is to achieve a level where you know-why. Learning new information "just because" does not make sense. With all that has changed in how we work, we need to work smarter, instead of harder and faster. Thus, it is important for the learning process that individuals know what they need to learn, what they think they are learning, and why the information is what it is. They must experiment with the new information, they must try it out, so they can trust it, and value can be added to their skills set. Keep in mind that for experiments to be successful, the focus must shift from justification and commitment to skepticism and doubt. Knowledge here should be regarded as provisional, and conclusions as tentative. Otherwise, prevailing views will not be subjected to testing, and experimentation will exist only in name. Beware of ambiguity: the higher it is, the less objective the insights taken from the experiment. Notice in Figure 5.3 that experimentation is the second step (number 2) in bridging the knowledge gap in the organization, as individuals are only able to share knowledge they have experienced.

5. In the fifth stage, reflection, the first revolution of learning is concluded, as individuals come full circle with the learning process. At this stage they should be able to look back on what they did not know, reflect on what they needed to know, and how they came to formulate a hypothesis about what they may get to know, and the results of the experimentation they undertook. Reviews and reflections must be conducted immediately, while the experience and memory is still fresh and data can be validated. Thus, at this stage the new information should have been validated, and a plan of action using this new information should be at work. Otherwise, the process should start again, back to observation.

6. In the sixth stage, action, individuals must be able to turn learning into action, to turn know-why into know-how. In the previous stage (reflection), the primary problem is passivity, an inability or unwillingness to act on new interpretations. Many times individuals will resist new information rather than restart the learning process, back into observation, as they feel

---

10. E. Lawler, *Adaptive Experiments*, New York, Bantam Books, 1979.

that this information *cannot be right*. That is why experimentation is important, but still, people tend to disregard hard facts when such information means a behavioral change, and most people are risk averse. As Jack Welch, former CEO of General Electric, stated, "change has no constituency."[11] Therefore, to turn leaning into action, a certain level of self-awareness is essential. The results of the experimentation stage, the current practices, must be understood, so action can take place. Watch for individuals' behavior, as often they are unaware of their own behavior, and do not always act the way they think they do.

7. In the seventh stage, recording in the (corporate) memory, individuals should record their newly acquired know-how, or know-how they learned they already had, into the corporation's memory bank. This stage is also very important, and its absence or underutilization is partially responsible for what I call the knowledge gap, which is what the small number 3 next to the box signifies. Recording and sharing knowledge is vital for knowledge transfer and management; without it, there is no learning organization. Arnold Kransdorff's book, *Corporate Amnesia*,[12] describes many organizations failing to codify and distribute their learning due to a lack of structured corporate memory, the digital nervous system Gates talks about. Without such recording practices, organizations will learn nothing, nor will they forget anything. Such organizations have not learned that history repeats itself, first as tragedy, then as farce! This stage emphasizes the vital importance of KM implementations and enterprise systems.

8. The eighth stage, knowledge transfer, is the final stage in the learning cycle, but the most important in bridging the knowledge gap within organizations. It is actually the first step (small number 1 in Figure 5.3), when knowledge is finally institutionalized within the organization. Unfortunately, not many companies take the time to reflect on their experiences and develop lessons for the future. KM professionals and managers in general must help individuals and work teams carefully review the new information learned and distinguish effective from ineffective practice. In stage seven, they must record their findings in an accessible form and in stage eight, disseminate the results to the other individuals in the organization.

Finally, ask yourself what strategies your organization is adopting to maximize the returns on your knowledge asset. Try to make better use of the knowledge that already exists within your organization by utilizing the action learning

11. J. Welch, "Former CEO Jack Welch Shares his Leadership Methods" *Fortune Magazine*, 1993.
12. Boston, Butterworth-Heinemann, 1998.

cycle discussed above. In my experience, I have heard several KM professionals and group leaders lamenting *if only they knew what they knew*. It is common to find individuals in one department or group in the organization reinventing the wheel or failing to solve customer's problems just because the knowledge they need is elsewhere in the company but unknown or inaccessible to them. Hence, CKOs and KM professionals typically focus first on installing or improving an intranet.

Consider focusing on innovation as well, creating new knowledge and turning ideas into valuable products and services. This is sometimes referred to as knowledge innovation. Do not confuse it with R&D or creativity, however. There is plenty of creativity in organizations, you just need to make sure that you do not lose it and that you allow it to flow throughout the organization and find its way to where it can be used. To do that you will need to invest in better innovation, knowledge conversion and transfer, and, eventually, commercialization processes. This thrust of strategy is the most difficult, yet ultimately has the best potential for improved company performance. It is effective commercialization of ideas that has taken companies such as Netscape and Cisco to multi-million dollar corporations in just a few years.

Taking Advantage of Smart Agent Technology

Smart agent technology is poised to transform the enterprise and integrate information systems. I decided to include this section here because I believe smart agent technologies are inevitable, and KM professionals, in particular CKOs, should be aware of them and take advantage of the technology for data and knowledge integration and sharing. The question you should be asking yourself when considering such technology is, "How can you conceive, design, and build adaptive, enterprise-scale information systems?" I strongly recommend the adoption of smart agent technology as an enabler of such systems.

Although a CKO myself, I have had my tenure as CTO in my career, and have been closely involved with the development and implementation of such technologies.[13] Thus, I must tell you that agent technologies can be very powerful in promoting interoperability of data, but they are not an end unto themselves. Nonetheless, when combined with the maturing disciplines of object technology and business engineering, their synergy is embodied in an agent-oriented framework for open redirecting content exchange (FORCE).[14]

---

13. The author is the inventor and co-inventor of couple patent-pending agent technologies architecture designed to extract, normalize (in XML), transform and redirect (deliver) data across heterogeneous platforms and multiple wireless devices, along with a crew of scientists and developers at Virtual Access Networks during 1999/2001.
14. Patent-pending technology developed by the author and other members of Virtual Access Networks R&D team.

I have envisioned, can take data interoperability, XML analytics, knowledge sharing, and, consequently, KM to a new level in the development of enterprise systems.

Virtual Access Network's (VAN) approach to building an agent-based system (FORCE) can be characterized in terms of three distinct, but related, topics:

1. A full lifecycle solution development process that explicitly addresses domain modeling, data interoperability and mobility – the effort spent in domain and problem understanding is leveraged to guide and accelerate application development.

2. Architecture – applications follow a consistent architecture approach so they can interoperate with each other.

3. Ontology-based domain models – fully understanding the domain is essential to understanding the problems in the domain. The richness of domain models allows the VAN to develop a flexible and reusable technology for its customers.

An Overview of Full Lifecycle Solution

Agent-oriented lifecycle models should be iterative and incremental. In my view, agent orientation benefits data interoperability and analytics by providing an active modeling paradigm and better analysis models that enable the reuse of code. Figure 5.4 depicts an agent-oriented domain modeling and architectural frameworks used on FORCE that enable the integration of best practice software engineering lifecycles, leveraging the contributions of artificial intelligence (AI), Semantics Web, and object-oriented software engineering. The technology enables adopters to preserve considerable intellectual capital while taking the next step in development methods for truly intelligent and adaptive information systems. In the twenty-first century economy, companies will no longer accept radical new methods; they are not in this to advance computer science, but business at the speed of thought.

Figure 5.4 – Smart agent-oriented lifecycle

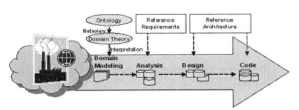

AN OVERVIEW OF ENTERPRISE SYSTEMS

Enterprise systems have increased in sophistication and complexity over the years. Through policies, standards, and procedures, centralized IT departments have improved the reliability, integrity, and consistency of applications under their control. The high visibility of system expenditures to these central resources could be straightforward and justified without too much effort.

Today, multiple platform systems are growing at a rapid pace, with personal computers on practically every desk throughout global companies making continued management and control very difficult. The complexity of modern IT environments has had adverse impacts on enterprise systems management, primarily due to the lack of comprehensive systems management tools. But also, it is sometimes difficult to justify very large software tool expenditures to the executive team when IT has often not delivered on their cost saving promises.

In developing an implementation strategy that includes selecting a product and vendor, it is important to spend time identifying quantifiable business results. Systems management efforts of this scope represent large implementation projects and certainly warrant the discipline and formal process called for in any large, complex undertaking. I would recommend the inclusion of at least the following quantifiable business results considerations:[15]

- cost to maintain and enhance the enterprise system

- cross-function usability

- development productivity

- dynamic requirement flexibility

- enterprise systems management (ESM), as the way in which IT management ensures reliability, availability, and performance of the IT infrastructure

- internal time to market

- workflow and integration gains.

The challenge of developing enterprise systems in this knowledge economy of the twenty-first century is to apply methodologies and tools that are truly enterprise-wide, and often across multiple sites and geographic borders. This is vital to KM managers because as the enterprise continues to evolve and become more complex, the effort of promoting collaboration and knowledge transfer will increase to the point that the expected return on investment from the new technologies may not be achieved.

---

15. Tivoli Manager for OS/390 includes many features that address many of such critical success factors in managing enterprise systems.

Modular Approach to Enterprise Systems

Most IT managers envision a simplified enterprise system model with multiple platforms viewed similarly. In simplistic terms all platforms run applications that are expected to behave in a desired and predictable fashion. A single view of the entire enterprise is often desired. In order for such a system to be effective in supporting KM initiatives, it must be able to:

- capture events throughout the enterprise

- produce warnings

- predict failures

- provide a management view that speeds problem determination

- increase problem avoidance

- enable KM process improvement.

Enterprise systems should be the result of an innovative combination of proactive integrated management tools, processes, and workflow automation and point technologies. Such a system should also include functions such as security, asset, application, problem, and network management tools.

Enterprise System Models

In order to progress beyond the traditional segmented enterprise system functions to a comprehensive KM-supportive solution, it is essential to have a model that acknowledges independent platforms and unified enterprise workflow. The model should encompass the traditional enterprise system's functions while demonstrating that the system actually consists of layers of functions to support KM activities, collaboration, and knowledge transfer.

DEVELOPING ENTERPRISE SYSTEMS

In today's information age, organizations are still struggling to turn distributed data into useful and powerful knowledge bases. At least in theory, enterprise KM systems attempt to address such issues by tracking resources, documents, and people skills, creating a company-wide, long-term memory that extends over its own employees. However, KM systems can be very complex to implement, and it is important to realize that there is no such thing as KM-in-a-box, as KM is not really a tool or set of tools; it is a discipline.

Enterprise systems are often developed and KM systems are typically part of them. However, when it comes to KM, one of the main challenges for such systems is not to manage a database containing millions of entries, but to bring all such information together contextually. That is one of the main roles for

KM. The challenge is to decide where to start. In addition, a number of preexisting technologies are being labeled as part of the KM umbrella, including document and content management, communities, portals, search engines, user profiling, and customer relationship management (CRM).

When implementing knowledge management, enterprise systems also must provide for the capturing of tacit knowledge, or the information that exists solely in peoples' minds. Enterprise systems must help KM implementations to facilitate the gathering of tacit knowledge by making it easier to capture, and sharing it in document form, or by directing requests to individuals that have that knowledge and collaborate with them.

For instance, some time ago, while I was still with ARC Advisory Group, the Ontario Store Fixtures Inc. in Toronto implemented a J.D. Edwards-based KM system. At that time, the retail store interiors manufacturer was using a multitude of reporting tools to compile data on sales order management, enterprise resource planning (ERP), and financials. It was a very complex setup because none of the company's systems were linked, forcing all basic data mining projects to require heavy in-house development. Hence the decision to implement a KM system based on J.D. Edwards' ERP system. After installing a new data warehouse and integrating its financial systems, the company added sales order, manufacturing, and document management software. Today, the company has a powerful end-to-end view of its workflow processes, and a goal to increase workflow efficiency by 95 percent through the combination of distributed data and tacit knowledge.

One of the company's first targets was to improve message management, as messages tended to sit in people's inboxes, and tasks did not get pushed through the system. The implementation of a KM system enabled the company to place gates at each end of the processes, so messages do not sit there for longer than a given period. One important aspect of enterprise systems and KM implementations is expressed by the managers of Ontario Store Fixtures, which consider their KM project a success. They attribute much of their success to choosing a system that complemented their existing platforms and back-end systems.

Even though it is difficult to measure the ROI on a KM implementation, adopters can gain significant advantage over their competitors just because information is readily available in many ways. If you are able to integrate the organization's information with supply chain and distribution channel partners, and provide customers with better information about what is going on with the status of their transactions, that should make your business much more competitive. And you do not have to implement all at once.

I believe the best way to measure KM ROI is by measuring your company's internal awareness and market responsiveness before and after an implementation. Do not expect an immediate ROI from KM implementation. It will take some time and effort before knowledge workers begin to embrace a philosophy that centralizes the data and knowledge that once solidified their corporate worth. Every organization deals with its own culture and baggage during a KM implementation, and it takes time. Make sure to approach the decision to adopt a KM mentality as you would any other strategic change.

Enterprise Systems and Data Warehouses

Building a data warehouse can be a very important step for any learning organization to capitalize on when implementing KM initiatives. However, projects like these take time and the last thing you want is to tackle them in a hurry.

Take for example the case of Jiffy Lube. The company relies heavily on repeat business, and to be effective, they must keep records of millions of vehicles, more than 35 million records, tracking all sorts of information, from how often a customer brings their car in for an oil change and other services, as well as what kind of service the customer will need in the near future and when. To top that, Jiffy Lube also makes sure to send its customers reminders and coupons 75 days after their last oil change. The company decided, in early 1998, to develop a data warehouse project to implement KM strategies focused on extending the use of its customers' database information to even better use. The use of data warehousing that provided historical business information enabled the company to group their customers into segments, and create special offers to meet their specific needs, or even encourage them to try other services, and then measure the effectiveness of the strategy.

It took Jiffy Lube more than six months of meetings, typically three times a week, to determine what their needs were and what it would take to complete the project. Any company developing enterprise systems, particularly those that focus on KM, collaboration, and knowledge transfer, will have to develop data warehouses of some sort. In the process, not only workflows and information sharing techniques need to be identified and planned for, but lots of technologies may have to be incorporated, and understood. But the most difficult part of developing such systems is that it is extremely time consuming to take any project from nothing to something and still fulfill the vision you have before you started.

Data warehousing and KM have enabled Jiffy Lube to profile their best customers out of about 55 million records and growing. The company is also using Web portals as a vehicle for sharing information with their service centers so they can custom design direct mailings to locals who match their best customers' profiles but have not yet visited them. Projects like this require careful planning. To make sure you do not widen the knowledge gap among the different groups within the organization, you have to be very clear about the parameters and know up front what questions you want the KM to answer. If you are not willing to do that, then gaps between existing infoislands inside the organization will continue to exist and the results of the project may not be what you want them to be. KM projects, in particular those aimed at bridging such knowledge gaps, take a lot of time and a lot of commitment to be successful.

Centralized Database Considerations

Centralized databases are still very much in use nowadays, but the dissemination and growth of personal computers in the late 1980s marked the beginning of an attack on host-terminal systems, and a major cultural change in how people used and retrieved information. Typically associated with mainframes, centralized databases were found on mainframe systems that had been tuned and polished for more than twenty years. Centralizing data storage seemed to be a very good idea, and there are many organizations that still think it is, be it because it offers a single point from which the corporate accessibility was conducted, or because of its high level of integrity, reliability, and security.

The problem, much emphasized by KM, is that once data has been disseminated to its users, there is no way to rein it back into a single, central system. Human activities and business processes abide, by nature, to a dispersed data regime. Thus, enterprise systems must take into consideration an architecture in which all these data stores are integrated with local procedures, with the capability of handling relations with a central control point to satisfy services requests such as compiling reports, satisfying queries, and complying with policies on indexing, security, recovery, and so on. This new paradigm of distributed technology enables information system groups to exercise their managerial responsibilities for enterprise data while allowing users to retain localized operations.

But interestingly enough, the advent of fast networks, server performance, and even improvements in mainframes continues to allow centralized models to snatch the momentum of development back from the desktops. Nonetheless, dispersed databases continue to gain momentum, much in consequence of several shifts in the technological background. As Internet applications keep on adding value to the traditional talking points of distributed databases, such as higher reliability and lower latency, compelling arguments for the use of centralized databases continue. By the same token, declines in processing costs are no longer driving technological change, and a major motivator to this concept is the somewhat familiar Gilder's Law, which advocates that the cost of bandwidth will continuously fall in even more dramatic curves, halving every nine months. Therefore, the cost advantage of distributing over centralized IT infrastructure doubles every year.

THE CORE OF ENTERPRISE SYSTEMS

This section is maybe the most technical, most IT-oriented of this book, as it discusses some of the most important technical aspects of enterprise systems.

I feel that the way enterprise systems are built directly affects the ability the organization has in bridging the knowledge gap that invariably exists. Thus, having an understanding of how such systems work can dramatically help KM professionals and IT groups to build or adapt such systems to promote the necessary collaboration and knowledge transfer throughout the organization.

But before we go any further, let me share with you two words of advice: Davenport and obsolesce. The first refers to Thomas Davenport and his book entitled *Mission Critical: Realizing the Promise of Enterprise Systems*,[16] which I strongly recommend for those seriously involved in developing enterprise systems for KM advantage, in particular for those wanting to take advantage of such systems as a platform for organizational information and Internet technology for gaining access to it. The second word, obsolesce, is a warning about this section, as well as any enterprise system you may develop or have developed. Make sure to always review the systems and technology being deployed as both Gilder's and Moore's Law's will make sure to keep you on your toes, otherwise, Murphy's will.

Enterprise Systems under the Hood

Enterprise systems must combine a very high level of functionality, which in turn carries an equally high level of complexity, and requires constant dependability and robustness. Some of the main technical capabilities affecting enterprise systems' effectiveness include:

- client/server architecture (with an eye on distributed systems!)
- common central database
- configuration
- modular construction
- open standards
- usability tests
- internationalization and localization.

Client/Server Architecture

Most of today's enterprise systems are client/server based. However, some vendors such as IFS and Datek are already offering Internet-based (I-net) applications, which are capable of running over the Internet, intranet, and extranet in a pervasive and decentralized fashion. The applications are allowing information to reach the right people at the right time so that they can make the best-informed decisions. These enterprise systems' applications are also

---

16. Cambridge, Harvard Business School Press, 2000.

providing a new vehicle for process control and monitoring, as well as client integration for enterprise resource planning (ERP) solutions, customer relationship management (eCRM), and support. In other words, in order to make them more maintainable and scaleable, these applications are being moved from the client to the server by some companies.

The strategy is benefiting organizations with heterogeneous environments, but latency can be a stopper. Industrial automation applications, for instance, generally cannot afford long communication delays. For example, for a web-based human machine interface (HMI) application, it takes too long to download a Java applet to the client before it starts up. Not surprisingly, Java has been disappearing from an increasing number of homepages and browsers. But whether it is a Java delay or bandwidth delay is not important. Mission critical applications typically require intensive user interface, and users simply are not willing to wait ten seconds for a form to animate. And the delays tend to be even longer on large intranets and on business-to-business extranets.

Nonetheless, increasingly more companies are deploying thin-clients architecture and enterprise systems are following suit. Mazda and Volkswagen have been adopting thin-clients as network stations instead of PCs, whereas the great majority of applications are stored on servers, and not on clients. Sysco, a $15 billion food-service marketer and distributor, has been installing several thousands of thin-clients in more than 60 distribution centers. Other companies such as AmeriServe Food Distribution, Allied Signal, British Aerospace, and Nike are following suit. Thin-clients are here to stay, and I believe the way corporate systems are built will have to change for thin-client solutions to be successful.

As applications are being re-architected from the monolithic mammoths they used to be, they are being split into multiple tiers. However, as depicted in Figure 5.5, this so-called "N-tier" usually breaks down into three tiers: the client, the business logic, and the data tier. Although the "N" indicates a system can have more than three computers involved, it does not necessarily mean that an N-tier solution could not be delivered all on one machine.

I believe the adoption of 3-tier applications to address enterprise systems, thin-client solutions is ideal, because this approach pushes processing to computers that have the power to do the work and makes maintenance and updates of applications much easier. The client tier reaps the benefits of the application and data tiers. Microsoft's Distributed InterNet Architecture (DNA) is a typical approach for N-tier solutions.

Most thin-clients use HyperText Markup Language (HTML) and Extensible Markup Language (XML) in a browser on the client, although Citrix offers its ICA (Independent Computing Architecture) technology to provide a thin-client interface with the server. For thinner Windows clients, Epicon's ALTiS service might be an alternative.

The middle-tier is where all application software is housed, as well as components such as Microsoft's Distributed Component Object Model

Figure 5.5 – Deploying N-tier applications

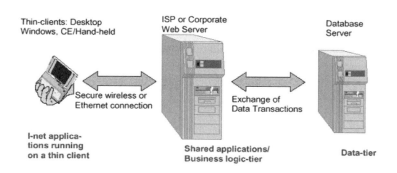

Thin-clients: Desktop
Windows, CE/Hand-held

ISP or Corporate
Web Server

Database
Server

Secure wireless or
Ethernet connection

Exchange of
Data Transactions

I-net applica-
tions running
on a thin client

Shared applications/
Business logic-tier

Data-tier

(COM/DCOM) or Enterprise JavaBeans (EJB) objects. Placing business objects in this tier on one or more computers also can provide substantial scalability for larger applications, especially for e-commerce.

Most database products available can handle the data-tiers. I recommend those that provide processing power through the use of stored procedures or triggers, and that allow the use of Java for customized projects.

I also believe that as thin-client deployment proliferates, Java will be leaving the client (or presentation layer), at least for a while. Thin-clients will have to be augmented to keep up with user demand. XML is already playing a major role in this augmentation. All rich-client technologies will have to move to mid-tier or server-side processing. As COM/DCOM becomes COM+ (or MTS), its application server will be fully integrated. Sun Microsystems' EJB model will continue to enhance and promote Servlets everywhere as a multi-platform alternative.

Common Central Database

Enterprise systems feature common central and non-proprietary databases, from which all application modules draw, manipulate, and update data. These databases are typically relational, but such a feature is not enough to cope with heterogeneous sources of information (infoislands) and to promote collaboration. Therefore, today's data-intensive applications and frameworks, such as enterprise resource planning (ERP), data mining, and enterprise application integration (EAI), require the integration of information stored not only in traditional database management systems, but also in file systems, indexed-sequential files, desktop databases, spreadsheets, project management tools, electronic mail, directory services, multimedia data stores, spatial data stores, and the list goes on.

To enable this level of integration, database suppliers and systems integrators (SI) usually rely on middleware and replication technologies. But as these applications grow, and mission-critical applications become more and more time sensitive, the need for real-time data will become critical. At the same time, hardware and system implementation costs to integrate and replicate data will climb as complexity and performance demands increase.

In the attempt to solve this problem, several database suppliers are pursuing a traditional database-centric approach, referred to as the universal database, as depicted in Figure 5.6. In this approach, suppliers extend the database engine and programming interface to support new data types, including text, spatial, video, and audio. But the supplier requires users to move all data needed by the application, which can be distributed in diverse sources across a corporation, into the supplier's database system.

Figure 5.6 – Universal database access architecture

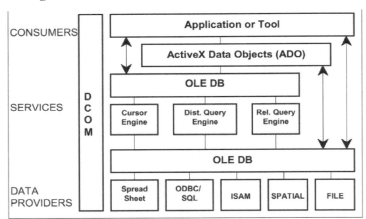

I believe this process can be expensive and inefficient. Universal Data Access (UDA) from Microsoft is an effective alternative approach to the universal database. UDA allows applications to efficiently access data where it resides without replication, transformation, or conversion. Open interfaces, such as COM/DCOM, allow connectivity among all data sources. Independent services provide for distributed queries, caching, update, data marshaling, distributed transactions, and content indexing among sources.

UDA provides high-performance access to a variety of information sources, including relational and non-relational databases, and an easy to use programming interface that is independent of tools and languages. This technology enables corporations to integrate diverse data sources, create easy-to-maintain solutions, and use their choice of best-of-breed tools, applications, and platform services.

While there are many benefits to using a universal database strategy, this approach may require expensive and time-consuming movement to and maintenance of corporate data in the DBMS. It may also require tools and applications to support it, as well as compromises in the selection of supporting products. Users' applications will need to either implicitly support this architecture, which is unlikely, or be customized to integrate with it, which could be expensive.

The UDA model does not exclude any data stores. This enables the two apparently competing strategies to actually synergize and cooperate. In fact, OLE DB suppliers for a number of new universal database products are currently developing UDA products.

UDA strategy allows enterprise systems to completely access data in its existing databases, universal database servers, desktop applications, mainframes, and so on. Organizations that combine UDA and universal database products will ultimately benefit from a broad choice of best-of-breed tools, applications, and DBMS products available from leading data access providers.

Microsoft has designed the UDA strategy to meet the needs of today's distributed, multi-platform organizations building client/server and Web-based data-driven solutions. As learning organizations continue to develop business solutions that leverage data from the desktop to the enterprise, and as data and access types proliferate, suppliers have an even greater challenge to develop customized business advantage solutions. By building performance and reliability features, making UDA a key part of the Windows DNA architecture, and by enlisting the support of a broad range of industry players, Microsoft is aggressively meeting customer needs.

In the process, Microsoft is also opening a wide array of opportunities for independent software vendors (ISVs) to use UDA as a tool to help organizations build on existing systems and data stores as they create new client/server and Web-enabled solutions. Therefore, I believe that Universal Data Access bridges the gap between existing systems and new technologies to create an evolutionary path for cost-conscious users when promoting collaboration and attempting to bridge the knowledge gap created by infoislands.

Configuration

Today's e-businesses must overcome the challenge of configuring enterprise systems for optimal performance. Reliability and flexibility are key to any enterprise system's success as a Web-based logistics service. Thus, enterprise systems' configuration must be versatile enough to allow translation capabilities that match all users' systems, as well as provide a solid integration platform to feed user's data into their application service. There are great technologies available on the market that enable the transformation of information from the organization's disparate systems into an XML-based front end.

Enterprise systems' configurations must be flexible, in particular when transforming data from different formats, point-to-point. So, whether an organization transmits data in EDI, XML, or a proprietary format, enterprise systems for the twenty-first century must be able to deliver the information to other networks in the appropriate XML format. In addition, these systems must be configured to also handle high transaction volume. Organizations should be able to have delivery of information integrated into their networks and have reliable and real-time access to their entire logistics operations, from contract management through execution.

There are several frameworks on the market on which you can build enterprise systems, mainly IBM's Network Computing Framework (NCF), Microsoft's Distributed InterNet Applications Architecture (DNA), and Sun's SunConnect. It is worth mentioning that Microsoft's .Net is being promoted as the next wave of enterprise computing over the Internet. Sun Microsystems is also betting on a new technology dubbed SunONE to counter .NET. But I chose not to cover these latest technologies here, as they are still in the early stages, and any more technical content would escape the objective of this chapter.

But a technology I would like to mention, and which would be compatible with either one of the new technologies being promoted by Microsoft (.Net) and Sun (SunONE), is a framework for agnostic server transcoding (FASTCloud), by iCloud. Although similar, these technologies are not equal. Therefore, understanding the enterprise system's integration requirements and the technology underlying these frameworks is very important when choosing and configuring them.

Especially for the financial environment, scalability is very important because it often includes support not only for horizontal systems, from supply chain to distribution channels, but also for vertical ones, including ERP and CRM systems. Frameworks also must be able to support enterprise systems' needs to scale across heterogeneous platforms and systems. In addition, manageability becomes critical when applied to the financial environment because services require tight integration and are often delivered by a multitude of suppliers.

When evaluating these frameworks, interoperability is the key issue. Both IBM's NCF and SunConnect solutions are based on open standards, primarily Enterprise JavaBeans (EJB) and CORBA, while Microsoft's DNA is based on Windows NT/2000 run-time environment as well as COM/DCOM. NCF runs on IBM platforms and relies on EJB as a port to the Internet, but its run-time environment is tightly integrated with IBM's platform, making interoperability with other platforms questionable. Unfortunately, NCF does not fully support Windows NT/2000, but IBM does plan to port it.

As for Microsoft, the company has market share in its favor. Microsoft's environment and application programming interfaces (APIs) are considered open, largely because they are widely adopted. Although Windows NT/2000 and COM are not easily ported to other platforms, they do support applications developed in any language. In addition, the solid COM/DCOM environment is the building block that will enable independent solution providers (ISVs) to develop complex applications very rapidly. Beware, however, of the integration between Windows NT/2000, Windows 9x, and Windows 3.1, which demands significant efforts, making the deployment of DNA in a multi-version Windows environment complex to maintain and administer.

Sun's framework is more customized for the financial industry than its contenders. Sun's goal is to persuade partners to develop their core components for SunConnect's framework, which allows for any core service to be supplied by any vendor, a feature no other framework has. Being completely platform independent, Sun's framework model also provides highly transactional applications using Java and CORBA, which enables a tight integration with other platforms and environments, including legacy systems.

Now, FASTCloud is a new, state-of-the-art technology developed by iCloud, totally based on open standards, namely XML and others such as SOAP, UDDI, ebXML, WSDL, and XHTML, which enables the creation of agents targeted at all kinds of online listings and databases, allowing them to be moved from one database facility to another, independent of its platform.

Today's heterogeneous business network environment requires framework solution not to be tied to any operating system platform, language, or even vendor. iCloud's framework is totally agnostic to operating systems platforms because its environment is fully Web-enabled. All it requires from a client is its ability to load and run a browser.

Financial institutions must take advantage of the pervasive state of the Internet and its ability to interconnect a multitude of platforms. Thus, the need for moving financial contents among several systems, within the same organization and across its boundaries becomes a desired feature. Nowadays, it is common for different financial organizations to exchange financial contents, either as partners or through a variety of alliances, as well as a result of a business merge.

To date, none of the frameworks discussed here are capable of fully and completely moving financial content across heterogeneous platforms. Java-based SunConnect does a great job crossing diverse business platforms, but it is not extensible enough to redirect contents dynamically from one platform to another. It works well with middlewares and established platforms, such as from a Windows NT/2000-based environment to a UNIX-based one, and so forth, but it has its limitations when more than one platform or content format (disparate databases, operating systems, wrappers, etc.) is involved.

iCloud's FASTCloud takes advantage of open technologies to format disparate contents and move it anywhere, across any operating system platform, over the Internet via HTTP protocol, and it is capable of safely traversing firewalls without the need to deal with customer's security policies. By taking advantage of its dynamic transcoding proxy technology, FASTCloud is capable of generating XML server pages (XSP) to intelligently and dynamically detect the format of the content a client requires, format it accordingly, and securely deliver it to the client. Contents are automatically compressed, encrypted, and delivered through a secure shell (SSH) tunnel to HTTP, WAP, PDF, or any required format.

With FASTCloud's smart agent application, financial institutions have a stable XML framework capable of gleaning data from any Web-centric environment, providing a powerful tool for any content extraction via a virtual agent for parsing of objects and records (VAPOR). FASTCloud agents can act as an Internet discovery tool, a content (or data) miner, and as an information integrator. FASTCloud's creation of RAIN enables smart agents to find out what sort of question they can ask a given XML domain. The use of XML allows them to dictate how entities like software agents can talk and exchange information, as well as redirect it.

Modular Construction

Enterprise systems should be developed as a collection of application modules. Object-oriented (OO) technologies address many of these needs. Their platform-independent and server-based architecture enables enterprise systems to be deployed across platforms that extend the reach to business partners, dedicated-use applications, and embedded operations alike. Thus, the techniques used to develop OO applications by many IT groups must address the needs of the new agile learning and knowledge intensive organization, with the focus on collaboration.

The use of non-OO application modules for knowledge-based organizations makes it difficult to maintain and especially to adapt to the ever-changing business model brought by the internet. Object-oriented technologies are, therefore, very important for this environment, since they allow for the reutilization of system components, reducing the development time for new applications, the total cost of ownership (TCO), and the maintenance of existing applications, as Figure 5.7 shows.

However, as knowledge-based organizations adopt OO technology for the development of modular enterprise systems, an important question arises: which object platform and component should be adopted? The impact of this decision will affect the enterprise system and the organization's future not only technically, but on its business decisions as well, since it will affect the base upon which all the new applications will be developed. Figure 5.8 provides a comparison table between the main OO technologies available, their applicability, and compatibility, as well as strengths and weaknesses.

In my former experience as CTO and enterprise application integration analyst, I have had the chance to evaluate the technologies in depth. The choice between COM/DCOM, or MTS for that matter, and Java/CORBA should not be up to IT groups alone to decide, since they tend to view it only from a

Figure 5.7 – Java promotes a reduction of TCO for enterprise systems through reusability of components

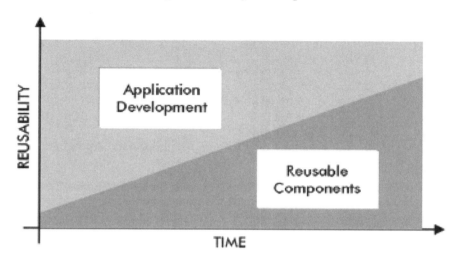

Figure 5.8 – The decision in adopting COM/DCOM/COM+ and Java/ CORBA for the development of modular enterprise systems is a very important one

COM/DCOM vs. JavaBeans/CORBA		
Aspect	COM/DCOM	JavaBeans/CORBA
Scalability	Limited. Middleware services are available only on desktops and midrange servers	Strong. Allows high volume of transactions and messaging.
Tools	Many options available	Only now are becoming available
Transport	TCP, NetBEUI, IPX/SPX	TCP
Languages	Much superior	Limited
Security	Still deficient (it may change with Windows 2000)	Stronger, if the OS platform is considered. Hard to use due to lack of standard among ISVs
Expertise	Easy to find since it's a natural evolution of the COM environment.	JavaBeans expertise is still scarce.

technical perspective. This choice must be a strategic one, and should include knowledge management professionals, to lay out the organization's needs, in particular for collaboration with other systems and users, as well as knowledge transfer. The decision will affect the choice of software, suppliers, training, and implementation costs. It will also affect transaction management, messaging queuing, and security.

I strongly recommend the creation of a taskforce composed of technical and decision-maker groups so that the organization's goals, both short and long-term, can be taken into consideration. The differences between both platforms must also be considered, which is not an easy task, since these technologies are constantly maturing.

Taking these considerations into account, IT groups should address the following issues when developing enterprise systems:

1. What is the volume of transactions expected for future applications? If high, JavaBeans/CORBA may be the standard of choice.

2. What is the groupware environment adopted? If standardized on Microsoft Exchange, COM/DCOM is the natural choice; if Notes, then CORBA is more adequate.

3. What is the infrastructure adopted? If the desktop, servers, and groupware are using MS products, then COM/DCOM is the OO platform of choice. If based on UNIX, Netscape, Oracle, and so on, then JavaBeans/CORBA is the choice.

4. What is the infrastructure adopted by key vendors, such as ERP? If they adopt CORBA, then the decision should be easy. If they have not decided yet, or do not have a strategy, you are better off changing vendors!

Open Standards

If you have had the opportunity to read Clayton Christensen's book, *The Innovator's Dilemma,*[17] and his discussion on disruptive technologies that encourage start-up companies to replace large, established firms (and technologies), the open standards phenomenon comes as no surprise. After all, open standards can very well crack any established technology by replacing the existing network of products with a new and larger one, one that promotes interoperability of data and processes. In this context, a larger network will consume a smaller network operating in the same space, because the value of the network increases exponentially with the size of the network. But open standard systems do not (initially) operate in the same space; they start by finding a new market with wants and needs that the old technology cannot

---

17. New York, HarperBusiness, 2000.

meet. I believe suppliers must understand the open standard trend, and strategically position themselves to take advantage of emerging enterprise systems based on it; otherwise, the risks of being sidelined by the market can be dangerous.

Open standards are in their essence a disruptive technology, and, as such, can initially compete directly against the existing proprietary and de facto standards for the original uses, even without taking the network effects into consideration. For instance, Microsoft is being challenged by a disruptive technology, the Open Source development model. Instead of relying on a team of highly trained professionals, the Open Source model relies on a loose association of hobbyists organized through the Internet as a kind of fan club. Often, this software development model tends to beat the old way of writing software, as the synergy created by a much larger development team motivated not by tangible rewards, but a sense of accomplishment and virtual community, is stronger. While traditional software development is motivated by the sale value of that software, Open Source development is motivated by the software's use value.

But an open standard, as an industry blueprint meant to ensure that competing products work together, may turn out to be a myth, and the example of it is the eternal standoff between America Online and Microsoft over instant messaging. While open standards still play an important role in disciplining enterprise systems, and in particular Internet software development, public discussion of standards has largely evolved into a corporate tool, where a firm can maneuver itself on either side of an issue depending on its position in a particular market, as in the case of Microsoft or Sun technologies adoption.

Therefore, when considering open standards for the development of enterprise systems, as a rule of thumb, always be aware that if a vendor, such as Microsoft, or even Sun, is a leader in its field, an open standard is not in their best interest because it could allow others to get a piece of the business. If a vendor is not a leader, then they will want to support it, as an attempt to level the field.

In my view, standards, in general, are useful to marketing and development efforts. If you look at it historically, an element of standards has always been used by underdogs in markets. But again, that is only one of the many reasons people get involved in standards efforts. Interoperability is so important, and companies cannot do it alone. If you recall the old days of Netscape, you will remember that the company implemented a number of features that did not hew to the HTML standard. A lot of it had to do with Microsoft's view of what Netscape was proposing, which was very negative. Netscape strategy with regards to open standard only slowed the company down and allowed Microsoft time to catch up.

Usability

The goal of usability tests when developing enterprise systems, in particular KM implementations, where it becomes vital that all knowledge workers adopt the system, is to achieve an optimal user experience for a given user type. Discovering this optimal experience, however, is often an elusive and complex process. Invariably, it involves users' interviews, observation and test of users while they complete standard tasks, application of heuristic analyses to product designs, write-up of users' scenarios, execution of ethnographic research, and creation of user flow diagrams that outline the ideal experience for the given user set. After all is said and done, however, you may often find yourself re-testing the enterprise system and its modular applications outside the methodological vacuum.

Rules and heuristics for usability evaluations can be effective measures for a product's usability. However, they do not take into consideration the idiosyncrasies of divergent user types, and applying strict heuristics to design sometimes breeds a new kind of user dismay: boredom. Some users like to be challenged. In fact, some need to be challenged in order to walk away with a sense of accomplishment. Just imagine if every single store at the mall had the same layout, the same sales associates, and the same products. Sounds extreme, but if we were to get our heuristic hands on every site and product out there, we would no doubt end up boring users into total apathy.

Usability testing of enterprise systems is important because you do not want surfers, browsers, and chatters on your KM portal, for example. What you need is people who are willing to work and to show you, and management, a positive bottom line. While this argument may sound a little harsh and seemingly contrary to the practice of developing enterprise systems usable to nearly everyone in the organization, the point is that sometimes only experienced, qualified users are desired in order to optimize business practices and customer service structures.

But in practice, neither approach is good or defined. While opening the doors of a KM portal to just any user via tested interface paradigms can bore high-end users and complicate the qualification process, creating an intimidating front door can repel those users who might be looking for a rewarding experience. That is why I typically recommend that with sufficient user research, a sense of *flow* can be achieved that challenges users sufficiently without boring them with the same old heuristically sensible approach. You do not want to develop an enterprise system usable for just any user. Rather, you want to make it usable for the right user.

Internationalization and Localization

The global nature of enterprise systems is also a very important aspect to be considered. The global economy and the Internet demand a global usability software development approach, one that can be developed independently of the countries or languages of its users, and then localized for multiple countries or regions.

One of the best tools available on the market is Sun Microsystems Java Development Kit (JDK) version 1.1, which provides a rich set of APIs for developing global applications. These internationalization APIs are based on the Unicode 2.0 character encoding, and include the ability to adapt text, numbers, dates, currency, and user-defined objects to any country's conventions.

Therefore, enterprise systems should be developed with internationalization in mind so they can be used by knowledge workers across the globe. An internationalized enterprise system should have the following characteristics:

- With the addition of localized data, the same executable can run worldwide.

- Textual elements, such as status messages and the GUI component labels, are not hardcoded in the program. Instead they are stored outside the source code and retrieved dynamically.

- Support for new languages does not require recompilation.

- Culturally dependent data, such as dates and currencies, appear in formats that conform to the end user's region and language.

- It can be localized quickly.

Localization is the process of adapting software for a specific region or language by adding locale-specific components and translating text. The term localization is often abbreviated as l10n, because there are 10 letters between the "l" and the "n." Usually, the most time-consuming portion of the localization phase is the translation of text. Other types of data, such as sounds and images, may require localization if they are culturally sensitive. Localizers also verify that the formatting of dates, numbers, and currencies conforms to local requirements.

The great majority of enterprise systems are not internationalized when first written. Many times, these systems may have started as prototypes, or perhaps they were not intended for international access or use. Thus, when internationalizing your organization's enterprise systems, focus on text messages, as they are the most obvious form of data that varies with culture. However, other types of data may vary with region or language. The following list contains examples of culturally dependent data:

- Colors
- Currencies
- Dates
- Graphics
- Honorifics and personal titles
- Icons

- Labels on GUI components

- Measurements

- Messages

- Numbers

- Online help

- Page layouts

- Phone numbers

- Postal addresses

- Sounds

- Times

The ultimate goal of enterprise systems and IT efforts in this knowledge economy is to support KM, collaboration, and the transfer of knowledge and best practices across the learning organization. The following case study exemplifies how important it is for a company to be able to transfer best practices, and their impact on the bottom line.

CASE STUDY: CHEVRON MAPS KEY PROCESSES AND TRANSFERS BEST PRACTICES[18]

By Verna Allee
    Companies that share and seek out best practices demonstrate visible dedication to the renewal of organizational knowledge. Chevron Corp., a leading proponent of this form of knowledge management, has already realized dramatic cost savings and important performance improvements through its "best practices transfer" initiatives. Chevron Chairman and CEO Ken Derr considers knowledge sharing of this sort "the single most important" employee activity at the $36 billion company. Chevron, which is based in San Francisco, has become a leading force in the emerging area of knowledge management by: strategically valuing knowledge; creatively using supporting technologies; specifically addressing and supporting knowledge creation, sharing and learning; and developing maps and frameworks that orient people to knowledge and information sources across the corporation.

---

18. I thank Verna Allee for allowing the use of this case study. For additional information on KM and her book *The Knowledge Evolution*, Butterworth-Heinemann, 1997, check her website at http://www.vernaallee.com.

Company executives expect such efforts to help it reach its stated aim of 10 percent annual earnings growth — a target that won't be easy to hit considering that the worldwide market for oil and gas is expected to grow at an annual rate of just 2–3 percent for the next 15–20 years. Chevron is relying on strong growth in the developing world and production-related innovations such as horizontal drilling and three-dimensional, seismic exploration in order to meet its objectives. New markets and new technologies, however, will not be enough.

If Chevron truly intends to meet its objectives, it must learn to effectively leverage and capitalize on knowledge on all fronts. Fortunately, Derr is a vocal advocate of knowledge management (though the language used by him and others at Chevron usually revolves around the more conventional term, Best Practices Transfer). The company's commitment to learning and knowledge is central to "The Chevron Way," a set of strategic statements that serve as a framework for company initiatives. One key element of the document is a commitment to learn "faster and better than competitors through benchmarking, sharing and implementing best practices, learning from experience, and continual individual learning and personal growth."

Chevron relies on benchmarking and Total Quality Management (TQM) to engage in extensive internal knowledge sharing. The tools and processes of TQM have proved a powerful vehicle for making tacit knowledge explicit. Process improvement techniques require in-depth, knowledge sharing in work groups and deliberate documentation of best practices and other critical corporate knowledge. Such problem-solving tools also provide a common language for creating and exchanging knowledge. Technology is also playing a key role in Chevron's knowledge management initiatives.

An important cornerstone for knowledge sharing is an innovative internal best practices database (which encourages people to contribute under the category "good practice" – so as not to stifle important insights – as well as "local best practice" and "industry best practice"). The company's Lotus Notes-based system allows people to pose questions to others throughout the company. They can also post learnings and insights using key words and categories.

Furthermore, Chevron encourages interest in knowledge sharing by tracking and measuring the impact of best practices. The company examines the impact on corporate performance in terms of dollars saved, customer satisfaction, public favorability, and reduced cycle time. Harder to determine but also addressed are the degree of integration of best practices, the number of improved processes and usage on the database.

Other knowledge sharing technologies include the Intranet, groupware such as Collabra Share, and e-mail. And while many of the company's technical professionals will continue to rely heavily on Lotus Notes, the corporate Intranet is expected to become the most important platform for communication and collaboration in the future. The Intranet incorporates such features as corporate and industry news, human resources information, resources (such as the best practices database and online training courses), financial information, and links to the home pages of many Chevron businesses.

Although employees are certainly encouraged to make use of networking technologies, yet another way of encouraging knowledge sharing is through informal networks that are the nucleus of "communities of practice." These groups are provided minimal funding for communication and occasional get-togethers.

On a more formal basis, the company sponsors regular internal conferences for best practice exchange. Networks and best practices groups may form either around technologies or around functional specialties. Some networks address future trends or focus on emerging developments in science and technology. Chevron was one of the first companies to experiment with knowledge mapping through the development of its "Best Practices Resource Map" – a powerful tool that serves as a kind of corporate "yellow pages." Roughly following the focus areas of the Malcolm Baldrige assessment, the map identifies (through color coding) knowledge-based resources, teams and networks within the company. The map not only identifies key networks of people (under such categories as "leadership," "strategic planning," "information and analysis," "human resource development," "process management," and "customer focus and satisfaction") but also helps users find more traditional forms of knowledge such as library services.

Roughly 5,000 copies of the original paper-based map were distributed. More recently, under the continuing leadership of corporate quality consultant Greta Lydecker, the resource map has been updated and adapted for the corporate intranet (dubbed "go.chevron.com") with hot links to individual e-mail addresses for easy and instant contact. This approach encourages strong demand-pull since it is interactive and real-time. Cost effectiveness is high since linkages can be built quickly and easily for enriched connectivity. "If you make it easy for people to network, they will," Lydecker says.

One key aspect of these efforts is their power to bring together a relatively dispersed and decentralized company. While the delegation of authority can lead to faster decision-making and greater customer-focus, it can also make it "harder for people to share knowledge," noted Derr in a speech on knowledge management. All companies, he added, "should be alert to conflicts between company structure and the imperative of sharing knowledge."

Strong Results

The implementation of best practices sharing initiatives has met with excellent results in multiple areas. For instance, the company has adopted a best practices approach to managing its capital projects, which is a task accounting for some $4 billion per year. After participating in benchmarking initiatives that enabled it to identify performance gaps, the company developed a new approach (known as the "Chevron Project Development and Execution Process") that has led to significant improvements. While Chevron admits that half its competitors used to manage capital projects more effectively than it did, it now claims to be one of the top performers. It claims to have saved $816 million in "downstream" capital projects since 1992.

Greg Hanggi, an internal consultant for Chevron Refining, points out that efforts to transfer best practices have helped his organization overcome political and geographic barriers that once stood in the way of widespread productivity gains. It's an initiative that has been embraced by the refining area for about five years, producing both qualitative and quantitative benefits. Among other things, it has helped the refining teams develop new technologies and processes that cut the costs of sulfuric acid usage, which annually cost the company $50 million in years past, by $10 million.

There are several teams in the refining function that are now facilitated by a so-called "master," a full-time participant hired by Chevron's Products business (which oversees the refining process) to ensure that tacit knowledge is made explicit and good ideas are shared. This individual is the driver and champion of best practices transfer — a knowledge manager that is considered "the first point of contact" for people seeking knowledge and expertise. Lessons learned? You can't "push" best practices successfully. You have to support and nurture communities of specialists so that they form what Chevron calls "self-discovering teams." Whereas companies have traditionally focused on "economies of scale," Hanggi points to the "economies of knowledge" that have been achieved by bringing together technical specialists throughout the organization. Such efforts, he says, have "helped us move toward the development of a high performance organization where people actively share information and knowledge." But there is more evidence of tangible payoff. Chevron USA Production reports savings of $30 million in 1996 on three best practices projects that focused on critical processes. Chevron also attributes much of its gains in energy-use management to knowledge sharing.

The company has saved more than $650 million in energy efficiency since 1993 – thanks largely to the efforts of a network of people that evaluates company-wide energy costs. Moreover, best practice initiatives have indirectly helped the company realize a $1.4 billion reduction in annual operating expenses in the last five years.

Finally, one must consider the way workgroups have begun to think strategically about knowledge. For example, the information management services group, which provides library and reference services for the company, developed a knowledge strategy to help it move from being a cost center to a profit center. It is an initiative that I [Verna Allee] personally participated in as a consultant. The unit faced a number of different challenges. Chevron employees were beginning to directly access corporate databases and other information providers.

The information service group, which was being bypassed, faced competitive pressures for perhaps the first time. The group also was challenged to understand and support increasingly sophisticated and complex knowledge requests. In response to these challenges, the group began to carve out a new direction – expanding its traditional library and information services to include value-added products and services that support knowledge building. As one team member put it, "We have been acting as data order takers, but what our customers need are knowledge navigators. We need to focus on the added value we can bring by doing more sophisticated knowledge integration and analysis." A key action step in this new direction was developing, publishing and distributing a service value "portfolio" featuring services supporting knowledge creation at various levels. I [Verna Allee] worked with team leader Mary Ann Whitney and the rest of the group to create a guide for building knowledge products. Our efforts revolved around the customization of knowledge. Understanding subtle differences in knowledge requests allowed the team to refine its services and provide higher value. It now offers packaged analysis, for instance, rather than mere information. Four of the group's eight strategic goals grew directly out of this new way of thinking about its role in organizational knowledge creation and sharing.

In addition, the group began to identify its own knowledge and performance gaps. It found room for improvement in its documentation of core service work processes, contracting and consulting skills, and its level of expertise in complex analysis. As the group began to understand the different levels of knowledge work required for each product, it improved its cost estimates and gained more consistency in its deliverables.

As a result of the group's efforts, employee satisfaction with its services has measurably increased, it is expanding internal and external partnerships to add value, it is achieving recognition for its vital role in knowledge creation and it is developing new individual and team competencies for the future.

Chevron is an example of a company that provides what can be called a good "practice field" for knowledge. The structures, technologies and processes being implemented at Chevron allow a wide range of knowledge "experiments" to take place. All of these efforts are supported by a culture of knowledge sharing. Through a continual process of experimentation and reflection, Chevron is generating the knowledge it needs for a competitive and profitable future.

As Derr sees it, knowledge management "is something all companies will have to master if they expect to compete in the global economy. Those who can learn quickly and then leverage and use that knowledge within the company will have a big advantage over those who can't."

Note that this Chevron case study was reported from the early stages of their initiative. Based on their early success, Chevron has continued to evolve their knowledge sharing practices. Jeff Stemke has continued their efforts and has led Chevron to over $1 billion dollars in business results by supporting dozens of practice networks focused on a wide variety of strategic and operational issues.

CHAPTER 6

Fulfilling the Vision: From Know-How to How-to

As organizations change ownership and structure at alarming speed, human relationships and informal networks often fail to keep pace.[1]

As companies transform themselves into learning organizations, senior management, in particular those executives responsible for facilitating knowledge transfer and organization learning, must be able to close the circle of knowledge by bridging the gap between know-how about the task at hand and how-to successfully execute and implement such a task. KM and organizational learning are blending together, complementing each other simultaneously, since organizational learning is a by-product of a properly implemented KM program. In turn, knowledge sharing becomes a key means of enhancing enterprise-wide learning.

To be competitive in the twenty-first century knowledge economy, companies must be able to effectively measure and leverage their information or knowledge assets and then turn them into action. The old paradigm of the 1990s, where IT investments were tied to traditional financial indicators and reengineering projects failed due to a lack of focus on information management, has contributed to a huge waste of knowledge capital. As Strassmann points out, companies should be focusing on identifying and increasing the level of what he calls Information Productivity, which he considers a key index of a company's strength or weakness. According to Strassmann, senior management should be measuring the value added by information.

(Net Profit − (Financial Capital Assets **X** Interest Rate for Borrowing)) **/** Cost of Information

Management or Cost of Sales, General & Administrative **+** Cost of R&D

Unfortunately, as confirmed by Strassmann, more companies are destroying knowledge assets than actively generating them. The problem is that our narrow-minded dependence on traditional accounting principles has failed to account for knowledge in any meaningful way, becoming one of the key reasons for

---

1. C. Collison, Knowledge Architect at BP Amoco, "BP Amoco's Knowledge Repository – Connecting the New Organization" *Knowledge Management Review*, March/April 1999.

the corporate world's continuing troubles. By contrast, companies such as Microsoft, Abbott Laboratories, and Coca-Cola have long ago grasped the vital importance of valuing and managing knowledge, and therefore have taken their industries by storm.

INVESTING IN KNOWLEDGE CAPITAL[TM2] PAYS OFF

I contend that the inability of many US and international companies to turn their know-how into effective action items is responsible for pushing information productivity to a negative level. Quoting Strassmann again, information is being treated as an instantly perishable commodity. Unfortunately, organizations are failing to recognize and measure the contributions of people to the generation of information and knowledge. None of these contributions to creating greater economic value are being recognized.

Furthermore, if you take a look at the annual costs of information, you will realize that it has long ago surpassed the costs of equity capital, except for some organizations, such as in mining, steel, transportation, and real estate. Nonetheless, it is through effective information management practices that the users of information are able to create all business value.

One of the main challenges in the process of capitalizing knowledge is finding out best practices for measuring and valuing knowledge assets. Actually this is an old challenge that has been around for more than twenty years. The literature on the subject is vast, as is the number of attempts at finding best practices. Back in 1991, Tom Stewart[3] made intellectual capital the attribute of an organization. But it is Leif Edvinsson, Skandia, and Pat Sullivan who define intellectual capital in a more pragmatic way, as knowledge that can be converted into value.[4]

Unless professionals can transform know-how into how-to, theory into practice, tacit knowledge into explicit, they will not only fail in the transference of knowledge, but also widen the knowledge gap within the organization. Again I point to Strassmann's excellent evaluation of the problem: that organizations try to work the problem of knowledge asset valuation from the bottom up; they point to software, patents, and trained people, and then try to estimate the value to come up with a total knowledge capital. Unfortunately, that is not what value is all about. Value is what the customers' demand values. It is a top-down issue, not bottom-up.

---

2. The term "Knowledge Capital" is trademarked by Paul Strassmann, and it is used in this book with his authorization.
3. B. Power, *How Intellectual Capital Is Becoming America's Most Valuable Asset*, Holland, CIBIT, 1991.
4. L. Edvinsson, Skandia, and P. Sullivan, "The Economies of Knowledge-Sharing Production and Organization Cost Considerations" *European Management Journal*, Vol. 14, 1996.

Very few organizations today are willing to put on the annual report a verifiable number that is recognized as knowledge capital. Senior management is still focusing on the conventional, deadly stuff – the old, industrial-age accounting. If there is any change in this attitude, management tend to add all kinds of fancy prose either in the reports sent to shareholders or in speeches. In this case, it becomes typical to hear statements such as "Our people are the most valuable asset we have." However, when their statistics are reported, return on equity (ROE), return on investment (ROI), or return on assets (ROA) are plain to see. The knowledge gap in the organization becomes very visible here, as what is said and what is done do not correlate.

This very same senior management is always open to any new ideas that can contribute to the increase in value of their companies. They have a keen interest in increasing stock prices, and the stock market clearly recognizes knowledge capital. This is true especially in the US where stock market valuations of equity are over six times the financial book assets. Only in the US are stockholders willing to pay more than six times book value for their stocks. The reason for that is often the amount of knowledge capital the organization has, which is added to the financial equity value.

If you are finding it hard to accept this assertion, just try to take any public traded company's knowledge capital valuation (KCV) according to Strassmann (as discussed earlier in this chapter), and then add it to the shareholders' book equity. You will find that it closely tracks the stock market. Not convinced yet? Do you remember when Wall Street paid almost 3,000 times earnings for Netscape? Surely, the dotcom era is over, but there are still many companies holding extraordinary valuations, and Microsoft, AOL Time Warner, Nokia, Cisco, Oracle, Siebel, and many other companies are examples of it. The bottom line is: people have been paying, and are willing to pay for knowledge capital, so why don't organizations really take advantage of it?

HAVING A MINDSET FOR KNOWLEDGE CAPITAL

You probably have heard it before, but in business, do you know what the definition of insanity is? It is to repeat the same business strategy over and over again and expect different results! To illustrate the motto in this context, take for example an event that I personally went through as a CKO of a start-up technology company a couple years ago: while teaming up with Gerry Lynch, the CEO at that time, and meeting with venture capitalists (VCs) trying to close a round B financing, I used to emphasize in every meeting the value and importance of our company's intellectual property (IP) portfolio.

Early on, when I joined the company only a few months after its inception and prior to the close of its round A financing, one of my first projects was to devise an IP strategy that not only took into consideration our current and unique technology, but also the need for raising market and technology barriers for new entrants. I worked so earnestly on this project that by the time we were raising our second round, almost one year later, we had already filed five patents and broken up our provisional one into multiple ones, in a way they all intertwined with each other, making it very complex (and expensive!) for any of them to be challenged in court.

To my surprise, hardly any of the VCs wanted to hear about it. And the patents applications were not our only intellectual capital (IC) asset. We had professionals sitting on important standards, committees, and consortiums that were very active in defining and building tomorrow's technologies, and consequently influencing the marketplace, including the W3C, OASIS/UN's ebXML, UDDI, and others. But IP (or IC) was not of value to these VCs, except for Lee Barberie of Stata Ventures. Stata Ventures had the fortitude of Ray Stata and his foresight about the value of IC in any organization, which began with his tenure as CEO at Analog Devices.

The truth of the matter is, since many of the financiers we talked to were from the old school of thought, very few were able to see any value in IC. Only the tangible assets got disproportionate attention, while the intangible ones sort of got sloughed away. Stata Ventures and another Boston firm were the only ones interested in our IC and IP. However, I believe there is an increasing recognition today that knowledge/intellectual capital is of greater significance to the success of a modern organization than physical capital.

The ratios of knowledge capital to book value and of market value to comprehensive value allow you to assess a corporate value (book value + knowledge capital = corporate value). Adding book value to knowledge capital produces a comprehensive picture of corporate assets. The market-to-comprehensive-value ratio measures market valuation's relationship to the aggregate worth of tangible and intangible assets with an eye to growth prospects. Comprehensive value is very useful, as it has the effect of making the balance sheet relevant in a period of sky-high stock valuations.

Do you want an example? Just consider the fact that market-to-book ratios of US companies in 2000/01 were roughly 2 to 1, which is double of the average between 1945 and 1990,[5] even though roughly 40 per cent of market value of the median US public corporation was missing from the balance sheet in 1996. In the relation of knowledge capital to book value, Dell Computer Corp. shows a very high ratio compared to the competition, a 37 to 1 ratio. Avon Products Inc. is another example, right behind Dell, chalking up a knowledge-capital-to-book-value ratio of 31 to 1.

Almost invariably, these ratios have the ability to predict superior prospects. Back in 1999, for example, Warner-Lambert Co. posted the highest ratio of

---

5. *The 21st Century Corporation: The New Leadership Q&A* with McKinsey's Lowell Bryan "Managers are Becoming Nodes" during a series of interviews for *BusinessWeek On-Line* (http://www.businessweek.com/2000/00_35/b3696034htm).

knowledge capital to book value, nearly 4.3 to 1. In November of 2000, two other pharmaceutical firms launched competing bids for Warner-Lambert, with their bids stemming in large part from expectations for the future of Lipitor, a drug developed by Warner that has become the most-prescribed cholesterol-lowering drug in the US.

If we were not to believe in the influence of such rations, how else could we justify the fact that AOL exchanged $146 billion in stock to acquire Time Warner, whose net tangible assets were valued at $9 billion? Or, on the negative side, take the Monsanto Co. example, which in 2000 also highlighted the predictive potential for knowledge capital. While still enjoying investors' favor early in 1999, Monsanto chalked up only an average calculation of knowledge capital to book value. Although this metric was somewhat surprising at the time, the company soon tumbled from grace. In an effort to boost slumped performance, it proposed detaching some of its assets, only to succumb in December to a buyout bid.

At Virtual Access Networks, where I began working on these issues, we realized that the value of a well-thought-out product architecture was not the tools and technologies we were using, but the people we had and their freedom to express and create what they were trained for – the knowledge capital we had accumulated. Fortunately, our lead VC, Stata Ventures, realized it too: only six months after the company inception, as a strategic move we decided to change the name of the company, its core technology and market, and yet Stata trusted that we knew what we were doing, despite all the appearances that we were being another victim of lack of focus and nonexecution of a business plan. Stata realized that if they disregarded knowledge capital because it did not show up in the budget they were likely to make very poor and costly decisions. Strassmann summarizes the principle well when he points out the fact that capital is now a small fraction of total input, and information is now the dominant input in the economy by far.

Measuring Knowledge Capital

As many companies evolve to this new knowledge-based economy, measuring knowledge capital is becoming increasingly important. Learning organizations will only be able to create a sustainable competitive advantage if they can successfully manage knowledge capital. The long-term success of any organization in the twenty-first century will come from their knowledge-based assets (physical assets may be important, but they are unlikely to be as effective a competitive weapon as knowledge assets), such as:

- customer relationships
- innovative products and services
- excellent process operations

- skills, capabilities, and motivation
- data farms
- information systems

Customer Relationships

For Alvin Toffler,[6] the customer is now a participant in the production process. According to him, the lines between producer and consumer have been blurred, as a result of a shift towards consumption. Under this new paradigm, it is the customer now that provides information as to what they need or want. Without that information, producers create a product that they cannot sell and no one wants. Furthermore, the Internet has radically changed and enhanced the customer and producer's relationship.

Consequently, the customer relationship has become crucial for today's business success and customer relationship management (CRM) practices will become even more vital in the knowledge economy of the twenty-first century. Therefore, any organization that reduces its customer relationship budgets also reduces its customer relationships and thus weakens its brand loyalty. Organizations must realize that customer relationship costs are hidden in all sorts of budgets, whether they are marketing, advertising, public relations, or transactions.

Those organizations that feel that they can get away with smaller customer relationship budgets are only fooling themselves, in particular if most of the interaction with the customer is done online. Online customer relationships may give a superficial impression of community and friendliness. However, it is in reality a very impersonal medium. Websites viewed from computer monitors lean towards being cold, lifeless environments. E-mail is informal but can as easily be impersonal. When you have to deal with 100 e-mails a day it is easy to become automatic in how you respond to practically everything. Such practice just widens the knowledge gap between the organization and its customers.

Therefore, organizations should develop brand communities online. Remember that brand communities are as much an attitude as a structure. Brand communities should be the environment in which the company and the customer carry out an online relationship.

---

6. *The Third Wave*, New York, Bantam Books, 1991.

Innovative Products and Services

When it comes to innovating products and services in a knowledge-based economy, senior management should step out of the boat. This is true especially for CKOs, which includes myself, as we have been far too introspective for far too long, so no wonder KM (and CKOs!) has had to prove itself over and over again. We have been spending too much time rearranging the furniture in our home and not enough with the people who enable us to pay the mortgage, so to speak. Focus should be given to our customers, both inside and outside the organization.

During the nineties, most of the organizational change initiatives, such as reengineering, organizational learning and total quality management, did not exclude customers, but they tended to de-emphasize their importance in practice. Unfortunately, customers inside and outside the organization are very important in the knowledge transfer process, which in turn is the key component in bridging the organization's knowledge gap.

Unless we become skilled at bridging knowledge gaps, investing in learning organizations will never succeed. No wonder Stan Davis, the world-renowned business consultant, still believes that investing in building learning organizations is a self-defeating job. In his experience, professionals focusing on learning organizations spend an enormous amount of time talking about the organization and lose sight of the business.

The problem is that learning organizations will never be successful unless knowledge transfer is effective. People tend to meet too much, present too much, and talk too much, when they hit knowledge walls. That is what makes them, and, consequently, their KM projects, so ineffective. In the process, as pointed out by Davis, professionals find themselves running in circles and never really achieving tangible, quantifiable business results, thus losing sight of the business challenge at hand.

Therefore, the vision every CKO and KM professional should have when developing organizations into learning ones is to successfully enable knowledge gaps to be bridged, in particular among the company and its customers, allowing knowledge to effectively be transferred. This process requires a reprioritization of the business goals, where focus should be given to customers, not business processes, not group integration, or even bottom line, unless directly related to customers. Customers no longer occupy the other end of the sale cycle stick. They are much more integrated in any successful business organization, influencing the development of new products and markets as never before.

Customers are no longer adapting to a market, but the market is adapting to the customers' demands. This does not mean, however, that companies need to be at customers' mercy. Instead, and this is where the power of KM comes in, companies' relationships with customers should be one of collaboration. In the process of developing learning organizations, customers' interactions with the company should also foster a learning relationship. Don Peppers and

Martha Rogers, of Marketing 1:1 in Stamford-CT wrote extensively about learning relationships with customers in their book *The One to One Future*,[7] which I recommend you read, as it emphasizes the need for companies to concentrate on keeping and growing their customers rather than merely accepting significant churn as a business reality. As Peppers so keenly states, "You have to manage customers and relationships, not products and brands."[8]

In focusing on bridging the knowledge gap between the enterprise and its customers, information technologies, including data farming and mining, and the Internet, can assist the development of this notion of one-to-one marketing relationships Peppers advocates. As the gap between knowledge stored in customers' infoislands and corporate silos is bridged, mass customization of products and services becomes possible. Learning organizations are taking advantage of this KM strategy with great success. Ritz-Carlton, which maintains a profile of each hotel guest, and Levi's, which now tailors the fit of its popular blue jeans to the needs of the individual, are examples of organizations succeeding with this approach.

Excellent Process Operations

As learning organizations reap the benefits of bridged knowledge with customers and internal groups, companies can now focus on improving process operations, so they can retain a greater share of the customer's lifetime business rather than just market share. After all, retaining existing customers is much more profitable than continuously spending resources on finding new ones.

By striving to achieve excellent process operations, the goal should be to improve dialogue with customers, as well as knowledge workers within the organization. Only through a continuous, dialog, a truly two-way exchange of knowledge between company and customer and every employee among themselves, the relationship is strengthened and true knowledge (not misinformation!) flows. That is when customers begin to invest time and effort in the relationship, and their willingness to share what they really need from the company and the product really happens. At this point, the company can learn about the customer's experience with their products and services, as they explain what they need, so that the company can personalize its product and service offerings to meet the customer's expectation.

Skills, Capabilities, and Motivation

While the general view about the inefficiencies of knowledge management and the lack of skilled knowledge professionals to lead learning organizations

---

7. New York, Currency/Doubleday, 1993.
8. Ibid., p. 139.

in America and worldwide is still strong, the fact of the matter is that there has never been a time that organizations were so much in need of such professionals.

The point is that KM professionals (and practices!) lie at the heart of innovation. Skilled knowledge professionals, in particular CKOs, should be considered a source of cutting-edge research and development — a wellspring of vital technology, information systems, human behavior, sociology, and market and business knowledge. Knowledge managers can be a dynamic force inside learning organizations in an interdependent value system that strives to tighten its relationship with and knowledge of its customers and their needs, in particular in the twenty-first century knowledge-based economy. In this new economy, the company's success is becoming a function of the success (not satisfaction!) of its customers. Knowledge management professionals are better positioned to bridge the gap between the company and the customer than any other professional, both for their eclectic background and multidisciplinary know-how, so vital in understanding and reaching out to the customers.

Typical marketing groups tend to become customer-led, focusing excessively on the existing needs of customers. However, these groups often fail in determining what the customers' unmet and unarticulated needs are. Knowledge management practices are a must to motivate learning organizations in collaborating with customers and promoting active dialogue that spurs innovation, enabling companies to create new and profitable customer solutions. Steelcase, for instance, capitalizes on collaboration with its customers by relying on its customer field test sites for insights into creating effective workspaces. Northern Telecom also capitalizes on collaboration activities with its telecommunications equipment customers in its activities from design to deployment.

I strongly believe that the most impressive breakthroughs of the future will not originate in complex research and development labs, or in visionary executive teams. They will happen outside the walls of the corporation, with CKOs and knowledge management professionals as catalysts, connecting the knowledge base of the organization with customers, wherever they may be found.

Database Farms

One of the main challenges in this new knowledge economy is that it relies intensively on the flow of information. For information to effectively flow it must rely on well-designed, open, and ubiquitous information systems and databases. However, the great majority of information systems today interact with legacy database systems demanding a lot of maintenance. A large amount of money is spent nowadays maintaining databases, varying from routine update of records all the way through continuously refurbishing old databases. This is because it costs a lot of money to repair poorly designed and badly organized translations of business processes into software code, and unfortunately, one of the core technologies for knowledge management implementation is data mining, which heavily relies on databases as a repository of vital and historical information about customers and the organization.

Therefore, the development of data farms should require special attention during knowledge bridging implementations, especially because the tendency today is for organizations to opt for developing new systems instead of supporting huge expenditures with information systems maintenance. The very high ratio of life-cycle maintenance costs to the original acquisition cost demonstrates that today's application software is one of the flimsiest artifacts that management will ever buy. Unless an assessment is made on how KM data farms are implemented, the whole project can be jeopardized due to inadequate fostering of data silos. In my opinion, the reason for the flimsiness of so many data mining applications can be found in the failure of most executives to understand that data mining has become an increasingly significant store of a corporation's knowledge capital. To make things worse, data mining development expenses are now wasted because senior management blindly accepts the view that data mining, and software for that matter, is largely unrecoverable every time technology, the organization, or business practices experience major changes.

That is why software asset management is becoming an important component in accelerating the accumulation of knowledge capital, as it provides an avenue for accumulated expert knowledge to be encapsulated and sold on the streets at a fraction of its original cost. Data farming, which encompasses data mining, sharing, and bi-directional collaboration, should be considered one of the best means for accumulating and preserving the vast amount of information about the corporation, its products, services, and customers, so vital in knowledge-bridging strategies.

Consequently, CKOs must take charge, as gatekeepers of data farming activities. They must insist that data mining implementations be preserved by means of technical designs that accommodate rapid changes in computer technologies. In addition, senior management, in particular CIOs and CTOs, must work closely with CKOs to make sure data farming implementations take advantage of innovations in operating systems, smart agent and business intelligence technologies and the pervasive ability the Internet and wireless technologies provide to virtual accessibility to data from anywhere.

Information Systems

Information systems are very important for KM implementations. The evolution of information systems has paralleled the growing size and complexity of businesses. If your organization relies on you to remember everything about the way it is run, then you are the information system of the organization. But as you probably already know by now, as the organization grows, it becomes very difficult to keep track of all the valuable information accumulated over time. It becomes more efficient to recreate something than to find it! In such an environment, institutional memory disappears on a daily basis, with dire competitive consequences.

With the virtualization of enterprises, largely promoted by the Web and its related technologies, information systems shortfalls were exposed, revealing that vast knowledge assets were locked in information silos that were unable to communicate with each other, let alone external partners, supply chains, distribution channels, and customers. Thus, in a knowledge economy, information systems must focus on information asset management at three levels:

• within the enterprise

• between enterprises

• between the enterprise and the world.

Learning organizations must be able to extract knowledge from anywhere in the organization to use it wherever it can provide business leverage, whether that leverage is the heightening of employee productivity, streamlining supply chains or distribution channels, reducing product development costs, or addressing future challenges. This requires an information system that can process and track literally billions of information objects, reuse, render, and publish them in different formats for multiple channels, control their revision and publication with workflow and life cycle processes, and permit access at varying levels of security. When developing information systems, make sure they are scalable so that they can accommodate growth. Also, make sure they are based on open standards such as Sun Microsystems' J2EE or Microsoft's .Net compliant and XML to incorporate new technologies.

Most importantly, information systems for knowledge management implementations must have provisions for Web Services, as the technology is a herald of where twenty-first century information systems are headed. Web Services are self-contained, modular pieces of programming logic that perform specific business functions. Their use relies on the adoption of three standards:

1. Web Service Description Language (WSDL)

2. Universal Description, Discovery, and Integration (UDDI) protocol

3. Simple Object Access Protocol (SOAP)

In the very near future, information system functionality will be described as Web Services. Information systems will also evolve to provide the versioning and management of Web Services, and the deployment of services to UDDI registries where they can be accessed. Web Services will transform learning organizations and their information silos into global knowledge repositories, or a Knowledge Ecosystem (KE). In a KE, business process integration, and information exchange and collaboration will function outside the firewall as fluidly as it does today inside the firewall, as shown in Figure 6.1. Information will flow easily and securely anywhere it needs to go.

Figure 6.1 – The bridging of knowledge and processed information will enable the development of community of practices and virtual marketplaces

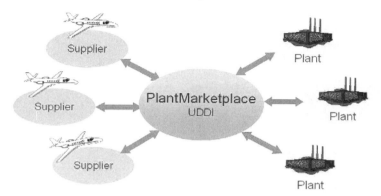

In this knowledge-based economy, information systems will have to move from a model where information used to be inert and acted upon to a model where it is the application that acts on the information and the information itself merges, as shown in Figure 6.2. When information becomes truly self-aware and can, on request, be extracted, transformed, replicated, automated, enhanced, and delivered/distributed by itself, and can interact with other self-aware units of information to produce compound, complex knowledge entities, then the KE will have truly arrived.

THE KNOWLEDGE GAP

As we try to work with the complexities of this fast moving, interdependent work environment, how well do KM tools and business models support learning organizations in new ways of thinking? How well do these tools enable the bridging of knowledge gaps within organizations? How long can we reconcile statements such as "People are our greatest asset," with our balance sheets, where they show up only as a liability and an expense?

In any learning organization, its people are indeed a core asset, and the way their knowledge and intelligence is utilized is a key strategy for the

Figure 6.2 – Interoperability of data is key for knowledge ecosystems to exist

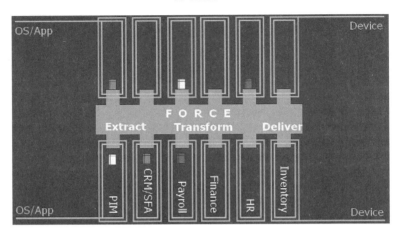

company's business advantage. Nonetheless, the great majority of professionals are bounded by golden handcuffs of business, financial, and economic models and frameworks that only continue to pull them in a very different direction. So, how long will organizations, in particular the learning ones, be able to cope with this disconnection between what its people know, their know-how, what they say is important, and the financial and economic models that drive all of our day-to-day decisions?

Today, almost all of our business and economic models, as well as our everyday management tools, are leftovers from the industrial age. Over and over again, I watch senior managers and executives try to move forward into new ways of working and managing only to be frustrated by tools and frameworks that are inadequate for the new economy. Many times when I attempted to emphasize the importance of KM to bridge many knowledge islands inside an organization, and to use effective tools to manage this burst of information flow, my words fell on deaf ears.

The bottom line is that, unless we find ways to work the emerging set of very different questions imposed by this new knowledge economy, we will continue to witness the failure of many businesses, including our own, and, consequently, dive into an economic recession. Curious enough, history shows that it is only during economic recessions that companies take the risk to innovate and reevaluate their business, their management, and their position in the marketplace. Business reengineering was the flagship out of the last economic recession. What will it be for this new one we are in? I'd bet, the bridge of knowledge gap through KM implementations.

Rethinking Old Tools

Senior management and executive staff must realize that this new knowledge economy we are entering, as we enter the twenty-first century, is rewriting the rules of business and forcing a radical rethinking of corporate value and business models. The old economy of the 1990s did not have the many perspectives of value and capital we now have in the new economy, such as intellectual capital, knowledge value added, and balanced scorecards. The industrial revolution did not have to deal with such "abstract notions" as knowledge management and learning organizations. But I strongly believe that the notions of value and capital we are trying to cope with today are only the starting point of a major business shift, where not even our standardized analytical tools will be sufficient to understand the complexities of value creation, preservation, and transfer.

In my opinion, in order to be successful, organizations must be able to incorporate intangibles and intellectual capital in the way they do business, leaving behind the Cartesian mechanistic view of the economy and business, so much based on Newtonian physics. In the new knowledge economy, a more dynamic interconnected view based on insights gleaned from quantum physics, chaos and complexity theory, behavioral science, and living systems must be adopted. As Verna Allee long ago asserted:

> [T]he economic and business world is struggling to translate this new understanding of life that has emerged in recent years in terms of what it means for the way we do our work and how we manage organizations. We long to heal the split between the strong human values we hold dear and old business models where they are irrelevant.[9]

To be effective, the major challenge CKOs face today is in trying to lead companies in adopting these new ideas, and finding themselves living the paradox of having their feet in two worlds: one foot is still stuck in the several decades old corporate world of management practice, and the other foot is stuck in the cloudy and fast-moving new waters of intangible assets and knowledge as the base for this new economic foundation of organizations and companies.

Unfortunately, a lot of what upper management thinks and does stems from old ways of thinking and an old mechanistic engineering-based approach, which means CKOs will have a tough time in convincing the executive group to rethink their way of doing business. Senior management and the executive staff are still unconsciously trying to stretch their old perspectives and tools to encompass new ideas, but as you might expect, they are not getting the results they expected. Many do not realize that the fundamental principles underlying

---

9. V. Allee, *An Emerging Model of Intellectual Capital (or Intangible Assets)*, Boston, Butterworth-Heinemann, 1997, p. 87.

intangibles and the knowledge economy are dramatically different from the way they have traditionally thought about how value is created and what makes organizations successful.

The major challenge here is that business professionals never had to deal with knowledge as they do today. Knowledge has never been as prevalent both with customers and suppliers as it is today. Knowledge simply does not behave like natural resources. Knowledge and ideas can replicate and multiply endlessly, but material resources cannot. Natural resources deplete with use, but a knowledge resource is expanded with use. As Allee comments, "if a natural resource is sold or given to another it is at the expense of whoever had to give it up. However, sharing knowledge allows both parties to not only retain the resource but to amplify and expand it through the exchange process itself."[10]

Further, the business practices and management principles that we are learning to operate by are very different as well. The industrial era enterprise models are no longer adequate to meet the dynamic conditions of an ever-changing world market. Knowledge intensive enterprises are calling forth a new approach to work, organizations, accounting, and business. In addition, there is a definite progression towards thinking about the enterprise from a more sociological perspective. To say the least, there is a strong appreciation from several companies, for what is known today as communities of practice. According to John Seely Brown, Vice President of Xerox, community of practice is comprised of peers in the execution of real work, held together by a common sense of purpose and a real need to know what each other knows. Companies such as British Petroleum, Buckman Laboratories, Chevron, General Motors, Hewlett Packard, Johnson & Johnson, Pillsbury, The World Bank, and the big consulting groups, among others, are all achieving outstanding business results by focusing on these internal communities.

Figure 6.3 illustrates a framework developed by Verna Allee that shows how intangible assets play an important role in the emerging perspective of wealth and value. Although these intangible assets have been addressed in management literature, the literature is inclined to focus on them in isolation rather than providing a whole systems perspective of how value is created in a way that is connected with the web of life.

While this larger perspective tends to appear overwhelming to address in most companies, in Allee's practices she finds that people respond positively to this framework at a fundamental human level. It is not so much a question of whether or not these things are important, as clearly they are; the real question is how will we address them? Can we bring coherence and integrity to our business models in light of the higher values that we hold dear?

---

10. Ibid., p. 68.

Figure 6.3 – Intangible assets: An emerging perspective of wealth and value

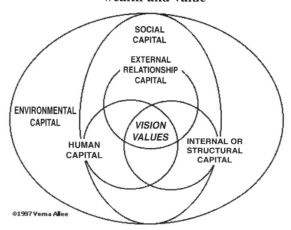

©1997 Verna Allee

Promoting Dynamic Exchange of Knowledge

In order to capitalize on intangible assets we must understand how specific exchanges, activities, or transactions contribute to both tangible and intangible value, and what conditions enhance those processes. This requires a paradigm shift in the way we look at knowledge flow and the sharing of knowledge in the organization. We must think about dynamic processes, where this interconnected universe of complex interdependencies of knowledge exists. The notion of knowledge flow tends to be unidirectional by nature, while the idea of exchanges suggests that for every action or transaction, there is some sort of reaction or response, one that can be understood, appreciated, and even measured.

While traditional models of enterprise value creation and innovation are based on the value chain, which is ingrained in an industrial-age, production-line model, in the knowledge economy the value chain model is evolving into a new enterprise perspective of the network. This new model is composed of a set of dynamic linkages among diverse members who are engaged in deliberate and strategic exchanges of services, knowledge, and value in order to generate economic wealth. Knowledge exchanges across these networks are clearly the foundation of innovation both internally within the firm, externally, across entire industries, and globally, across national boundaries.

Further, this network view positions organizations as consisting of multiple, interconnected, and overlapping knowledge networks. By not focusing solely on a successful network activity, companies can improve performance of an organization, while it interacts between the networks. Ideas, events, and domains of expertise can become visible and compelling to these networks and evolve due to network interactions and social affinities that create particular viewpoints, interpretations, or patterns of understanding.

An important factor in the exchange of knowledge is that it must be accurate, complete, and easy to exchange. Thus, when dealing with a knowledge base stored in data warehouses and marts, you might combine it with unstructured sources, and then make it available to the broad range of users. Make sure to take into consideration their level of expectations about the content and how information is delivered to them. Do they want a report, a flight deck-like display showing critical business metric, or some sophisticated query with drill-downs? Knowledge sharing tools, from reporting to analytical solutions based on online analytical processing (OLAP) and personal query, can help tremendously. These solutions, when combined with enterprise information portals (EIP) can enable users to incorporate and combine information from unstructured sources into their overall knowledge base, and then share and collaborate.

How knowledge creates value is yet to be understood by the industry, but my hope is that this book will bring about enough tangible key results to prove its importance. I hope this book provides you with many insights and breakthroughs about the complexity of KM practice. I emphasize the role of CKOs in turning knowledge into action. CKOs today have a unique opportunity to help organizations shift from the mechanistic, linear thinking of the industrial age to a more dynamic view of the world being ushered in by discoveries from a wide variety of scientific and human behavior fields. They must question and rethink underlying business models in order to incorporate the new fundamentals for the emerging knowledge-based economy. This process will require a reshape of assumptions and beliefs, as well as mental models about the significance of success.

When discussing knowledge exchange, I recommend you read Verna Allee's latest book, *The Future of Knowledge: Increasing Prosperity Through Value Networks.*[11] In this book she demonstrates a simple but powerful approach for mapping knowledge dynamics in value networks.

TURNING KNOWLEDGE INTO ACTION

In this new knowledge economy, the best knowledge management application in the world will not be enough to completely meet the challenge you have in turning knowledge into action. A KM application can help you in collecting, organizing, and sharing information among knowledge workers, thus promoting collaboration. But where its true value lies is in unearthing the real problems that we were probably aware of at the outset of our KM projects, but were unable or too afraid to challenge head-on.

---

11. Butterworth-Heinemann, 2002.

Knowledge management implementations can only be successful if contributors care about and are motivated to own the content in the first place. In order to do this the content needs to become an inextricable part of their daily working lives, and KM implementation will not be enough. We need systems and ways of organizing knowledge that reflect the incredible diversity of people and how they interact within the business itself. Knowledge sharing and management technologies are no longer enough.

Without a doubt, KM systems have helped organizations to bring order to the chaos of complete free-structure and non-distributed knowledge content mismanagement. Previously, knowledge would be anywhere, in any form, created by unknown sources and with unknown use and control over its lifecycle. To fix this, most KM implementations have applied a rigid rule of control where compliance to rules set centrally is foremost and the flexibility to react to the all too frequent exceptions that break the rules goes unsupported.

To effectively turn knowledge into action we must get to a point where KM systems will work with people's quirks, strengths, weaknesses, short-comings, and specific variances of style and use of IT tools before we can realistically expect buy-in from knowledge workers to the idea of total knowledge sharing and collaboration within the organization. Demanding that people use a templated view of their knowledge creation and delivery, and insisting that all knowledge workers adhere to this is merely a great way to let some people shine whilst others just lose interest and give up contributing their knowledge. Somehow we have to embrace the unstructured and at times downright chaotic within knowledge/information/knowledge cycle, which I call the knowledge tornado.

Current KM approaches are a great start, this is good. These approaches allow learning organizations to put rules around the things we know about, and encourage knowledge workers to create more of the things we already understand, thus tapping into this precious tacit knowledge in everyone's mind. What these systems absolutely do not do is allow learning organizations to grow outside of what they already know and understand, into areas of business and intelligence that may actually be of massive benefit. It is those areas of "uncharted and dynamic knowledge" that will allow learning organizations to become innovators rather than knowledge producers operating merely in a sausage factory manner.

Another challenge is with regard to teamwork. Turning knowledge into action requires collaboration. However, in my view, collaboration is a fiction, a verbal convenience, rather than a useful description of how people in a firm cooperate and collaborate to create value. I am not alone in this view. Michael Schrage, in his book *No More Teams!*,[12] writes that the word team has been "so politicized, so ensnared in the pathology of the organization, that we don't really know what it means anymore." Schrage contends that we have become

12. New York, Currency/Doubleday, 2000, p. 98.

so obsessed with the composition of the team and the capabilities of its individual members that we have lost sight of how innovation really happens.

Therefore, in line with Schrage thinking, I strongly believe that knowledge can only effectively be turned into action through innovation, and innovation requires what Schrage calls "cutting-edge teams," which are composed of knowledge workers drawn to innovative prototypes. Thus, creative collaboration becomes essential for business strategies and innovation. In this context, collaboration is not about communication. Effective collaboration does require successful communication, but it can only be achieved through the creation and maintenance of a place where the people can freely interact with each other, play, and represent models of their ideas. This is what Schrage called shared space, which is key for the creation of shared understandings, an extension of knowledge sharing.

When PowerPoint Misses the Point

Very often you find in organizations a huge amount of know-how. However, knowing how does not necessarily mean how-to. The reality of things is that knowing what to do is no longer enough: writing about how to execute an elaborate PowerPoint presentation on how a task must be executed does not add to any solution, any action; calling meetings and assigning tasks does not mean execution either. It is not the presentation that creates solutions; it is the solution that creates the presentation. Or, if you prefer, it is not the soldiers that make the war, as conventional wisdom believes, but the reverse: war creates true soldiers.

If you apply this paradigm to the corporate world, it is not the executives and entrepreneurs that create the business and the market, but the market that "asks" for products and services, and true executives respond by innovating and delivering. Thus, past successful experience as well as pre-conceived successful ideas seldom guarantee any great result. That is why there is so very little evidence that PowerPoint masters, aka MBA graduates, bring any tangible increase in organizational performance. If you need examples, look at known successful companies such as Southwest Airlines, SAS Institute, Starbucks, and many others. What they all have in common is that business degree credentials are not emphasized. Honestly, if you were to assess what you learned in college, how well do you feel it prepared you for the function you exercise today, as you read this book? I would bet, very little, regardless if you are a fresh graduate or not.

To be successful, learning organizations must develop new and bold strategies in order to ensure that its knowledge is turned into action, and that innovation becomes a frequent event. This will require companies to reevaluate what they do when they confront business challenges and complexity. If companies will continue to follow the traditional paradigm, they will break a task into its component parts and then delegate it to several professionals.

Here we see the first mistake, as delegation is inherently anti-collaborative. The challenge resides in creating communities that foster collaboration and eventually innovation. This will require the involvement of suppliers, distribution channels and customers.

Technology is very important in bridging the knowledge gap, but it is a cyclical variable, which will require revision every so often, as software versions are upgraded, new collaboration features become available, and so forth. But the level of commitment you make in promoting knowledge sharing, collaboration, and, ultimately, shared spaces should always be the overarching driver. Instead of focusing on groupware solutions such as Lotus Notes, Microsoft Exchange, and many others, the focus should move from using technology to structure data and information to structuring interactions and relationships among people. Here exits the CTO/CIO and enters the CKO. Of course, the success of turning knowledge into action depends on the utmost commitment of the CxOs of the organization, but it no longer becomes a matter of technology or information management alone.

The goal here is to focus more on thoughtful action, by spending less time and effort on contemplation and PowerPoint presentations about the organization's problems, and more time on taking action, even if mistakes are made in the process, as this is the only way to learn. The ability to act on knowledge is power, but unfortunately, the majority of people inside organizations do not have the ability to act on the knowledge they possess.

Leading by Example: The Power of Parables and Analogies

One of the largest, most successful, international organizations in the world with a huge customer base that continues to grow year after year since its inception hundreds of years ago was established by an uneducated man. This man never traveled more than twenty-five miles from his hometown and his whole organization rested in the hands of twelve executives, most of them also uneducated. The organization was very flat, with him as the head, the CEO. His product never changed (although today you will find cheap imitations offered by its competitors), but the company never stopped growing.

The uniqueness of this CEO is that he always led by example, focused on relationships and successful collaboration, as well as the development of communities of practice. Knowledge transfer was always practised during meals, parties, walkabouts, and story-telling, or parables. Most amazingly, every member of his organization was willing to work long hours, incorporating their business as part of their lives, and without the requirement of, or desire for, any corporate perks (i.e. BMWs, six-figure bonuses, stock options, etc.). Much to the contrary, they gladly returned part of their salaries to the corporation, to foster its continuous growth. The case in point is Jesus Christ and Christianity.

Today, not only parables, but also anecdotes, myths, fables, archetypes, and metaphors are being used to help companies manage knowledge, and turn it into action. Much like the practices of Jesus with His apostles, KM consultants draw hypotheses and try to get the client to fit those answers, while anthropologists go in as unseen observers and watch the stories flow from person to person.

This enables them to observe people using knowledge they were not aware of. I believe Jesus was so successful with His ministry because by using parables He could tell the truth in a fictional form, He was not attributable. For instance, while Jesus told His disciples parables while standing by an Olive tree, while in a boat, or having a meal, archetypes could be constructed to represent certain types of people within the group. The same is true in any organization. From these archetypes a learning organization can anticipate how it will react to change. The cartoon "Dilbert" is a modern example of archetypes in action, much like disciples were and are still today among Christianity.

By speaking in parables Jesus could provide his disciples with an illustration of the task at hand, assess alternatives to resolve it, as well as the consequences of a wrong or right action. Such an approach is very important in bridging the knowledge gap, which makes Christianity so successful. In today's corporate environment, time after time knowledge professionals understand the issues and what needs to be done, but they fail to do the things they know they need to do. That is why the concept of mentoring (or discipling, in Jesus' time) is so important in any organization.

Jack Welch, while CEO of GE, advocated that, "above all else, good leaders are open. They go up, down, and around their organizations to reach people. They don't stick to established channels. They are informal. They are straight with people. They make a religion out of being accessible." [13]

The new economy of the twenty-first century is capitalizing on knowledge flow, in and out of organizations and knowledge workers. It is an economy characterized and differentiated by services, even at the most basic level of retailing or manufacturing. Nonetheless, consultants and KM professionals must realize that knowledge is more than an asset that can be acquired, measured, and shared. Knowledge cannot always be quantified or adopted explicitly; many times, it is tacit. Even though, in some circumstances, knowledge could be qualified as tangible, the organization must be able to turn it into action, otherwise, its value is underestimated, wasted, even at the level of intellectual property.

In addition, the unmatched velocity of change and innovation we are now witnessing is leaving many corporate executives spinning without answers. They are being told (often by self-interested parties) to invest heavily in technology, training, and education if they want their companies to survive in the fast-paced knowledge era. However, it is seldom true that throwing technology on a problem will produce results. Again, no formal system can

---

13. R.T. Pascale, *Managing on the Edge*, New York, Simon & Shuster, 1990, p. 12.

effectively capture or store tacit knowledge. Therefore, most of the knowledge being captured today by all the technology available is not quite so useful. Instead, it is under the trees, at the breaks, during meals, company's outings, stories, parables, and jokes that tacit knowledge is actually being transferred. Therefore, informal brownbag at lunchtime is often much more efficient than searching for structure (and dead!) data on data warehousing server farms.

Knowledge professionals must constantly upgrade their knowledge and skills in order to thrive in the new economy, but investing large sums of money in classroom-based programs and training bureaucracies is ludicrous. Unfortunately, according to Edward Shaw, former trainer and now consultant, "as much as half of the $50 billion American corporations annually spend on formal training is being utterly wasted, squandered on training that's unnecessary, training that's aimed at non-training problems, and training that's doomed to fail by its poor design."[14]

Coping With High-Velocity Learning

Turning knowledge into action is at the heart of the emergence of the knowledge era, which places a premium on agile and productive knowledge work. Thus, high-velocity change demands high-velocity learning and consequently high-velocity knowledge sharing. KM implementation, therefore, must incorporate the development of information architectures that facilitate the real-time acquisition, exchange, and generation of knowledge. As performance support technology expert Gloria Gery rightly contends, knowledge should be made available at "the point and moment of need."[15]

Instead of shuffling employees off to classrooms to absorb more training-related, T&L expenses, companies should be investing in knowledge networks that enable individuals to share expertise, exchange knowledge, and learn on demand. They should be investing in intranets, groupware, interactive multimedia, maybe tele-learning technologies, and performance support systems.

Many companies have begun to realize that they must focus on managing customers and relationships. While it is important to create truly excellent products and services, what good are they if they are not what the market wants? Total customer management (TCM), to coin a phrase, is now eclipsing total quality management (TQM) as a corporate priority. For similar reasons, there are numerous reasons why CRM is now in vogue. The fact that companies are finally realizing the strategic importance of long-term loyalty is one of the main reasons, as satisfied and loyal customers buy more and attract new customers through word of mouth referrals. Since it costs a lot more to replace

---

14. E. Shaw, "Corporate Knowledge Nets" *Training Magazine*, 2001, p. 37.
15. In Britton Manasco's *Enterprise-Wide Learning: Corporate Knowledge Networks and the New Learning Imperative* Knowledge Inc, Austin, 1997, p. 51.

a lost customer than retain one, by cutting customer turnover, you can dramatically improve your company's profitability.

Do not underestimate the fact that customers are becoming increasingly sophisticated. Customer knowledge is becoming one of the most valuable resources in modern economic life, and in order to win their loyalty, you must now identify and understand their interests, preferences, needs, and demands. Otherwise, they know they no longer depend on any single vendor, especially now that markets are viciously competitive, so you will surely lose them.

Therefore, CKOs and KM professionals, as well as the whole senior management staff, must realize that customers – and this includes the corporation's internal customers, the employees – are the beneficiaries of the knowledge economy. They are the ones calling the shots, and the corporation must adapt. In this new economy, we all are not only providers and producers, but customers as well.

STRATEGIES FOR BRIDGING THE KNOWLEDGE GAP

One of the major obstacles in developing strategies for bridging the knowledge gap inside an organization is that knowledge in itself is very complex. The many artificial intelligence initiatives of the 1970s, as well as the data mining and warehousing of the 1990s, showed us that we cannot easily package knowledge into a black box and have it perform miracles. Moreover, many KM professionals are mistakenly confusing the concept of knowledge for information. Information is very important to any learning organization, and IT plays a major role in collecting, cataloging, and sharing the banks of information residing in data warehousing silos. But managing knowledge, in particular tacit knowledge, is not an easy task.

Often, the most valuable resource of any successful (and I would venture to say unsuccessful ones as well!) organization today is the knowledge in the minds of its people and its customers. So, how can we attempt to capture such knowledge, and subsequently transfer it? First, let's take a look at two typical and complementary approaches used today:

- Knowledge conversion: this is one of the most typical attempts, influenced by IT organizations and CTOs assuming KM roles, to convert tacit knowledge into a more explicit form, through documents, processes, databases, etc. This so called decanting of human capital into a structural capital is the main emphasis of many European and US knowledge projects.

- Tacit knowledge enhancement: this is an attempt to promote and generate tacit knowledge flow through enhanced human interactions. The idea is to facilitate the diffusion of knowledge around the organization, preventing it from being held inside the minds of a few. One of the fastest growing churches in the US and the world, the International Churches of Christ (ICOC), adopts such an approach by promoting weekly meetings, where various social activities are supported by the leaders to promote this kind of knowledge flow. Those leaders in turn promote similar group gatherings, informally called d-groups (or discipling groups) to extend the dynamics through other members of the church.

In Japan, an approach similar to that of ICOC is taken (used by early Christians 2000 years ago – Acts 2:42), whereby community of practice activities support the knowledge flow through a very natural spark of insights for the generation of new ideas and knowledge.

It is important to observe that some of the fastest and most successful learning organizations heavily rely on knowledge management tools and practices for competitive advantage. Take for example the ICOC, which heavily relies on the knowledge of the Bible to spread the gospel and grow. Its leaders understand that it is people and processes, rather than the content of a strategy, which will determine its ultimate success. Tetra Pak Converting Technologies have developed learning networks, where people from across the organization update and develop their expertise in key technologies, such as laminating and printing. The company understands that knowledge sharing is very important for innovation. Thus, they develop innovation workshops, expert and learning networks, as well as communities of practice.

ICOC and Tetra Pak are only two examples taken from the many organizations that exhibit best practice in knowledge innovation, but all of them show a number of recurring characteristics, including:

- Clear and explicit vision of their business strategy: does your organization have a clear vision of your business strategy? Is the knowledge strategy something separate or is it simply another layer or view of existing business strategy? How does knowledge or know-how add value to your business strategy? Conversely, what exploitable knowledge products, processes or expertise emanate from your business strategy?

- An understanding of what knowledge is: it is very important that your organization understands the knowledge advantage. Thus, you must discuss knowledge in your organization and make sure you differentiate knowledge from information, and that your people understand the advantages of nurturing and harvesting knowledge. Therefore, make sure the knowledge dimension becomes a key element of every product plan, marketing plan, strategic initiative, annual budget, and personal development plan.

- A clear vision and architecture: what guides the business decisions in your organization? Is it the knowledge facet of your business framework? If so, how clear is the vision? Would an investor give you millions for your intangible ideas?

- Knowledge leadership: do you have, or are you, a knowledge enthusiast proponent of the knowledge agenda throughout your business? Does your CEO visibly reiterate the importance of your organizational knowledge to your business success?

- Methodical knowledge processes: do you have a process methodology for capturing, organizing, and sharing knowledge throughout your organization? Do these processes enhance the creation of knowledge and innovation? Do you have policies and procedures to protect your knowledge assets?

- Proficient hard and soft knowledge infrastructures: can the people in your organization readily communicate and access each other, as well as share information over the network? Do these networks extend outside the organization to reach supply chain and distribution channels, as well as partners and customers? Can you find what or who you want quickly and efficiently? Does your organization's culture promote innovation and learning? Are your organization structures flexible and adaptive? Are your personnel systems geared to recognizing and rewarding individual and team knowledge contributions?

- Appropriate and realistic bottom line measures: is the contribution of knowledge rewarded? Are intangible assets valued? Are financial performance indicators balanced with non-financial measures that underpin value creation? Do you measure knowledge flows? Do you use some of the new metrics, like those in Skandia's Navigator or Karl Erik Sveiby's Intangible Assets Monitor?

If you can effectively and realistically answer these questions, you have probably already developed strategic advantage through the application of knowledge, and are ahead of most organizations in the world in this process. If not, then you should seriously consider starting it. Just like quality-defined success in the last decade, innovation through knowledge will be a key success factor in this knowledge economy.

Ideas must be Turned into Assets

More than ever before truly learning organizations understand that the greatest source of innovation and creativity for competitive edge is its own people. Hitting at the foundation of KM, the success of these organizations is greatly influenced by how well the ideas of its people are tapped and turned into valuable and tangible assets.

As part of turning knowledge into action, people must generate ideas, so innovation can take place. Thus, everyone in the organization must be able to think creatively. I do not mean the developers and engineers only, but all groups within the organization, including sales, marketing, administration, shipping, and so on. If you plant the creativity seed right, you will have a flood of ideas coming from everywhere in the organization. At this stage, your goal should be to harvest these ideas by creating an intellectual property strategy that is valuable to the organization.

Planting the Seeds of Creativity

Planting the seeds of creativity throughout the organization is a very important step, as it involves not only encouraging people to share their ideas but also recognizing that their ideas could be valuable. Often, rewards and recognition programs are very effective to motivate the groups.

When someone in the organization has an idea, they can get one-half of a monetary reward (say $50) for filing an idea registration form. If that idea turns into material for a provisional patent application of an invention, then an invention form is filled and the complementary reward is given. If the provisional application then turns into a full patent application, then the person could receive a greater reward, one that will not only provide recompense but also motivate others to put their creative hat on.

Encouragement to be creative begins with the right attitude. There are several steps to creativity that any learning organization can follow, basically including:

- Attitude: this first step begins with creating a positive environment where people feel grateful going to work everyday and being part of a team.

- Expectation: people also need to have a level of expectation set for them. What the organization expects from them, to be creative, is very important in setting people up for success.

- Awareness: this is a vital tool for generating great ideas. People need to be aware of where they can tap into new ideas. Some of the sources may be customer complaints, industry trends, business challenges, workplace challenges, etc.

- Subconscious: help your people to be aware and trust their instincts. Tell them to pay attention to their dreams, daydream included! Instruct them to think of a problem they want to find the solution for right before going to bed, and tell them not to be surprised if next day, or overnight, they wake up with a solution for it.

- Documentation: be it at the office or sleeping, make sure to ask your people to document their ideas. They should have a notepad next to their beds, so they can document their insights and submit them next day.

- Self-praise: praise is also a very important part of idea generation. Make sure to motivate people to personally give themselves a slap on the back.

- External praise: make sure to be quick to also praise those generating ideas by recognizing them publicly.

CHAPTER 7

Chief Enchanter Officer and Chief Knock Out: Business in Wonderland?

We can do as partners what we cannot do as singles.[1]

The knowledge economy of the twenty-first century brings a very elusive future. Business executives do their best to proactively prepare for what is to come. However, often, by the time they hear it approaching, they discover that it is still quite some distance away, or worse, it already passed! The speed of business today brings about what Evan Schwartz called a Digital Darwinism.[2]

More than ever before, CEOs need to be smarter, faster, more innovative, and more adaptable. They must be able to lead their executive staff and company with unprecedented vision and execution to keep pace with the evolving technology and customer needs, as Figure 7.1 suggests. As Schwartz writes in his book:

> The world's biggest companies are gazing toward a future in which much if not most of their purchasing, invoicing, document exchange, and logistics will be transferred from stand-alone computer networks connected by people, paper, and phone calls to a seamless Web that spans the globe and connects more than a billion computing devices.[3]

To succeed, CEOs must be able to surf the waves of business at Internet speed. Therefore, to be able to succeed, convince investors, and get the loyalty and buyout from their staff and employees, chief executives must become chief enchanters, a sort of wizard of odds, not to mention of Oz! They must be able to understand and take advantage of quasi-magic events such as "sending a wireless fax from the beach; read, if not produce, a customized multimedia newspaper on a portable electronic tablet; conduct a due diligence on a proposed corporate acquisition from a plane 35,000 feet in the air and then beam the report to the board of directors in advance of his/her arrival."[4]

1. D. Heenan and W. Bennis, *Co-Leadership: The New Constellation of Power*, New York, John Wiley & Sons, 1999.
2. E. Schwartz, *Digital Darwinism*, New York, Broadway Books, 1999.
3. Ibid., p. 23.
4. D. Burstein and D. Kline, *Road Warriors: Dreams and Nightmares Along the Information Highway*, New York, Penguin Group, 1996, p. 45.

Figure 7.1 – To succeed, CEOs must be able to surf the waves of business at internet speed

Any CEO knows how necessary and important leadership is. Leadership is the main reason why some companies, teams, and business ventures succeed when others fail. The credit or blame of any endeavor most often goes to the CEO, the coach, or principal of any organization. Thus, the factor that empowers the work force and ultimately determines which organizations succeed or fail is the leadership.

However, one must not confuse management with leadership. Management can be defined as a mental and physical effort to direct diverse activities with the objective of achieving a desired result. In this process you may include the practice of planning, staffing, directing, and controlling. Leadership, however, is having the natural and learned ability, skill, and personal characteristics to conduct interpersonal relations that influence people to take desired actions.

GOING BEYOND LEADERSHIP: THE ART OF ENCHANTING

In the twenty-first century, customers are more educated and aware of products and goods than ever before. They can go to the Internet and compare prices, specifications, develop a competitive report among the vendors who supply the product they want, and even discuss the technology and features of these products. Furthermore, customers are rating their experience and posting it on the Internet, influencing future customers to buy, or not to buy, your product.

Therefore, I believe CEOs today must do more than lead. There was a time when the hard-line style of CEOs like Lee Iacocca was necessary and would pay off, as it did for some time at Chrysler. But then, as the third wave of knowledge began hitting the shores of business, hard-line traits had to be replaced with traits of persuasion, of cohesiveness, of non-bickering, and self-aggrandizement. Instead of commanding, CEOs today must be able to coach, counsel, manage conflict, inspire loyalty, and enchant subordinates with a desire to remain on the job, beginning with his own executive staff. In the words of former President Harry Truman, "[the] definition of a leader in a free country is a man who can persuade people to do what they don't want to do, or do what they're too lazy to do, and like it." That takes enchantment, as Figure 7.2 suggests!

Figure 7.2 – CEOs today must do more than lead; they must enchant!

Not convinced yet? According to Roget's Super Thesaurus,[5] to lead is to direct, show the way, conduct, usher, head, spearhead, and escort. To enchant a person is to mesmerize, captivate, hypnotize, and sweep them off their feet. Which traits do you think make a more successful CEO? Competence alone is no longer sufficient for a CEO's success. They must be able to enchant followers to accept their leadership by gaining, through ethical means, the followers' consent to be led. Thus, leadership becomes an activity, an influence process, in which the CEO gains the trust and commitment of his staff and every employee in the company, all without any recourse to formal position or authority to induce the organization to accomplish one or more tasks.

To be successful in the twenty-first century, chief executives must become chief enchanters. They must be able to get people excited; otherwise, they will lose them. People willingly sign up to serve under chief enchanters. Ask Steve Balmer of Microsoft, and Bill Gates' first generation of executive staff, and consequently the whole company. At Microsoft, people work long hours, under pressure, and in a very challenging and competitive environment. Yet, their loyalty and commitment to the company is unprecedented.

Another well-known example is Jack Welch, the recently retired CEO of GE. Addressing GE's corporate officer,[6] back in 1987, he commented,

> [T]he world of the 1990s and beyond will not belong to "managers" or those who can make the numbers dance. The world will belong to passionate, driven leaders – people who not only have an enormous amount of energy but who can energize [enchant!] those whom they lead.[7]

INVISIBLE BUT INVALUABLE: CHIEF KNOCK OUT

The importance of cooperation and collaboration in the business environment is growing every day. More than ever before, top executives, in particular CEOs, are in need of exceptional deputies. Co-leadership, where power and credit are freely dispersed throughout the enterprise, capitalizes on the contribution of subordinates, which typically is depreciated by many, but very much needed by successful leaders. To these leaders, cooperation and collaboration is not only desired, but also vital to their everyday success.

The partnerships of successful leaders enable them to do as partners what they could never do by themselves. When leaders put their talent in tandem they redefine leadership as a true partnership. It does not take much insight for us to realize that all successful companies are the fruit of true collaboration

---

5. Roget's Super Thesaurus, 1st edition.
6. In Crotonville, NY, 2 February 1987.
7. The emphasis on "enchant" is mine.

among leaders. To be successful these organizations rely on teams working together with a common goal. Shrewd leaders of the twenty-first century are those that recognize the importance of developing alliances with partners sharing the same goals, be they internal or external partners.

Typically, CEOs tend to have an array of options among the executive staff in choosing a co-leader. At Microsoft, Bill Gates has Steve Balmer, and at Chrysler, CEO Robert Eaton chose Bob Lutz. Former President of the United States, Bill Clinton had Al Gore, and co-founder Charlie Merrill, of Merrill Lynch, had Win Smith. The list goes on and on, and I am sure you can identify many other dynamic duos, aside from Batman and Robin. But you must look beyond the Batman's and Eaton's of the world to fully understand what will make companies succeed in this new knowledge economy.

To begin with, in order to become truly successful, CEOs must become truly collaborative. They must abandon the notion that the credit of any significant achievement can be attributed to them or the senior staff. They must acknowledge that success is a result of a joint effort of several contributors throughout the organization. No matter how effective the sales group is, that group can only exist if the organization exists and without the many other groups sustaining it, there would not be any organization.

The Right Combination of Skills

By trade, successful CKOs should be professionals strongly connected to the business world around them. They should be conscious about their needs to recycle their knowledge and skills on a periodic basis, by competing with themselves daily. But most importantly, their ability to manage knowledge makes them the ideal co-leader for CEOs, becoming the chief knock outs in almost every situation a top executive such as a CEO may face.

The point is, CKOs are capable of doing much more than managing KM implementations. Managing knowledge extends beyond data and information manipulation. CKOs and CEOs, every one of us for that matter, are a personal store of knowledge with experiences, training, and informal networks of friends and business acquaintances whom we often seek out to gain knowledge in the form of information when we need to resolve a problem or explore an opportunity. With CEOs the situation is no different; on the contrary, CEOs get things done and succeed by knowing an answer or knowing someone who does. Nonetheless, no one is better fitted for the job than a CKO, as managing knowledge creates value by increasing productivity and fostering innovation.

However, before CEOs can enchant, they must establish a close relationship with their co-leaders. No matter how competent a CKO might be, unless a tight relationship is developed between the duo, no true co-leadership would have been established, as suggested in Figure 7.3. Co-leaders are not a fuzzy-minded position designed to make CEOs feel better about themselves and their careers. Rather, they carry the responsibility of full commitment to the

Figure 7.3 – CKOs ability to manage knowledge makes them ideal co-leaders for CEOs, becoming the chief knock outs in almost every situation a top executive such a CEO may face

leader, the CEO, independent of tough times and/or political correctness. A case in point is Bill Clinton and Al Gore, during the Monica Lewinski case: Al never compromised his co-leadership commitment with the President.

Therefore, a co-leader must be able to devise a tough-minded strategy that can unleash the hidden talent in every organization. In other words, co-leaders must be able to transform the organization into a learning organization and in the process become the CEO's armor bear, the one holding "the great general's armor." Their ultimate goal should be to help chief enchanters to knock out business opportunities in the wonderland, or the global knowledge economy.

BUSINESS IN WONDERLAND

The new knowledge economy is characterized by high levels of uncertainty and inability to predict the future. Thus, the use of the information and control systems, as well as the conformity with pre-defined goals and objectives may not necessarily accomplish long-term organizational competence. As we enter the twenty-first century, businesses are being conducted in a sort of wonderland, where executives are being challenged to reevaluate the assumptions underlying their best practices and way of doing things. In this new economy, executives need the capability to understand the problems afresh given the ever changing environmental conditions. In wonderland, unlike business in the twentieth century, executives must not only focus on finding the right answers but also on finding the right questions.

Having spent the last fourteen years designing and managing information systems, I believe technology is the easier part of the information system equation, as well as for any knowledge management implementations. There are two real challenges. The first is to keep technology, as well as the reengineered business processes and models built upon it, in sync with the radically changing business environment and the evolving motto of the twenty-first century. The second challenge concerns the questions CEOs will have to ask CIOs, CTOs, and CFOs, such as:

- How do we justify investments in new technologies?

- How do we ensure information systems deliver the expected business performance?

- How do we define the critical success factors necessary for information systems and KM to deliver the expected business performance?

- How can knowledge technologies and management facilitate adaptability of business models and business processes to prevent business failure?

Dr. Yogesh Malhotra, from Syracuse University, published an excellent book, entitled *A Case for Knowledge Management: Rethinking Management for the New World of Uncertainty and Risk*,[8] that addresses all the above questions. It helps executives, in particular knowledge managers, to track all these vital indicators before, during, and after the implementation of information systems and technology to ensure that they do not get relegated to the heap of project failures and missed targets that increasingly characterize the landscape of organizational transformation.

Another challenge CEOs face in wonderland is one inherited from the late 1990s, often responsible for the failure of information systems and technology projects: the unsuspected clashes and differences of opinion between CEOs and CIOs. This is another reason to have CKOs involved in the technology and IS projects. As first defined by Computer Sciences Corp., CEOs are from Mars and CIOs are from Pluto, and more than 50 percent of them are fired from their position mainly for failing to establish a working relationship with the CEO.

Therefore, open communication between CEOs and CIOs is very important; once broken it is very hard to fix. CKOs typically understand that CEOs tend to be interested in technology only when they see tangible value to the

8. For more information, check Dr. Malhotra's book site within Brint.com at www.kmbook.com.

organization, and, therefore, can help CIOs to focus not only on the technology and service delivery, but also on the bottom line and strategic aspects of the business. CKOs multidisciplinary background can be very useful in helping CIOs bridge the gap between business and technology, by helping them to constantly think and talk about it.

Business in wonderland imposes the need for variety and complexity of interpretations of information outputs generated by computer systems, which is necessary for deciphering the multiple global views of the uncertain and unpredictable future. CKOs must be capable of knocking out successful strategies for surviving in this knowledge economy, which cannot be predicted based on a static picture of information residing in the company's databases or individual mindsets. Rather, such strategies will depend upon developing interpretive flexibility based upon diverse and multiple interpretations of the future. Thus, CKOs are well positioned to help CEOs in establishing business strategy objectives for this new economy, not by indulging in long-term planning of the future, but expecting all plans to have a high level of adaptability and flexibility as they are challenged by changing dynamics of the business environment, changing market trends, and shifting competitive landscapes.

Such co-leadership among CEOs and CKOs, however, is not another buzzword to help CKOs to feel better about themselves and the typical allusive nature of their positions. Rather, it must be a well-thought-out strategy to unleash the hidden talent of the learning organization. Great examples of coequal CEOs include Citigroup and Daimler-Chrysler. These companies are proven testimony of successful power sharing. Unfortunately, many organizations are still resistant to this model and look at those successful experiences as exceptions to the rule, or, in terms of business in wonderland, a rabbit in the hat.

The Rabbit in the Hat

Co-leadership, in particular among CEOs and CKOs, is not only a very new concept, probably mine (hopefully not!), but also an inclusive one. The Bible records that Jesus was already practicing it 2000 years ago; so was God, through His leaders, both empowering Their co-leaders to bind decisions on earth that would also be bound in Heaven.[9] The US Marines have been practising it for more than 220 years. Both accounts have always recorded excellent results.

Business in wonderland, or the new knowledge economy if you prefer, is characterized by power being distributed, not concentrated in a single person, allowing the organization not only to share values, but also aspirations, all working for a common goal. In wonderland, corporations must become farsighted, which requires their leaders to do more than put effective systems

---

9. Mathew 16:19, NIV Bible.

in place. These companies must be able to take rabbits from their hats, that is, be capable of spotting the next trend and responding to it before the competition. Such competitive advantage relies strongly on knowledge management not only from knowledge workers, but also from the market and adjacent industries. Thus, in wonderland, organizations are like living organisms, constantly adapting to changes within them and in the global markets.

In such an environment, chief enchanters, or magicians, need first-rate co-leaders. I believe no complex organization should rely on a single leader. Robert Goizueta, former CEO of Coca-Cola is a vivid example of how important it is for companies to have co-leaders. After his death in 1997, Goizuela's successor, M. Douglas Ivester, made sure the company continued its successful course, regardless of the change of command, which often comes as a major shock to business continuity and success in a typical organization. The reason for it is that Goizueta was a proactive leader, and had prepared Ivester to take over his place when the time arrived. Not only was Ivester a co-leader at Coca-Cola, but he also had a dozen other co-leaders under him, all trained by Goizueta.

Co-leadership is the rabbit in the hat; it is the magic (do you believe in magic?) that takes place when developing business in wonderland. Chief enchanters must realize that co-leadership is a strategy for unleashing talent throughout the learning organization. In this context, I believe chief knock outs (or CKOs) are key in translating co-leadership as more than rhetoric about teamwork, but as a commitment to partnering at multi-levels, to address the constant changing needs of the organization.

SELFLESS LEADERSHIP

A significant issue related to business in wonderland is the impact of the background belief-system or tradition that the organization may identify with. Thus, co-leadership roles tend to be structured according to tradition, be it prior experience acquired as a protégé of a CEO, or the dictates of a parent body organization. However, as co-leadership roles do have a significant impact on the organization's success, I argue that there needs to be some exploration of what co-leadership involves. A book I recommend is one by David Heenan and Warren Bennis, entitled *Co-Leaders: The Power of Great Partnerships.*[10]

Advantages of Co-Leadership

As discussed earlier in this chapter, co-leadership is particularly useful if the organization is a large and complex one, with several groups, or departments, requiring careful monitoring or support. Also, co-leadership can provide mutual

10. New York, John Wiley & Sons, 1999.

support, particularly when one of the leaders is lacking confidence or needs to work on their group skills. Again, due to their eclectic background, CKOs can effectively impact discussions prior to, and after an organization's meeting, being useful for mutual support, development of the organization, and in planning and evaluating the company's activities.

In a difficult organization's situation, the presence of both leader and co-leader can act to diffuse feelings of anxiety and tension, as well as providing practical support. Another advantage is that co-leaders can learn from each other, both in the organization and in feedback sessions. This can be useful if part of the relationship is aimed at transferring knowledge and leadership skills, as Coca-Cola's former CEO went on to prove.

However, co-leadership may have a negative influence on the organization when it is uncoordinated. If CEOs have different opinions on and approaches to the direction and the organization, then this can lead to confusion and unease, particularly if an argument blows up between CEOs and their co-leaders. This can easily escalate into a situation where co-leaders feel that they have to take sides with one co-leader or another. It is important in this type of situation for co-leaders to be seen as supportive of each other. This usually entails some negotiation and discussion between leaders and co-leaders about how they wish to present themselves to the organization. Effective co-leadership requires:

- Leaders that feel comfortable with each other. It should be obvious that, for this relationship to be effective, the co-leaders need to feel comfortable with each other and develop a relationship of mutual trust, which takes time. Otherwise, any distrust between leaders and co-leaders can give rise to a feeling of relief among organization members when leaders are not present, or may leave co-leaders feeling guilty that their leaders might disapprove of what went on in his/her absence.

- Leaders need to work together and respect each other's contributions. Co-leaders need to meet regularly in order to structure group activities, give each other feedback and identify any problems that might arise in the organization. The partnership needs to be one of equality. The employees of any organization can easily perceive an unequal relationship between leaders. Situations where there are two leaders yet one partner is obviously doing all the work, or where leaders compete with each other will have detrimental effects.

- Leaders share common aims and objectives regarding the group. Leaders do not need to necessarily share the same beliefs and perspectives in all areas – different skills, approaches, and perspectives can broaden the resources of the group. However, if leaders' different approaches result in attempts to pull the group in different directions, this can quickly lead to confusion and tension in the group.

In addition, the size of the organization and the number of groups it has will also influence the co-leadership dynamics. The situation of having two co-leaders and one other member may sound rather strange, but from my own experience, I would suggest that this is not uncommon in the wonderland. Unless the leaders are able to re-negotiate their status as regards the other person present, this situation can quickly become frustrating for the other member.

THE REALITY FACTOR: ASSESSING GOOD LEADERSHIP

Successful changes in any organization will depend on leadership excellence. Leadership is a vital catalyst for individual, team, and organization success. As we enter the twenty-first century, co-leadership partners have a unique opportunity and an enormous responsibility to shape the future of their organizations in a direction they want rather than be slaves to it.

One of the major traits of successful leaders is to always create a climate of trust among their peers and people reporting to them. Trusting relationships are vital in the new economy particularly because leaders cannot be sure about anything more than a few months ahead. Thus, when these leaders ask their team to move ahead they are actually saying that they believe this to be the right action to be taken, but that they are not yet certain about how it will work out.

Consequently, those being lead will only be able to buy into it if they trust the intent of their leaders. The following is a list of key behaviors and attributes successful leaders portray:

• Staff's interests come first: before you can win the trust of your followers you must give them reason to trust you. Thus, you must give, give, and give, before you can receive. When followers can truly see that their leaders are aware of their needs and care about them, they commit. At this point, instead of hired hands, leaders will have willing followers. If you are this kind of leader, you will take tremendous satisfaction out of your team's success – not your own! In addition, as you care for your team players and inspire them, they will tend to be more successful, have stronger commitment to you and the cause, and have feelings of support. There is nothing more powerful than a team player that volunteers his work and sees the financial remuneration just as a consequence of it.

As a leader, if you are not an enchanter and do not lead by example, then you are using people to further your own end and you will quickly be exposed. In this context, CKOs can help CEOs by helping them understand the people they work with. As CKOs are typically involved in building communities of practice throughout the organization and acting as pollenizers across the several groups, they tend to have (should!) much more rapport with the organization as a whole than CEOs.

I once worked for a CEO, John Blunt of Info/Ed, who, over a period of two years, built a very effective team of IT education consultants. With the crash of the stock market in 1987, and the eventual closure of the company, he helped all members of his team to find a new job, even though his own future was uncertain.

- Talking the talk; walking the walk: it takes time for a team to trust their leaders. Although team members can act in the spirit of trusting their leader, only their behaviors and actions over time can really attest to their character. Thus, it is very important that CEOs keep their commitment and hold their team accountable to it as well. There will be times, however, when leaders, or team players, will find themselves in situations where they feel that they have not kept their commitment. In this case, CEOs should be upfront as early as possible about the reasons. As for judging their own team members, co-leadership is very beneficial, as CKOs may be in the best position to address, admonish and council the individual, while the CEO works on helping the individual to recommit, to regain the vision, to re-engage…to be enchanted.

Acting as CKO (and an unofficial co-leader of the CEO), I was able to persuade a key employee already with a resignation letter in his hand. He not only decided to stay, but since then became a key player in the group, with renewed vision and commitment. He actually willingly agreed to become one of the "samurais" of the R&D group in the development of a codenamed project called Unagi.

Therefore, CEOs can only continuously enchant and CKOs co-lead if they consistently live the message they preach and consider it a gift when someone points out inconsistencies in their role as leaders. Followers take a great account of what you do, or do not do, and not what you say.

- Being aware of people's feelings: as pointed out earlier, real motivation and commitment comes from the heart, not from the head. That is why volunteers are powerful players. To reach your employees' hearts you must care for their feelings. In bridging the knowledge gap within organizations CKOs must help CEOs to bridge the gap between the head and the heart of everyone in the organization. Otherwise they may fail on their mission by about thirteen inches – roughly the distance between the heart and the head.

Do not underestimate the power of reaching for your people's hearts, for being interested in what they do outside work, their families, their likes and dislikes, their fears, their personal goals. This is definitely a win-win situation. Just like the stock market, you must make consistent deposits into the hearts of everyone in the organization. This way, in times of green pastures and emotional commitment (emotional heart = profit), you will have a fully committed professional. But in times of hardships, be it through your mistakes as a leader, economic downturns, or business realignment, their trusting level will sustain disappointments, hardships, and even a business failure.

I was CEO of TechnoLogic, a system integration (SI) company, back in the late 1980s. We were all traversing hard times in the American economy, in particular with the savings and loans scandals. I eventually had to realign the business and close down the SI activity of the company, but through the end, my team remained committed, more than I would have expected. A couple of them, my right arm, a Brazilian woman, Beatriz Salles, and another Brazilian SI, Victor Murad, stood behind me all the way. They forfeited their salaries for more than a couple of months, and at the end were even willing to lend their own money to the organization.

Even as I wrote this chapter, and we were traversing another financial downturn during early 2001, I saw Virtual Access Networks facing similar financial constraints as I did back with TechnoLogic little more than ten years ago. Fortunately, through friendship, genuine concern for people is paying off again: a key senior staff member approached me and volunteered to have his salary cut to help the organization survive these times. Not only that, but during business trips he took the initiative to stay with friends, to cut cost on lodging, and even shops for cheaper gasoline when driving a rental car! There is no money, BMW, or any other type of corporate perk that could buy this level of commitment.

- Handling pressure and crises calmly: enthusiasm is an emotion every executive staff should portray, in particular the CEO. However, while fear and panic are emotions generally understood among the organization, its leaders should never display them, even if they are feeling them. Instead of running around like headless chickens, leaders and co-leaders should save their energy for thinking the situation through.

   When leadership runs into quick and major decisions, there is no time for enchanting to work, no time for thinking the situation through and preparing the organization. It is very hard, if not impossible, to remain calm in situations like that; as I typically say we should worry about crossing a bridge when we come to it, not before. Thus, in crises, co-leaders should focus on action to relieve the situation and continue to move forward. One of the main challenges in bridging the knowledge gap in any organization is worrying about tomorrow, trying to anticipate the outcomes of innovation. But if we could anticipate the end result of an innovation, then it would not be innovation, but a reinvention.

- Being honest and truthful: leaders must have high integrity, which should be based on clear knowledge of their own values. They should be genuine about their discussions with their team, even and especially in hard times and uncomfortable situations. Again, CKOs can help here, as their experience with collaboration projects in the past would have included honest and open discussion with relevant people and senior staff, rather than secret and closed-doors conversations.

   Derailed corporate leadership groups are often the result of a betrayal of truth. The lack of honesty among senior staff, deceit, and dissention are the cardinal sins of leadership and management. When reality does not match expectation, leadership is faced with a number of disappointments and disillusions on business results.

- Not taking personal credit for other people's work: if leaders want to lose the trust that team members and the organization have in them, all they need do is take credit for something they did not do. Credit must go where credit is due. Nonetheless, within knowledge organizations of the twenty-first century, collaboration, and teamwork are essential. Effective leaders will work as a team and be leveled with the team. They should have a hands-off approach, leading from within or behind, as much as from the front. Recognition should come from the success of the team and the growth of the individuals within it.

    Acting as a CTO at Virtual Access Networks, I was responsible for the research group and innovations in the area of virtual access technologies and wireless. However, as a group, we were pretty flat. We used to call ourselves musketeers and charge the motto, one for all and all for one. But since that group was hooked on sushi, we decided to call ourselves samurais. As a group, we all worked together, trying to build on our strengths and weaknesses.

- Always being fair: to be effective enchanters, CEOs must always be fair, not exhibiting personal favoritism, inconsistent behavior, status, or perks. Leaders must also make sure to stick with the code of ethics and best practices of the company.

    Watch for your own biased opinions. In wonderland it is very easy for us to believe in whatever we want to. Thus, look for feedback. In my case, once a month or so I used to take my group for sushi and we used to go around the table asking each other how could we better serve each other, both at the professional level with the project in hand, as well as on the personal level, so we can continue to grow in our friendship. It has paid off, and we have always been able to under promise and over-deliver in our projects, often two weeks ahead of schedule and more than expected.

I am personally proud of that group of samurais, in particular because we have managed to accomplish such a high accolade despite the fact that each one of us is from a different nationality and culture. Vijay Gummadi is from India, Thavoring Heng is French, of Japanese descent, Rick Castello is American, and I am Brazilian. As individuals and professionals we are many, but in wonderland, under a chief enchanter, we are one.

CHAPTER 8

Helping to Move the Cheese:
Closing the Circle of Innovation

Change before you have to.[1]

The title of this chapter was inspired by acclaimed book *Who Moved my Cheese*, by Spencer Johnson M.D.[2] The book tells a simple and amusing story of four characters that live in a *maze* and look for *cheese* (a metaphor for what you want to have in life) to nourish them and make them happy. The story reveals profound truths about change that give people and organizations a quick and easy way to succeed in changing times.

In the story, two *mice* named Sniff and Scurry, and two *little-people* the size of mice, Hem and Haw, who look and act a lot like people, are the protagonists. In the context of the story, *cheese* can be a good job, a loving relationship, money, a possession, health, or spiritual peace of mind, while the *maze* can be depicted as where you look for what you want, such as the organization you work in, or the family or community you live in.

In the story, the characters are faced with unexpected change. Eventually, one of them deals with change successfully, and writes what he has learned from his experience on the maze walls. When you come to see *The Handwriting on the Wall* you can discover for yourself how to deal with change, so that you can enjoy more success and less stress (however you define it) in your work and in your life.

Unfortunately, innovation has always been a primary challenge of leadership. Today we live in an era of such rapid change and evolution, that leaders must work constantly to develop the capacity for continuous change and frequent adaptation, while ensuring that identity and values remain constant. They must recognize people's innate capacity to adapt and create – to innovate.

The twenty-first century promises to be an exciting time, much like Figure 8.1 suggests, with the course of action changing all the time with the wind of innovation. While there are many management, leadership, and economic theories on what the future holds, we can all agree there will be a great deal of

1. J. Welch, *Excellence in Management and Leadership Series*, MICA Group, Canada, 2001, p. 56.
2. http://www.whomovedmycheese.com.

constant and revolving changes. Leaders must be prepared to successfully guide their groups and organizations through change to survive, innovate, and prosper. This preparation should first begin with an understanding of organizational culture and the levels of culture. Analyzing a group's artifacts, values and beliefs, and basic assumptions will bring insight to the actions and reactions of a group.

Figure 8.1 – The 21st century promises to be an exciting time, with a great deal of constant and revolving changes

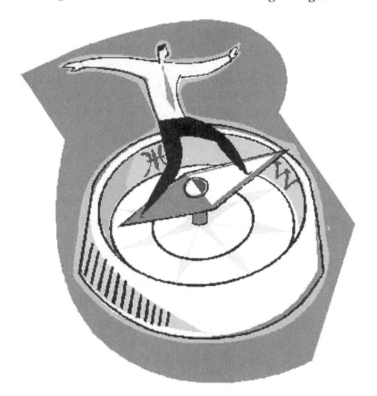

Leaders, in particular the executive staff, should understand they are the most important players in the organizational change process. Using culture, creating or imbedding mechanisms, especially what the users are interested in, sets the tone for the organization. Thus, to be most effective, leaders must consistently act in ways that reinforce their values and the desired end state.

Through a human perspective, leaders can look at how to best match people's needs and skills with organizational goals. Power and competition for scarce resources give a view from the political frame of reference. Finally, a symbolic frame of reference sheds light on portions of a group's culture including symbols, rituals, ceremonies, legends, heroes, and myths.

Change should not be seen as disruptive or threatening, as it provides new opportunity and resources for organizations to improve themselves through their own creative initiative, by generating innovation. It will take continued leadership effort and attention at all levels to complete the job, and leaders must be completely committed to creating an environment of trust, teamwork, and continuous improvement. It is only then that the organization will be an enterprise that allows each of its employees to achieve their full, God-given potential.

As discussed throughout this book, to thrive in the knowledge economy, organizations must continually renew their competitive strengths. Dorothy Leonard-Barton,[3] a consultant specializing in innovation and a professor at the Harvard Business School argues that every *core capability* that leads to success is also a *core rigidity,* and strengths can quickly become weaknesses. According to Leonard-Barton, organizations must consciously invest in activities such as collaboration, experimentation, prototyping, and the acquisition of technological knowledge from outside the firm. She also adds, "[If] all employees conceive of their organization as a knowledge institution and care about nurturing it, they will continuously contribute to the capabilities that sustain it." [4]

ANTICIPATING AND PROMOTING CHANGE

While everyone would agree that the twenty-first century holds many unknowns, to effectively manage KM and support chief enchanters CKOs must realize that the knowledge economy is characterized by vast and dynamic changes. New technologies, in particular the Internet and knowledge technologies, as well as new regulations, directives, and resource restrictions, will be catalysts of change. Why do I believe CKOs are one of the most indicated leaders to hold the flag of organizational change? What can CKOs do to prepare for and successfully implement effective and lasting organizational change?

Strategy in itself is a powerful tool in bringing clarity to any organization, as it can help integrate and focus energy, efforts, and resources. My emphasis on charting CKOs to lead change in organizations is because these professionals can take advantage of knowledge strategies where three other critical leaders in the organization would be brought together, as members of the changing management process: the CTO or head of IT, the COO, or head of HR, and the

---

3. D. Leonard-Barton, *Wellsprings of Knowledge*, Cambridge, Harvard Business School Press, 1995.
4. Ibid., p. 69.

CEO. By bringing these leaders together, who rarely have sat at a strategic table together, except for staff meetings, organizations are able to bring an integrated, focused, strategic force to their efforts.

The optimal structure of KM efforts in change management will vary enormously according to the size of the organization, the degree of change and the challenges it faces, as Figure 8.2 suggests. One concern leaders have in charting CKOs with change management projects is the fear that new bureaucracies may be created. Thus, to be successful in this endeavor, CKOs must not add any more red-tape to an organization attempting to morph itself into something new, as business process will definitely be affected by the changes impacting policies, procedures, and consequently the existing bureaucracy. In addition, CKOs must possess excellent entrepreneurial traits and be influential and persuasive enough to meet the knowledge economy business challenges. That is why I emphasized in chapters one and two the urgent need for a new breed of CKOs that is more business oriented, more focused on the bottom line of the business and not so much on data mining and warehousing, database marketing, or even e-commerce. These activities, with advanced software application and business intelligence tools, are best

Figure 8.2 – The optimal structure of KM efforts in change management will vary enormously according to the size of the organization, the degree of change, and the challenges it faces

taken care of by IT professionals and the CTO/CIO, with the cooperation of
the CKO, of course.

Therefore, as opposed to launching corporate-wide knowledge initiatives
without clear business objectives at the outset, one of the main roles best tailored
to CKOs under change management is to first identify the business
competencies that can be enhanced by KM, as organizations develop different
knowledge strategies depending on whether they are competing on cost, product
innovation, customer relationship management (CRM), partner relationship
management (PRM), or even supplier relationship management (SRM).

Another key challenge CKOs are better equipped to address is the need for
systems that integrate knowledge, technology, and people. This has been
pointed out by Jim Bair, research director with the Gartner Group, where he
comments that we now have technologies at our fingertips, particularly the
Web, that promise to enhance access to information and make it more pervasive
and ubiquitous. Bair argues that organizations must now incorporate people
into their KM efforts. Bair also contends that firms should place more emphasis
on capturing the knowledge and expertise of their employees, and then ensuring
it is effectively shared. "It is the uncaptured, tacit expertise and experience of
employees that will make a big difference",[5] he adds.

Notwithstanding, any organizational theory research will tell us that to
change an organization, leaders must first understand how an organization
operates. That also requires an understanding of the organization's culture,
how it was developed, as well as how it was analyzed. Further, leaders must be
able to view their organization from several points of view to understand how
it really functions. CKOs can play a major role in this process by helping
leaders to unfreeze, restructure, and refreeze their organization's culture as
necessary. Or, if you prefer, remove, reshape, and reposition the cheese inside
their organization as necessary, in order to promote innovation.

I believe CKOs are the most indicated professionals to help to move the
cheese because of their exposure to knowledge management techniques,
knowledge technologies, and the generators of knowledge: people, the Sniffs
and Scurrys, the Rams and Raws of every organization. This is a time-
consuming process, which requires a great deal of effort and consistency. Often,
senior management, in particular CTOs and CIOs, underestimate and
misunderstand it, and try to address such cultural issues with total quality
management (TQM) implementations, which can be very expensive, lengthy,
and ineffective. The United States Air Force, for instance, overestimated their
TQM implementation, and as a result, more than six years have gone by and
they are still working to complete their cultural change. While changes may
be implemented fairly quickly, it takes consistent leadership commitment at
all levels to complete the institutionalization process.

---

5. J. Bair, "Knowledge Enabled Enterprise Architecture" *White Paper*, http://strategy-
    partners.com.

Organizational change can be seen as a double-edged management sword. Any major economic, social, or professional event in an organization can disrupt the flow of business and other functions within the organization. When changes occur, they can promote unity and tighten integration throughout the organization, or unleash a backlash of unrest and turbulence. Changes in a large enough organization can affect an entire industry. For instance, when we look at the late 1998 sharp decline in crude oil prices, we see that such an event caused a significant reduction of business opportunities for oil service companies. More recently, the burst of the dotcom bubble also brought hard changes to marketing companies, and the whole concept of real estate on the Internet. The knowledge economy is being characterized by an economy that capitalizes on change, and unless organizations get ready for it, the price to be paid can be very high, as this new economic condition calls for boldness, innovation, and risk taking.

One of the best places in the world I like to spend time in is Brazil. After I spend some time with my family and friends, I always get amazed with the Brazilian economy and how it positions itself with the global market. What I admire is the willingness and ability of Brazilian entrepreneurs to adapt to change. With the economy in a challenging and ever-evolving position, in particular as its neighboring Argentina's economy collapses, it is amazing to see how promising that market is. As I write this chapter, early 2002, one of the best ETF funds available at iShare[6] is a Brazilian fund, symbol EWZ. How can that be? How do Brazilian leaders pull this one off over and over? The answer, very likely, is heavily focused on innovation, as executives respond to the challenge by trying to improve their marketing focus and *selling their way* out of the downturn. They see the moving of their *cheese* – by global market forces, inflation, and hyperactive cultural changes – as an opportunity to innovate, to re-invent themselves. The same goes for Mexico, one of the leaders in the use of smartcard technology in the world. I am definitely convinced that Brazilian entrepreneurs are always aware that they must change, or adapt to new market forces, when the market environment changes, in order to continuously bring business success. That is why I believe it is the scariest markets that prove the mettle of a fund and its managers.

CKOs should use their deeper knowledge about KM, communities of practice, and organizational change to help learning organizations to navigate the *maze* of change and reorganize their organizational groups, much like an NFL coach reorganizes the team over and over again, as many times as necessary, according to the game at hand. Thus, organizational positions, reporting lines, and responsibilities of all executive staff, senior managers, and departmental groups must be modified according to the challenge, to better address the situation. Under Spencer's analogy, that is when the organization must *move the cheese*.

---

6. http://www.ishare.com.

Changing One Step at a Time

Changes in an organization not only take time, but also many steps. In the process, any attempt to shorten the steps or develop short cuts will only produce a false illusion of speed and the results are never satisfactory. Change is at the core of the gap between know-how and how-to in any organization, and I believe the gap often exists because leaders know-how to implement a change, but do not feel easy about how-to implement it, as they avoid dealing with change. Thus, CKOs must help executives and leaders to realize that change is not just necessary to bridge the gap, but it is also the only constant they can count on when turning knowledge into action.

Whether it is bridging the gap between the know-how about a new technology and how-to incorporate such technology, about the know-how of achieving compliance with a new regulation and how-to implement it, change is the bridge that makes it possible. Know-how must generate strategies, but only change strategies will provide the execution plans of how-to create effective and lasting organizational change to meet these challenges, as depicted in Figure 8.3.

Figure 8.3 – Change is the bridge, the constant connecting know-how and how-to in the transformation of knowledge into action

Changes can come in many forms and forces, originating from both inside and outside the organization. Bridging a knowledge gap within an organization will always require the implementation of new organizational structures, realignment and often consolidation of roles and responsibilities, and even the revision and restatement of the company's mission. Thus, change is always at the core of bridging knowledge gaps, of turning knowledge into action. The problem is, very often, leaders and senior executives have the tendency to postpone change, typically through actions such as "crossing the bridge when you come to it," which often turns into not crossing the bridge at all, or worse, burning the bridge! That is why expensive consulting recommendations seldom lead to change, as executives, despite knowing what needs to be done (often even before hiring a consultant!) are not ready to embrace the changes that will come about as they begin crossing the bridge of knowing-how into how to execute it.

As John Kotter states, one of the major mistakes corporations make is not to establish a great enough sense of urgency in changing. "Most successful change efforts begin when some individuals or some groups start to look hard at a company's competitive situation, market position, technological trends and financial performance,"[7] Kotter says. Surprisingly enough, according to Kotter, more than 50 percent of companies he saw failing in the changing process did so because they did not have enough sense of urgency. Executives either underestimated the hardships that come with changes, in particular taking people out of their comfort zone, or they overestimated the sense of urgency they had placed in the process. Lack of patience, immobilization in the face of downside possibilities, concerns about defensiveness from senior employees, lowering of morale, outlooks of short-term business results, are all reasons for not embracing change, not wanting to cross the bridge, or as Spencer would put it, not wanting to deal with the fact that something or someone has moved the cheese.

CKOs are leaders, and leaders lead, or co-lead, in particular during times of change. To do so, they must be aware of the intricacies and inner workings of the groups they interact with, or lead. Although leading can be exciting and challenging, at times of major changes it can be very frustrating, as organizations are made up of people and human behavior can be very difficult if not impossible to predict. Change always requires the creation of new systems; it requires innovation. Innovation is a great thing, but it demands leadership. Therefore, before CKOs can readily help the implementation of change in a group or organization, they must first understand what makes an organization tick.

Needless to say, if of the right breed, CKOs can very well be the best

7. J. Kotter, "Leading Change: Why Transformation Efforts Fail" *Harvard Business Review on Change*, 1998, p. 48.

professionals for the job, better suited than CIOs and CTOs, as hopefully they are aware of the organizational culture, including artifacts, values, and assumptions, and framed to gain an insight and understanding of the organization. Of course, CKOs can be great co-leaders, but they rely on the support of their leader, namely the CEO. Change will only really happen when the organization has a good leader, often a new leader, who genuinely sees the need for major changes.

Dealing with Resistance to Change

One of the primary sources of resistance to change is the organization's culture. CKOs and other KM professionals involved with organizational learning are typically well aware of it. But unless senior staff and leaders understand what organizational culture entails, very little can be accomplished in dealing with the resistance to change. By definition, it is commonly accepted that organizational culture is a pattern of common and shared basic assumptions that the organization learned as it solved its problems of external adaptation and internal integration, that has worked well enough to be considered valid and, therefore, to be taught to new members as the correct way to perceive, think, and feel in relation to those challenges. David Drennan simply states it as "how things get done around here."[8]

When dealing with the need to change, to know who or what caused the need for change is important, but not so important if you look at it proactively. Of course, it is important to know who or what *moved your cheese*, so you can both run after it or them and compete to get it back. This is what I call a reactive approach to change, which does not necessarily lead to innovation, as chances are your cheese was moved as a result of innovation, only not generated by you or your organization. Thus, you must move your cheese before someone does it for you, or as Jack Welch once said, "change before you have to,"[9] as illustrated by Figure 8.4.

Successful change must lead to innovation. Otherwise, your organization is only playing catch-up. Often, failed attempts to change are a result of lack of vision. In such cases, you do find plenty of plans and programs, but not vision. Success is the result of a vision in action. If your organization is pursuing change based on a vision, but is not being successful, verify your action plans, as very likely there is not much action in place, typically caused by resistance or fear. By the same token, if you believe you have a good action plan, have the support of the organization, and still you are not being successful in implementing changes, and consequently innovate, you must check your vision, or lack thereof, for that matter.

8. D. Drennan, *Transforming Company Culture*, London, McGraw-Hill, 1992, p. 29.
9. J. Welch, *Excellence in Management and Leadership Series*, MICA Group, Canada, 2001, p. 56.

Figure 8.4 – As Jack Welch, former CEO of GE once said: "change before you have to"

Always remember, innovative success is the result of vision in action. Some immediate actions that can be taken when managing change should include:

• create a new vision

• define a mission statement, core values, basic principles, and an operating style.

• create a quality council of senior leaders to oversee the change process.

Removing, Reshaping, and Repositioning the Cheese

Organizations deal with change differently, depending in the stage on which they find themselves. For that reason, knowledge managers whose organizational change projects start with great promise, may fail to live up to that promise, and, eventually, do not make the grade as successful reengineering, or plain change, is unfortunately more common than one would expect.

Creative individuals stand out from the rest of us, and often have odd reporting relationships, but somehow they instinctively insert themselves into organizations wherever they are needed, and the changes and innovations they bring are often more like leaps than the small steps most of us experience. They think of the world in large terms, and their creativity comes from the novel connections they make between their work and their experience or observations. They are usually curious and need a field in which to exercise that curiosity. Leaders can work to bring the special and creative gifts of these people to bear on the efforts of a group.

Chief knowledge officers and knowledge managers are catalysts in this process, as knowledge strategies enable organizations to enhance their business competencies, whether they are focused on efficient operations, product innovation or customer intimacy, thus becoming an important component of removing and reshaping the cheese. By strategically managing and acting on knowledge, organizations can generate tremendous value for shareholders and customers.

In order for CKOs to become effective instruments for change in organizations, they must attend to the fact that any organization in growth stage has its leaders focusing on the development of group values and assumptions. Thus, what leaders pay attention to, control, and reward, as well as how they allocate resources, select, promote, and eliminate people, is very important during this stage. This is a phase in the organization when there is a lot of personnel recasting, mission focusing, and the establishment of business processes. Chief knowledge officers are even more important in the change process when the organization matures, as leaders begin to lose their ability to manipulate the organization, thus making it more difficult to enforce changes. This is a very sensitive stage for any organization experiencing change, as earlier strengths can turn into liabilities, and often what leaders had believed to be an organization's weaknesses can very well become strengths in a different context.

Therefore, I propose that organization leaders tap into CKOs use of their KM skills, as well as their desirably eclectic background, to help them promote change in the organization. Chief knowledge officers are the most adequate senior professionals for the task, mainly because changing deeply held values and assumptions in any organization requires considerable understanding of human behavior and culture in organizations, effort, and time. Nonetheless, as discussed in chapter two, we need a new breed of CKOs in order to be successful in the changing process. CKOs must posses two or three of the following characteristics listed below, and help their executive peers, in particular the CEO, to also posses as many as these traits as possible:

- *Ambitious.* Do people in your organization perceive you as someone that has managed your career well over the years? Do they have confidence that if they stick with you they too can benefit from your successes?

- *Excellent motivator and team builder.* Are you a team leader? Do people easily follow your dreams, your directions, despite the clarity of your vision at times? In other words, do people have faith in you? You should always be able to develop visions of the future that are relatively easy to communicate, and appeal to customers, employees, and stockholders. However, there are times when one must believe in what cannot yet be seen.

- *Loyal, with proactive management habits.* Are you willing to make sacrifices for the organization and its members? Would you be willing to temporarily sacrifice your salary so that you could make ends meet in the organization?

This is a trait a CEO must posses if they are to conquer the respect and loyalty of employees, especially in though times.

• *Outgoing, well-liked (enchanting)*. Are you, and in particular the CEO, a true enchanter, a person that people like to hang out with, listen to? Are you or your CEO seen as charming?

• *Outstanding reputation*. Do people in the organization perceive you and, most importantly, the CEO as people with a high level of competence and potential for success?

• *Survived organizational restructuring or change of management*. Do you have a history of surviving corporate shakeouts, which may indicate an inherent value to the organization and an above-average emotional intelligence (EQ)?

• *Technically savvy*. Do you or your CEO have a reputation for being technically brilliant, insightful, and visionary?

Having two or more of the traits listed above positions leaders for success in promoting change in their organization. However, as Edgar H. Schein[10] comments, leaders should be able to understand how culture is created, embedded, developed, and, ultimately, manipulated, managed, and changed. Often, many problems that were once viewed simply as communication failures or lack of teamwork are in essence a breakdown of intercultural communications. For instance, many companies today are trying to improve their designing and manufacturing process, as well as the delivery of new products to customers. However, the coordination of the marketing, engineering, manufacturing, distribution, and sales groups requires more than the organization's willingness to change and improve. It also requires more than good intentions and a sleuth of management perks. Such a level of integration and proactive change requires a much better understanding of the subcultures of each of these functions, and the structure of the typical group interaction processes that allow communication and collaboration across sub-cultural boundaries. KM practices are key in this process, as KM professionals, in particular CKOs, can develop the necessary cultural analysis to better understand how new technologies influence and are influenced by organizations.

In this context, a new technology tends to be a reflection of an occupational culture that is built around new core scientific concepts. CKOs have the responsibility to develop cultural analysis for the executive staff across national and ethnic boundaries. Thus, organizational learning, development, and planned change cannot be understood without considering culture as a primary source

---

10. *Organizational Culture and Leadership*, New York, Jossey-Bass Business and Management Series, 1997.

of resistance to change. As Leonard-Barton asserts,[11] leaders must increase their study of culture and place the research on a solid conceptual foundation. She also alerts that superficial concepts of culture will not be useful. We must come to understand fully what culture is all about in human groups, organizations, and nations so that we can have a much deeper understanding of what goes on, why it goes on, and what, if anything, we can do about it.

Since cultural issues cannot be understood on the fly, changes in the organization can be very complex if conducted in a single, process-oriented fashion. Thus, change must be conducted in a three-step approach, very similar to Spencer's model in his book, *Who Moved my Cheese*:[12] removing, reshaping, and repositioning.

Removing the Cheese

Removing the cheese from the organization is the first step in seeking out changes and promoting innovation. The process of removing the cheese should be backed up with information or data showing negative trends or tendencies, proving that the current *cheese* is no longer healthy for the organization or its individuals. For instance, the organization is failing to meet some of its goals, or its systems are not working as efficiently as required.

Leaders, CKOs I would add, must make sure that this negative information is fully recognized and explicitly linked to important organizational goals to produce a feeling of guilt or anxiety within the organization so important in promoting change, as no settled professional wants to change. By using the community of practice approach, peer-group discussions, and other KM tools, leaders then must provide a new vision to serve as a psychological bridge from the current situation to the new one. Here again, bridging the knowledge gap created by changes in the environment or business landscape is very important. At this stage, CKOs must act very cautiously though, with much regard for the well being of the organization's members, much like dealing with a relative that has just lost someone or something very close and dear to their hearts.

A leader connects creative people to the entire organization. A leader does not demand unreasonable personal or corporate loyalty, understanding that creative persons are loyal to an idea and often appear to others as not so feasible. Their work arises from discovering and connecting. Remember the story of Archimedes' discovering the principle of displacement while taking a bath: Creative people have insights in all kinds of contexts: Art Fry realized the potential of Post-it notes while singing in his church choir; Hewlett-Packard began in a garage. Leaders understand the potential of connections like these, and make it possible for creative persons to discover them.

---

11. *Wellsprings of Knowledge*, Cambridge, Harvard Business School Press, 2000.
12. http://www.whomovedmycheese.com.

The word *removing* can be a negative word in itself, pointing to a notion of loss, emptiness, void, and despair. Thus, it is here, at this first stage that most organizations give up on changing. At this point, all the organization knows is that the current state of affairs is not healthy, no good, and needs change, but it is part of human nature to resist changes. Therefore, reshaping the cheese is a very important stage, one that will determine the success or failure of change in the organization, on which the pure essence of innovation depends. Quality programs must be developed during the reshaping stage to review:

- the establishment or refocus of mission statements and objectives

- the creation of a new strategic plan

- the development of quality councils, to assess and re-evaluate the quality of the staff in line of new mission and goals, thus preventing the miscasting of staff, personnel, and team training

- the development of process action teams and measurement indicators or metrics

- the development of individual and team quality awards programs to be implemented during the repositioning of the cheese.

Also, during the removing of the cheese, make sure to include training as one of the basic thrusts of quality programs. Training courses and workshops ranging from awareness, team member, and team leader programs, as well as customer satisfaction, teamwork skills, and continuous process-improvement programs, should be included.

The organization's and employees' visions, missions, credos, and core values serve as cultural embedding mechanisms. Thus, it is important that throughout the change project leaders continuously refer to, and reinforce, management actions, by providing directions to guide action and change. A good idea is to develop frames and small posters to be affixed on the walls of the organization, as a constant reminder that they are all engaged in the changing process. It is when these espoused concepts and values are continually reinforced and discussed that the organization and its employees begin to move deeper into the new organization culture and impact basic values and shared assumptions of the group. This takes conscious commitment over time.

Also the concept of commitment during the removing and reshaping of the cheese is very important, as at all levels it is critical to institutionalizing change. If overlooked, lack of commitment turns into resistance. Commitment can also be lost when employees see leadership not walking the talk, which includes but is not limited to:

- canceling staff meetings, quality council meetings, or continually sending replacement attendees

- demanding unrealistic leaps in productivity over short periods of time

- continually overriding team recommendations

- forcing change, or not enforcing it at all when the excitement and fervor of the new initiative quickly ware off.

Reshaping the Cheese

With the organization's current (or obsolete!) knowledge system *removed*, leaders now must think about restructuring the organization's basic assumptions, the employees' basic belief system, their basic knowledge base. Leaders now must reshape the organization's cheese, as illustrated by Figure 8.5. This restructuring process, chaotic by nature, is what I called the *eye of the knowledge tornado* earlier on in this book. As the organization attempts to move out of the eye, the chaos, it begins to develop a new, and often adjusted, set of basic assumptions and a change in behavior.

Figure 8.5 – In face of constant change, leaders now must reshape the organization's cheese!

At this stage, a clear vision for what the organization wants to achieve is very important. Without one, the changing effort can easily dissolve into a very confusing project with many incompatible initiatives, which can dangerously take the organization in a completely different and wrong direction. Furthermore, a blurry vision will produce lack of cooperation from the individuals in the organization, which will not be willing to make any sacrifices, especially if they are unhappy with the status quo. At this stage, everyone must believe that useful and fruitful change is possible. Thus, credible communication, consistently delivered, is a must if leaders want to capture the hearts and minds of the organization as a whole. More than ever, at this stage, success will be the result of vision in action.

CKOs can be very effective here by using gentle and consistently applied pressure on the organization about the vision, the actions to take the organization there, and the rewards that await them once they get there. Some strategies may include:

- Lively articles about the new vision, delivered through the organization's newsletter. If you do not have one, create one!

- Replace the boring and ritualistic weekly staff meetings with exciting discussions on the changes being undertaken.

- Make change the core objective of the organization. For instance, instead of discussing sales pipelines, discuss what needs to change this week so that the organization can be more profitable. Instead of discussing performance planning and reviews, discuss how individuals in the organization can obsolete themselves on a daily basis, on all fronts.

- Most importantly, talk about how everyone in the organization, beginning with the CEO and the executive staff, can walk the talk. How can everyone consciously attempt to become a living symbol of the new organization's culture?

Keep in mind that communication comes in both words and deeds, and the latter are often the most powerful and effective form. Be careful with the leadership behavior, as well as the posture adopted by the employees during this process of reshaping the cheese, refocusing the vision. Nothing undermines change more than behavior by senior staff that is inconsistent with their words.

Repositioning the Cheese

This new behavior and desired set of assumptions and beliefs must be continually reinforced until there is no more anxiety throughout the organization and in the system. At this point, the organization should be stabilized. Thus, in successfully repositioning the cheese, make sure to continuously involve large numbers of supporters as you progress.

Make sure to encourage employees, emboldening them to try the new approaches and develop new ideas in line with the new vision. The more employees you get involved, the better will be the outcome. However, do not rely on communication alone. Repositioning also requires the removal of obstacles. Often individuals in the organization see the new vision and want to be part of it. But very often they get immobilized by a wall that appears in front of them, turning the effort ineffective. Most of the time, these walls are imaginary, present only in their heads. Thus, the challenge is to be able to convince them that there is nothing, or no personal risks, to stop or prevent them from changing. Such walls tend to be very real, as the human self-preservation instinct tries to avoid actions that can be detrimental to their job, image, or career.

Another important aspect in repositioning the cheese is timing. Change takes time, so it is important the leaders keep the organization motivated throughout the process. Most employees will not stick around waiting for the benefits of change for very long. Thus, make sure to plan for at least some small results within twelve to twenty-four months. Without these short-term results, employees might begin to give up on the vision, and even display resistance against the changes.

CKOs again bring an advantage to the change process as leaders are pressured to produce short-term results. Since CKOs typically are not so involved with the management of employees and their everyday responsibilities in keeping up with the business processes, they fit very well in the role of *bad cop*. Direct managers do not like the fact that they may be forced to produce short-term results for the changes taking place. At this stage, pressure can be very useful in achieving this goal, particularly because once managers and employees realize that major changes will be slower to materialize, the urgency level tends to drop. By not being directly in the line of fire, CKOs can help to keep the urgency level up, while promoting business intelligence activity that may enable the clarification or revision of the vision.

Finally, a successful repositioning of the cheese or a successful change in the organization is measured by how well the changes become embedded in the organization's new culture, seeped into the way its employees conduct their everyday business. As discussed earlier, an organization's culture can be summarized by the way things are done. By the same token, a successful change would have been institutionalized through the organization and become part of its culture.

To ensure changes are institutionalized in the organization's culture, knowledge about the change and the new way of doing things has to be turned into action. One way of verifying that is by consciously attempting to show employees all the positive results the new approach, behavior, and attitude have brought to the organization and its performance. It is very important that leaders make an effort to communicate such accomplishments as employees may not realize it, or, many times, establish very inaccurate views of the results.

For instance, at Virtual Access Networks, I was once asked to manage the research group working on a new wireless technology concept that had failed under previous management. This was an unusual situation for a CKO to be in, but I believe management understood that most of the challenges the group faced were not of a technical nature, but of a multicultural and motivational one. It was clear that several changes had to take place in that group if it was to be successful, which was not a choice.

As I began removing the cheese, the team member's characters began to clash with the new vision. At some point, one half of the group even threatened to resign if they were forced to change. But after much communication, group lunches, peer-quality reinforcement meetings, and the development of a unique identity, the group finally began to turn around, accepting the new shape of the cheese. We were finally able to successfully reposition the group, its goals and deliverables in record time. However, the group did not naturally take ownership of their success, and few even expressed that the reason they stayed around was out of consideration for me. These team members at first clearly missed the point, as there was no way one person alone could change a group, unless each element of the group did their part, beginning by believing in the new vision and doing their best to succeed. It was necessary for us to meet as a group a few times, as well as individually, to emphasize the glory for the accomplishment was theirs individually and as a group, and not just their leaders'.

The group today is self-sufficient and successfully operates under that new vision. Furthermore, at least one successor rose up from the pack and is ready to lead that group. Leaders must breed new leaders.

CLOSING THE CIRCLE OF INNOVATION: FORGET THE CHEESE!

In the knowledge economy, innovation is not only a necessity, but it is king. Unless learning organizations gain access to new ideas that in turn can help the generation of innovation, timely dialogue cannot be established, promising ideas cannot be disseminated. But conducting business at the speed of thought gets more complicated than this, as different industries operate at different levels of change and thus need to use different approaches to succeed.

The innovator must forget about the cheese they have, or used to have. Such cheese, be it a technology, skill set, customer base, current product, or service, has been moved by market forces, competition, obsolesce, or economic shifts. Thus, the challenge now is to forget the old cheese and focus on creating new cheese, which will require more than simply chasing the old cheese or responding to its demands. Think about some of the many times cheeses were moved in the past few decades:

• Chrysler moved the automobile industry's cheese in 1993 with the introduction of the minivans. At that time, a van mounted on a car chassis with folding seats and cup-holders moved the cheese of every automaker and car buyer.

- Sony moved its customers' and the industry's cheese when it told them to strap its tape players around their heads, giving birth to Walkmans.

- Napster moved the cheese of record label companies when it forced them to adapt to a new way of distributing and selling music tracks over the Internet.

- Audible is moving the cheese of hardcopy book sellers and readers by making it available over the Internet on MP3 format, allowing people to enjoy a book even if they are driving, flying, jogging, with the lights off in bed, or in a group.

In this new economy, successful companies are not those capable of surviving the move of their cheese, which is very important, but those capable of letting their cheese go so that they can search for more enjoyable and gratifying cheese. Thus, innovation is the main ingredient to spark new sources of revenue based on changing and disruptive technologies, demographics, and consumer habits. Just like a new kind of cheese can destroy the demand for old cheese, new business models can also destroy old models.

Therefore, moving the cheese to promote innovation is a threat to every traditional, uninspired business. Never before have strategy life cycles been shorter and market leadership counted for less. If you or your company is not pursuing innovation, rest assured that it is only a matter of time until you become overwhelmed by it. Strategy innovation is the only way to deal with discontinuous – and disruptive – change.

Demystifying Innovation

Innovation is not something that can be predicted or scheduled. Thus, existing orthodoxies and obsolete business models must be revised, if not let go all together, if innovation is to be promoted. True and insightful innovation bursts that prompt new ideas are never bound to predictability or corporate brownbag and strategic meeting calendars.

One of Nokia's most successful cellular phones, the rainbow-hued, emerged from an afternoon at the beach in California, and not out of a strategic meeting in an air-conditioned think tank room at the company's head quarters. The innovation also gave birth to the inspiration that would further Nokia's success with cellular phones: mobile phones are not only a communication tool, but also a fashion accessory. But very few companies follow Nokia steps, especially in the US where a hierarchy of organization dominates a hierarchy of ideas. Innovation can only be fostered if the encouragement for new ideas is unlocked across the organization. One way of doing this is by bringing together a cross-section of employees at all levels and groups of the organization to share their ideas and any new perspectives that may contain the kernel of a fruitful and even market disruptive new idea.

Developing an Innovation Paradigm

The process of innovation cannot be anticipated or predicted, but it can be consciously developed, as long as learning organizations are willing to dump the cheese that is preventing them from being innovative, such as old policy and procedures, old culture and habits, and upend cherished conventions. As a rule of thumb, past achievement imposes resistance against future adaptability by developing policies and subtle ways of doing things that cause the organization to undermine and even totally ignore innovative insights.

Therefore, one of the major threats for organizations in the ever-evolving knowledge economy is their past successes. The laser focus of the past becomes the set of blinders of today, lessening an organization's ability to discern what is truly new and what it already knows. Glimmers of great ideas are evident in most organizations. However, people, from upper management down, tend to be resistant to change and will tend to target those new ideas as a foreign variable to the organization's culture or know-how. Thus, instead of welcoming new insights, most organizations attack those ideas as foreign enemies threatening the status quo of their organization.

In the UK, for example, where knowledge management and innovation are seen as catalysts to competitive edge, some organizations are capitalizing on the shift of an innovation paradigm. Richard Branson, CEO of Virgin Enterprises, encourages every one of his employees to call him and share a new idea. They all have his cellular phone number. A successful example of his strategy is the wedding planning boutique Virgin Bride, which was the result of one of Branson's Virgin flight attendants who was having problems planning her own wedding. She called Branson and the boutique was created. In the US, seldom will you find a CEO who is willing to share his cellular number with his employees. Believe me, I have tested it, and as a senior staff member!

In developing an innovation paradigm, you must also institutionalize innovation by building a safe place for people to think new thoughts. In some companies, new ideas are in short supply, muffled by an organization climate that deprives the intellectual oxygen, discourages change, and demands conformity. An innovation paradigm should promote plentiful generation of ideas, and then make sure that those ideas can be turned into action. More precisely, ideas generate new knowledge, new know-how, which is not worth anything unless your organization knows how-to convert this knowledge into action.

Bridging the Knowledge Gap of Innovation: From Ideas to Action

The institutionalization of innovation is the bridge that needs to be crossed to turn ideas into actions. Such a bridge enables the creation of an internal constituency for change, and again, CKOs should be at the forefront of such initiatives, inspiring a new breed of *innovation activist* to find an ear and an outlet for creative new concepts within the organization. Unless such a bridge exists, organizations will become innovation-unfriendly, and eventually push their iconoclasts out, to an organization that welcomes their new ideas.

In the twenty-first century economy, organizations need more than chief enchanter officers, chief knock outs, and a core of co-leader executives. These executives must be innovation-minded, capable of developing a culture that sees change as a normal event, a necessary event. Just like God equipped us to deal with daily changes in nature and accept and take advantage of them, so should innovation-prone executives. A rainy day or a sunny day, especially when unexpected, does not necessarily mean good or bad news. The opportunist will use the sunny day to go to a beach and the rainy day to plant or water his lawn. We must look at changes in business as an opportunity to innovate, to evolve, to recycle, and to grow.

Therefore, instead of chasing existing markets and the competition, close the circle by promoting innovation:

- Stimulate new ideas and discussions around creative topics related to your industry. Beware that new ideas will not flow under systematic approaches and charts. You must promote an environment where people feel free to speak their minds. The best strategy for innovation sessions is no strategy at all. Let free associations flow. If anything, spark conversations between executives and employees so the hierarchy chart can be broken. Ask people to tell stories about how their products/services could better be utilized IF...(let them fill the blanks with a story).

- Look for new alternatives. To be innovative is to evolve, to become new again, to anticipate or impact the future. No one is better suited to do that than young people. Ask your kids, and encourage your employees to ask their kids for input. That is why I say focus groups never work! If you really want to pick at your consumer's mind, find them by the pool, or in their neighborhoods; ask them informally. Nokia does it on a day at the beach. Have fun and make sure your people are having fun. It is only when the psychological barriers of human insecurities fall that people will really feel part of a team, and, most of all, that they will make a difference.

In my lectures on information systems (IS) management at Boston University/MET graduate program, I am always enticing the students to think creatively about IS. After all, the new economy will require new IS management approaches. Thus, I am always the first one to laugh out loud at my past mistakes and urge them not to commit the same mistakes by questioning how they can do it differently. The great thing about it is that the class is always very diverse, with students from all over the world, so you really hear a variety of viewpoints. I actually even show a small movie, a cartoon, that illustrates the necessity of thinking out of the box, called Joshua in a Box, not only to encourage them to think out of the box, but also to persuade them to be persistent and hang on when opposition and resistance arrives. The results are amazing and I realize its impact when I receive e-mails from former students exercising innovative approaches at the marketplace, and being successful in coming up with solutions that are simple and that no one ever thought of before. I have a collection of such e-mails in my archives.

- Be passionate and spark passion. Innovation and inspiration hang out together. They do not originate in the brain, but always come from the heart. That is why it is so important for CKOs to take advantage of their cultural and interpersonal skills to help people to be passionate about what they do and how they do it. Unless people volunteer their work, their mind, and, ultimately, their hearts, you will have a team that is together out of duty and not out of desire.

  If your innovation initiative has restrictions, forms, and does not allow for free association of ideas, you will be sure to fail by about thirteen inches: the distance between your employees' hearts and brains. Innovation comes from the heart! Companies that are not afraid to innovate engage employees' energy in a new and profoundly different way. When people are part of a cause and not just a cog in the wheel, then their emotional quotient (EQ) skyrockets, promoting a level of success never experienced by high intellectual quotient (IQ) figures. In the twenty-first century, EQ will be much more important than IQ.

- Good ideas are more important than great capital. Companies that look to incremental change to generate additional revenue will tend towards subsistence at best, being eclipsed by companies that create an environment of innovation, spawning the new ideas that generate new wealth. A culture of continuous experimentation embedded broadly and deeply throughout a company.

  As an example, take Schwab, which controls about 30 percent of all the stock trading that takes place on the Web, with a market capitalization back in 1995 in excess of $3.5 billion, about less than half that of Merrill Lynch. Well, not so today, as the company has now pulled even with Merrill's, which instead of engaging the Internet, pursued until recently a policy of digital denial.

Keep in mind that you will be creating value for your organization when you help employees transform inputs of resources into products and services of greater worth. The patterns of interaction, coordination, communication, and decision making through which they accomplish these transformations – the processes – will be of great importance to any innovation *movement,* as processes are often very hard to change. By processes I mean not just manufacturing processes, but all of those by which product development, procurement, market research, budgeting, employee development and compensation, and resource allocation are accomplished.

Steven C. Wheelwright and Kim B. Clark[13] talk about the formation of structures called heavyweight teams to break the inherent processes that often resist innovation. Much like the *special teams* in NFL Football, diverse companies such Chrysler in the automobile industry, Medtronic in cardiac pacemakers, IBM in disk drives, and Eli Lilly with its new blockbuster drug Zyprexa have used heavyweight teams as vehicles within which new processes could band together.

To create new cheese, to change or innovate, organizations must do more than assign the right resources to the problem. They need to be sure that the organization in which those resources will be working is itself capable of succeeding. In making that assessment, leaders must analyze whether the organization's processes and values fit the problem, and how they are coping with resistance to change.

---

13. *Revolutionizing Product Development: Quantum leaps in Speed, Efficiency and Quality,* Free Press, 1992.

CHAPTER 9

So You Want to Become a CKO?

What is necessary for someone to become a CKO? Like anything else in life: Talent!

This chapter is about nurturing a new breed of CKOs. The proposition is mine, the deliberation is yours, and the action needs to start with you. Since nothing in life is free, you must invest in it, so you can achieve the desired results. Just as the CFO manages a company's fiscal resources, and the CTO manages all aspects of information systems and technology, often sharing the information management with the CIO, the CKO is responsible for developing processes that facilitate knowledge transfer. As such, you must possess hard technical skills and soft interpersonal skills; that is, as CKO, in particular in the knowledge economy, you should have two main duties:

- championing an internal culture of knowledge sharing

- designing enterprise information portals or other IT knowledge infrastructure.

This chapter focuses solely on the qualities and attributes CKOs should have or develop in order to be successful in the knowledge economy, once their organizations are learning entities. Some of the specific qualities discussed in this chapter include how to:

- set realistic expectations about the value of knowledge and its application

- gain personal and professional respect within your peer groups and the organization as a whole

- bring to your organization something that is not always definable

- be capable of conceptualizing valuable and doable situations

- have a reservoir of information that could be useful as a resource

- have a full understanding of the interaction of technology with people

- be perceived as creating value within the organization

- become a thinker who can think through issues.

But before we can talk about qualities and attributes of this new, and necessary, breed of CKOs, it is important to understand the role CKOs should play in the twenty-first century learning organizations, which can often be viewed as very controversial.

A NEW AND CONTROVERSIAL JOB

Without a doubt, the job of a CKO is a new and controversial one. Many organizations have yet to even hear about the job title, much less its attributions. To say the least, the CKO title and role as part of the senior management staff have brought up a good deal of skepticism. Many critics, for the past few years, have been saying that KM is a transient management trend, and that CKOs perform insignificant work. But what many critics do not realize is that knowledge is the key differentiator in today's business.

As discussed earlier on, every organization goes through what I call the knowledge tornado. There is no way around it! Just like in the movie *The Perfect Storm*, the business world is experiencing today the much-anticipated clash Alvin Toffler warned us about in his book *The Third Wave*.[1] Toffler talks about three great advances or waves in our society/economy:

- The agricultural wave began thousands of years ago, forcing people to move away from nomadic wandering and hunting, to begin clustering into villages and develop culture

- The industrial wave, where machines flexed their muscles, much characterized by the Industrial Revolution of the eighteenth century, which gathered speed after the Civil War in the US. During this wave, people began to leave the peasant culture of farming to come to work in city factories, which culminated in the Second World War, a clash of smokestack juggernauts, and the explosion of the atomic bomb over Japan. But machines, as reality showed, were not as invincible as was once thought, and the third wave began to form, one that set the stage for a "perfect storm," a wave based not on muscle, but on mind.

- The knowledge or information wave was co-driven by information technology, and by new social demands worldwide for greater freedom and individuation.

As the international business borders fall and the Internet (e-business, e-commerce, and m-commerce included) enables the share of information and feedback almost in real time, information overflow walls are raised. Today, a typical executive no longer has months to make a business decision, as in the 1970s, or weeks, as in the 1980s, or even days, as in the 1990s. Business

---

1. New York, Bantam Books, 1991.

execution today is done in minutes, even seconds. The advent of the Internet gave birth to data repositories, information silos, spread and available all over the world. The amount of information, both explicit (reports, statistics, how-tos, best practices, economic indices, etc.) and tacit (multicultural, instinct, ability to detect which wave you are dealing with, as many countries are still riding one of the two previous waves…), makes up this perfect storm that is trapping several businesses in the US and abroad.

Approximately 500,000 businesses are started each year in the US, and about 400,000 fail. The problem is, despite the huge amount of business investment, technology resources, and academic preparedness (the market is overflowing with MBA graduates!), business executives are unable to break through the three-wave walls generated when the Toffler waves clash. Although Toffler's paradigm proposes a sequential wave evolution from agriculture to information, because other countries and regions of the world are still on the first or second wave, and because the Internet brings these cultures and economies together, the conditions are ideal for a perfect storm, or, if you prefer, a real information chaos.

This means that any piece of information in the twenty-first century must be checked for context, and the correct information or advice in one area of the world could be a recipe for failure in another. Corporate executives are not prepared to deal with such a storm, as they did not learn how to in school; even if they had, they would have no time to ponder, make sense out of information, and make decisions in a timely fashion. It is no news that most executives already rely on instinct, or gut feelings to one degree or another when making decisions. CEOs today are in need of partners – call them co-CEOs, chief strategists, or, my favorite, knowledge officers. These knowledge officers could help the CEO make decisions, and help their organizations become aware of the "knowledge storm" affecting every business today, as well as how to face and survive the storm, without sinking their careers, their businesses, and the economy.

ENTER THE CKO

CKOs are agents of cultural transformation. In this knowledge economy, information is power, but only if you can capitalize on it; otherwise, it becomes a distraction, a challenge for business execution. Unfortunately, much status goes to those who own knowledge and not those who share it. Thus, one of the main roles of CKOs is to work against this mindset inside the organization (and out!), beginning by fostering an environment of trust.

In an economy fueled by knowledge and information, workers must be able to trust that the information they receive is accurate and the information they give will be used in an appropriate manner. Thus, knowledge becomes a greater component of value added to any service and product. It becomes a key commercial imperative of this new economy, where the agility in the use of information is one of the determining factors of success.

Such a proposition is easier to be undertaken by small organizations that have little trouble being agile. However, as organizations grow, it becomes less easy to make proportionate use of what it collectively knows and yet be agile. To be a large organization that is agile and actively knowledge deploying is a challenging prospect. Furthermore, whereas most activities in complex organizations were once conducted around their internal affairs, they are now increasingly extrospective, dealing as equals with partners, others in the value chain, knowledge holders, and assorted gatekeepers.

It is under these environments that CKOs operate. Although they are still spending part of their time fighting against the ambiguities of a new, ill-defined corporate role by carefully linking KM projects to a company's bottom line, successful CKOs are fully aware that KM is not an end in itself. Knowledge management implementations should be deployed in the interest of business models and overall corporate strategy, but the role of CKOs goes beyond these boundaries. Nonetheless, the CKO's contributions to any organization should be directly linked to the bottom line of their business, with very specific tangible results.

For example, the former knowledge manager at British Petroleum plc (BP), Kent Greenes, now CKO at Science Applications International Corp., develops KM programs for his company that explicitly drive corporate profit and market share. Greenes gained fame as a CKO because he saved BP $260 million in 1998. If you want to become a CKO, and live to talk about it, you must justify your presence within your organization by pointing to just this kind of cost savings and increased productivity. A job security for a CKO depends on the ability to show measurable results. I personally always kept a WSIGAR (why should I gain a raise?) file in my iPaq, so I could always be in touch with the measurable contributions I bring to the organization as a CKO.

Designers and Architects

Every successful CKO should also be a successful designer and architect. They should be able to develop comprehensive knowledge-sharing systems that reach throughout the organization, and also be able to establish procedures that coordinate and integrate diverse communities within the organization. It should be the CKOs, working together with CTOs and CIOs, the ones responsible for designing routines that knit together the information in databases, legacy applications, file cabinets, intranets, and employees' informal knowledge.

As they implement their designs and new architectures, CKOs typically change the way work is done in an organization, as KM strategies are embedded into the everyday business processes. For instance, very often, to further the exchange of tacit knowledge, CKOs tend to design spaces that facilitate conversations and chance encounters between workers, as discussed in chapter six. In the process, learning centers may be built, relaxation areas with appropriate furniture may be implemented, and virtual communities that allow employees to mingle and share ideas may be fostered.

Unlike other IT executives, CKOs are often aware of the fact that addressing the cultural issues without the systems and processes required to collaborate and share knowledge is only half the solution. If you want to become a CKO, or if you are already one, you should know that one important goal to be accomplished, with the help of KM implementations, is the creation of an online collection of documents such as former project proposals, best practices, meeting transcripts, and so on that are useful to future projects or aid with employee training. Thus, partnership with the IT groups, in particular the CTO and CIO, is very important, as you cannot develop such a project alone.

The Role of CKOs in Globalization and Agile Business Cycles

As discussed earlier in this chapter, globalization and faster cycles are two consequences of the three waves that collide in the process of moving from an industrial-age economy to an information-age economy. Business in the twenty-first century is being characterized by rapid change and increased competition at global levels. One of the most effective ways senior management can respond to these challenges is by consistently creating new knowledge, circulating information throughout the organization, and quickly updating products and services. CKOs are the most indicated professionals to create the conditions that speed the rate of innovation and spur products to market.

CKOs also play an important role at the level of e-business and e-commerce strategies. As the Web disseminates information more widely throughout the organization, it breaks up its hierarchies as well. Consequently, organizations are moving to team or project-based models, which are often cross-functional and geographically dispersed. CKOs can develop strategies to help these team-based organizations to communicate and learn from each other, but certain skills are necessary. The following discussion highlights such skills.

Developing the Necessary Skills Set

Typically, CKOs have (should have!) a wide-ranging skills set. Such skills should combine IT expertise, an understanding of cultural and multicultural issues related to personnel, and a feel for interpersonal factors that facilitate knowledge transfer. In addition, CKOs should be able to unite a pragmatic business sense with a visionary belief in the power of knowledge management and knowledge technologies. To achieve this goal, CKOs should, at the very least, nurture the following skills:

• *Business Acumen.* It is essential that CKOs posses a keen understanding of business strategy. CKOs with business acumen should work with CEOs and the heads of IT, HR, and marketing, in an attempt to align KM with overall corporate strategy and define it systematically by deploying organizational knowledge to answer a specific business need. To be successful at this level, CKOs must understand the organization's business model and accurately identify what kinds of knowledge will generate value. They should concentrate on achieving concrete, measurable business results in a specific length of time.

- *Being a Visionary.* CKOs must have lots of stamina available for new ventures, in particular the potentially risky ones. Further, not only should they be visionaries, but also be able to convince the executive staff and have change management skills to move the company towards that vision. They should be able to clearly define and communicate their vision, and then help people understand how sharing their collective knowledge can help them individually, as well as help their organization.

- *Having Interpersonal Skills.* CKOs must be their organization's cheerleaders. They must possess the social skills necessary to forge coalitions among a company's different communities. In addition, it is important that CKOs have relationship management skills, as they operate most effectively through influence and persuasion. Thus, empathy is an important skill for CKOs, as well as listening to the needs of the people that deliver the organization's products and services. They should address the organization's needs with improved systems and processes that make it to their advantage to collaborate and share knowledge. After all, KM should never be imposed on an organization from above, and CKOs can accomplish very little on their own.

- *Technical Knowledge.* To design and maintain the necessary digital infrastructure, CKOs need a broad background in technology. However, traditional IT professionals are not well suited to becoming CKOs, as they are not trained in business models and market strategy, and lack an understanding of the cultural issues associated with KM. While IT managers are experts in the acquisition and retrieval of explicit knowledge, CKOs typically concentrate on the strategic aspects of knowledge that are realized through digital tools. While CTOs are focused on storing, benchmarking, and retrieving data, CKOs are focused on organizational learning and knowledge transfer.

The Challenges

Not every organization believes they need a CKO – and they are right! For organizations where the organizational structure is decentralized, having a CKO can be very much counterproductive. Take the examples of companies like 3M and Hewlett-Packard, which have a very loose culture of relative divisional autonomy. A CKO or even a centralized knowledge manager would not be in sync with the rest of the company.

To top the hardship of the CKO market, several organizations choose not to hire CKOs because other managers are already performing these duties, often CTOs or CIOs. Selling KM has become a little tougher over the past few years, as upper management has begun demanding greater proof of return on investment (ROI). The emphasis on ROI is likely to continue driving KM spending decisions in the years ahead. This is not surprising, and it proves my point that a new breed of CKOs, capable of delivering on tangible results, emerges.

I believe ROI will be the driving force for deciding whether or not an organization moves forward with any KM project. Also, I believe organizations will rely on KM-oriented solution providers, such as the Delphi Group of Boston-MA, for strategic orientation in helping make the ROI case to senior staff. This is true because due to the overall spending constraint of many companies coming out of the economic downturn of early 2000 and 2001, organizations do not have the expertise on staff for every KM nuance and implementation. Thus, organizations might decide to rely on solution providers, instead of hiring a CKO, although I believe the CKO should be an integral component of this effort.

Nonetheless, consulting arms such as the Delphi Group can help their clients in focusing on ROI methodology in its KM – and even IT – assessments and pilot programs. These types of assessment, pilots, and evaluations will be increasing for the years to come, as every industry sector attempts to make sense out this new knowledge economy and the perfect storm it creates. Consequently, expect a lot more pilot projects, where CKOs and consultants will jointly develop. Also, expect CEOs to continue to make the most of the KM spending decisions, with the input of CIOs/CTOs and CFOs, as well as CKOs, if existent. Thus, a lot of signatures will continue to be gathered before a project gets signed off.

Compensation

As an officer or a corporation, CKO salaries are typically in line with other executives. CKOs with MBAs or Ph.D.s being hired at companies with revenues less than $100 million should typically expect compensation from $125,000 to $225,000 per year. For companies with revenues greater than $100 million, CKOs will typically have a Ph.D. and expect a salary around $200,000 to $350,000. In addition, most CKOs receive company stock as part of their compensation package.[2]

CKOs assume a demanding set of tasks, and finding the right person is important. Beware that many CKOs are often internal appointments at the senior management level. Because they design enterprise-wide knowledge

---

2. According to a July 2000 survey in *CIO Magazine*.

systems and ask employees to adopt new behaviors, ideal CKO candidates should have already achieved credibility within an organization.

IS THERE REALLY A NEED FOR CKOS IN ORGANIZATIONS?

As discussed earlier in this chapter, whether or not an organization needs a CKO is relative. So, let's take a look at why an organization should (or should not!) have a CKO. To begin with, the issue tends to be controversial and bipolar. While some organizations see the appointing of a CKO as prudent and foresighted, others see it as bizarre and ridiculous.

Therefore, I cannot stress enough that CKOs should be persuasive if they are to thrive in an age as skeptical as the one in which we are now living. Leadership skills are also very important to have, as corporate knowledge initiatives and programs will not succeed without decisive and determined leadership. However, while some organizations believe knowledge-based leadership must be widely distributed, others are convinced that it takes a leader to ensure that knowledge is effectively highlighted and capitalized upon. That is why I believe companies will increasingly look for the inputs of management consulting firms for guidance on this issue. But do these firms believe in the CKO concept? Ernst & Young, Coopers & Lybrand, and Booz Allen & Hamilton all have CKOs. However, Andersen Consulting and McKinsey & Co. do not. Despite their huge commitments to the growing field of knowledge management, these two companies have decided that knowledge leadership is best left to a network of leaders.

While I believe CKOs fly in the face of agile organizations, CKOs should recognize that the deep cultural changes necessary to create high-performance knowledge enterprises cannot be centrally imposed. Thus, if you want to be a successful CKO you must have the organizational skills to encourage business unit leaders, who possess the underlying financial power, to support knowledge initiatives.

Having a CKO

Having a CKO does not guarantee success in promoting learning organizations or KM implementations. Often, having a CKO does not result in substantial positive results. Thus, whether an organization can benefit from having a CKO often will depend on corporate culture. Also, execution is a determined factor on the success of CKOs in any organizations. In addition to being a knowledge leader, CKOs must be able to become a vital and dynamic force in the organization rather than the figurehead of yet another corporate change program. As CKO, you must be able to achieve real success, to the point where the position becomes, at least apparently, no longer necessary.

THE NEED FOR LEADERSHIP

CKOs must have a good head for business – global, that is! The current wave of globalization in this twenty-first century knowledge economy has pushed companies past the point where CIOs with international responsibilities can simply carve the world up into territories and put managers in charge who are primarily technologists with a second language and a flair for regional etiquette. Thus, CKOs can help CIOs aiming to partner with business management who understand the global strategies of the company and can partner with business at the regional level to consummate those strategies.

Multinational organizations are employing a variety of strategies to ensure that they have the star leaders they need, and CKOs can help, as long as they posses technical astuteness, business understanding, cultural sensitivity, and the ability to communicate well. Of course, that is hard to find, as cultural issues are not as clear-cut as one would desire. Different cultures tend to view some fundamental processes, such as coming up with a vision or strategy, through very different lenses.

For instance, in my experience consulting overseas, the kind of leadership behavior I had to adopt varied from one region to another. Although leadership tasks typically do not change, how you get the job done does. In Brazil, for example, in particular Rio de Janeiro, goals and task lists must be fully supported by consensus over administrative/operating meetings. However, in Costa Rica, you can order it done and the executive team will typically trust and support you. I have experienced the same in my consultancy in the Middle East.

Needless to say, there is a huge difference between running a KM implementation in North America and globally, in particular in Central and South America. This can be easily revealed in approaches to project management. Latin American corporations look to a starting point and build to the logical conclusion, while Americans start with an end in mind and work backward. While this generalization may not always hold true, it is a great example of the variances in how people of different cultures exhibit the traits that are considered hallmarks of leadership. If North American CKOs are looking across a multinational workforce for individuals who have vision, for example, that quality may show itself differently in potential leaders who are not from the US. Given the short supply of professionals with the right credentials, CKOs cannot afford to have their cultural blinders on when searching the globe for the next crop of KM managers and leaders. Rather, they must broaden their own cultural understanding so that they can recognize leadership in many contexts. Otherwise, they may overlook those who lead in ways that are appropriate for their own cultures but not typical of US style.

BECOMING A BETTER CKO BY FINDING THE LEADER WITHIN YOU

Finding the leader within you can dramatically enhance your ability to become a successful CKO. Although this premise is true in any role in life, it is very important for CKOs. This is true because you must have passion for what you do as CKO. You must be committed to a cause, have a vision, energy, and courage. If you look back in history you will find that all the great leaders shared the same trait. Take the examples of Jack Welch formerly of GE, Lee Iacocca of Chrysler, Ray Stata formerly of Analog Devices and now of Stata Ventures, Bill Gates of Microsoft, Michael Dell of Dell Computers, and many others. I suggest that you make your own list of successful leaders, as one of the best ways to become an inspirational leader is to study those who already are. If you can, work for one and learn from them.

Early in my career I had two experiences with what I would classify as inspirational leaders. One was my favorite boss, while I was with Recoll Management Corp. First, she was always accessible. No matter how busy she was, she made time for me. To me, it meant I mattered. Second, she never solved my problems. Instead, she gave me guidance in the form of principles that could be used over and over again for different situations. Some examples: "Don't speed up the river, it runs by itself"; "Always take the high road – in the long run, it is the winning strategy"; "Win the war, not the battle;" "Success is vision in action." Third, she encouraged me by praising my strengths. It was up to me to use them to succeed. Lastly, and perhaps most importantly, she "lifted me up." She made me feel I could do anything. Isn't that what inspiration is all about?

If you want to find the leader within you and as CKO inspire others, here are some characteristics to emulate:

- Authenticity: say what you mean and mean what you say. Meet commitments. Be predictable. Set the example of what you want people to be.

- Caring: the ability to empathize with others and understand their individual motivations is a hallmark of leadership. Great leaders find many ways to meet people's needs. They care enough to expect a lot from their people, and they believe in them. They engender tremendous loyalty as a result. When someone cares about you personally it creates a solid bond.

- Charisma: there are leaders with low-key personalities who inspire great devotion, and there are also many who have great charisma and their social, extroverted personalities draw people to them like a magnet. Either way, great leaders manage to find a common ground with people and build rapport.

- Confidence: fear of failure is not an attribute of inspiring leaders. They take failure in their stride. The best leaders can readily describe their failures; only the mediocre have none to remember. Learn from these great leaders and try again. Have the confidence to make the big decisions and move on.

- Connectedness: inspiring leaders connect with ideas by listening intently with open minds and learning from everyone. They connect with people by looking at them directly. They see people for who they are and what they know, and not what they are and who they know.

- Courage: according to Aristotle, courage is the first of all virtues because it makes the others possible. There is an element of personal risk-taking in the deeds of great leaders. There is also a willingness to take a stand even if it is controversial or politically incorrect. With this goes the willingness to take responsibility and accountability for results.

- Determination: some people commit to accomplish, others try to accomplish, but great leaders are determined to accomplish. They will know no boundaries. No matter the number of distractions, they keep their eye on the target. They see obstacles as only those things you need to get past to reach the target.

- Passion and vision: people are drawn to those who have a vision and a passion for their cause. If you really want to become a CKO, in the field of KM, being a visionary and strategist this should be an easy one. The mix of the new technology and the transitional state of business as this knowledge economy unfolds before our eyes makes exciting opportunities easy picking. If you like what you do passion surfaces with no difficulty. You should then create the vision for others to see. Finding the words, drawing the pictures that capture the imagination is a skill that can be learned and practiced.

As CKO you should also be ready to take up the reins of leadership, as Michael Useem points out in his excellent book *Leading Up*.[3] That includes calculating risks, voicing concerns, and guiding uncertain superiors.

MASTERING PEOPLE MANAGEMENT [4]

An unexplored yet critical side of leadership is upward leadership, or getting results by helping to guide your boss. Rather than undermining authority or seizing power from superiors, upward leadership means stepping in when senior managers need help and support in a way that benefits everyone.

Leading up is a matter of offering a superior your strategic insights or persuading a boss to change direction before it is too late. It requires an ability to work in two directions at once, of stepping into the breach when nobody

---

3. New York, Crown, 2001.
4. This section was written by Michael Useem, which kindly contributed to this chapter. Mr. Useem is a professor at the Wharton School of the University of Pennsylvania and director of its Center for Leadership and Change.

above you is doing so – and of listening to those below you before you step off a cliff yourself.

The Ups and Downs of Leading People

Upward leadership is not always welcomed. Many managers have worked for a supervisor who ran the office with a fine level of detail or misjudged the future. To come forward when a superior does not encourage it can be risky, but if the upward leadership works – whether welcomed or not – it can help transform decline into growth and, occasionally, turn disaster into triumph.

Upward leadership is not a natural skill, but it can be mastered, and there are few better ways to appreciate its exercise than to study those who have had to apply it. Watching their efforts can provide lessons for leading up when it really counts.

Bold Subordinates

A few years ago, Al Gore, then US vice-president, defeated Bill Bradley in the campaign for the Democratic presidential nomination. Many factors contributed to the defeat, but among them was Bradley's reluctance to reply to stinging attacks by his opponent. His instinct had been to run his campaign above the fray – less as "a twenty-first-century politician, than as an Old Testament prophet."[5]

Although his campaign suffered defeat after defeat in the early stages, Bradley might have recovered his momentum had he hit back hard. To do that, though, the candidate needed to be led into the fray, a form of leading up that no one working for him proved willing to risk.

Bradley tended to take his own counsel more than that of campaign advisers. For their part, they did not always say what he needed to hear. An aide summed up the problem just after Bradley withdrew from the campaign in March following defeats in two states: "These people were always concerned about what their relationship with Bill should be, as opposed to just doing what it takes to win."

The apparent inability of Bradley's staff to distinguish between leading up and currying favor may have contributed to the aspirant's decline. However, the cause goes back to the man who had created such a mindset in the first place. Had Bradley pressed those who worked for him to do their best by him, even if it meant voicing criticism, they might have bolstered his run for the party's nomination.

Leading up can require fortitude and perseverance. Managers might fear how superiors will respond and doubt their right to lead up, but all carry a responsibility to do what they can when it will make a difference, and to tell a

---

5.   J. Dao and N. Kristof, "Bradley's Fatal Mistakes" *New York Times*, 8 March 2000.

superior what they ought to hear. Many strategies and more than a few organizations have failed when the middle ranks could see the problems but hesitated to challenge their command.

From the other point of view, there is also an obligation on managers to encourage people below to speak up and tell them what they need to know, to fill in for their shortcomings when future success is threatened.

A culture of upward leadership is built, not born. For that, managers should regularly insist that more junior staff examine proposals and challenge errors. Asking those of lesser rank to say what they candidly think and complimenting them for doing so are among the small measures that can make for a big improvement in attitude.

Risk and Reward

Some individuals begin with a head start but everybody can improve their ability for upward service. In 1997, David Pottruck, COO of broker Charles Schwab, faced a critical decision in his career, in which the outcome depended greatly on his upward leadership skills. Could he convince his chief executive and company directors to make a radical move into Internet-based client trading? It would be expensive and risky, but it could also be highly advantageous.

Founded in 1974, Schwab's annual revenue exceeded $2 billion by 1997. Through its thousands of customer service representatives, the company bought and sold shares for a million clients, and in the astounding bull market of the 1990s everyone seemed to benefit. The rise of the Internet, however, threatened to undo all that, undermining a rich network of relationships painstakingly assembled over many years. The web furnished free and fast access to company information that had long been the broker's province and it opened a way to trade stock at a fraction of the time and cost required to call a broker.

For those willing to forgo personal contact, Schwab had built an electronic trading service, charging just $29 a trade. Many customers, however, still wanted real dialogue with real people and it was from these people that the serious money came – as much as $80 a transaction. For how long, though, would these clients continue to pay $80 when they knew other clients were trading for just $29?

One solution would be to bundle full-service and online trading into one offering and so give all customers the combination that many increasingly wanted. In the spring of 1997, Pottruck decided that the two-tier system had to go, even though he was personally responsible for building much of it. In its place, he would create a single full-service offering with Internet trading and he reasoned that it could cost no more than $29 a trade.

Pottruck turned to his boss, Charles Schwab, for approval. Charles Schwab had already embraced the Internet. He had appreciated the power of the web early and had pushed the company to move online in 1995. The founder was known to have a feel for market trends and as Pottruck explained his thinking, Charles Schwab immediately affirmed his interest in the proposed move. However, he also posed hard questions: how much would it cost, how would it affect the organization, and how soon could benefits be expected? Charles Schwab was willing to take large risks and place big bets when the odds were known, and he pressed Pottruck to nail them down.

Pottruck instructed his staff to assess the effect of slashing the full service commission of $80 and providing full service to everybody at $29 a trade, including 1.2 million customers using the limited-service Internet option. The strategists came back with a shocking conclusion. If the company allowed account holders to migrate, it would depress the company's revenue in 1998 by $125 million and its earnings by $100 million, more than a fifth of its projected pre-tax profits. Stock markets would be likely to drive down Schwab's share price with a vengeance.

Although he was sure of the long-term chances of the new offering, Pottruck was less sure if returns would arrive quickly enough to avert financial disaster. The plan would require vigorous support from the chief executive and board members if it were to succeed. Pottruck himself was in the best position to make the case.

He gave Charles Schwab the financial implications of the low-price full service and warned of the effect on profits in the short term. Following weeks of discussion, Schwab endorsed the plan. The founder always insisted on putting customer service first and Pottruck had made that his guiding principle; Schwab had consistently stressed careful analysis, which Pottruck had done; Schwab had delegated much to those he trusted and Pottruck had already earned his confidence.

The next stop for Pottruck was the company directors, without whose wholehearted approval it would be foolish to proceed. Pottruck brought his plan to the board in September 1997. Some directors wondered why any change was needed since the year was already proving to be the best in company history. After-tax profits were approaching $270 million, and what Pottruck was now proposing would slash them by a third or more. Others wondered if the options had been thoroughly studied. Still others asked if the downside could be weathered. Pottruck's confident response was, "It will be fine but it will take some time, possibly a year and a half or more." The directors duly agreed on what would be the company's most fateful decision of the era.

On January 15 1998, Schwab announced it was offering web trading for $29 a time and was extending all services to all customers – consultations at branches and by telephone, and personal advice.

The first quarter's results, as Pottruck had forecast, were devastated. Schwab was indeed cannibalizing its full-service, high-priced accounts. Quarterly revenues had been growing at 6.5 percent per quarter in 1997; now they had declined by 3 percent. Pre-tax income had been rising by 8 percent per quarter in 1997; now it had dropped by 16 percent.

Yet the expectation that the world was moving to the web proved prescient. By the end of 1998, the number of Schwab customers with online accounts nearly doubled and Schwab finished the year with 20 percent growth in revenue and 29 percent rise in profit.

Meeting the Internet challenge at Schwab required keen insight and a reasoned capacity to risk much when others doubted the proposed path. It also depended on a boss ready to be persuaded and a board ready to be moved. However, that readiness was not automatic. Rather, it was the product of steps that Pottruck had earlier taken to establish a relationship of confidence with those above him.

Learning to lead up is a lifelong endeavor and it is greatly helped by a willingness to learn from past mistakes and superiors who are willing to suggest how it is done. Taking risks is a defining element of any leadership, and calculated management of risk is essential. To succeed as a risk-taker on behalf of superiors, decisions need to be taken quickly and accurately. In spite of the uncertainties and large stakes that may be involved, if decisions are for managers to take, it is essential for them to do so rather than kick the responsibility upstairs.

The first step in winning the support of superiors and the board is ensuring accuracy. The second is to communicate carefully why the proposed course of action is necessary and how it can be accomplished with the minimum upheaval.

The Cost of Failure

When organizations foster upward leadership, the benefits can be great. Conversely, the costs of ignoring or discouraging it can be enormous. Consider a recent example. In February this year, the nuclear submarine USS Greenville suddenly surfaced and collided with a Japanese fishing boat, the Ehime Maru. The boat overturned and nine passengers were killed. A navy investigator reported that a visiting officer on the Greenville had sensed that Commander Scott D. Waddle was rushing preparations and cutting corners to give a demonstration to sixteen civilians on board – but the visiting officer had said nothing to the commander about his concerns.

Similarly, Waddle's second-ranking officer, who carried the most explicit obligation to challenge questionable procedures, had failed to voice his own doubts about his commander's pace, including an abbreviated periscope inspection of the horizon just before the surfacing. The subordinate officer, the investigator found, "was thinking these things, but did not articulate them to the commanding officer."[6]

The investigator concluded that the crewmembers so respected their captain that they were reluctant to challenge him. Commanding officer Waddle, he

---

6. E. Walsh, "Sub Commander Reprimanded" *The Washington Post*, 24 April 2001.

found, "doesn't get a lot of corrective input from subordinates because he's very busy giving directions and the ship has experienced a lot of success when he does."[7] Had the institution more effectively stressed its principle of upward challenge, had the visiting officer and the commander's subordinates been emboldened to question their commander's actions, the fatal event may never have happened.

Even short of the loss of life, the cost of failure for upward leadership can be huge. Consider the price of such an error for the chairman of Samsung Group, Lee Kun Hee. In 1994, he decreed that Samsung should invest $13 billion to become a car producer, aiming to make 1.5 million vehicles by 2010. Car manufacture was already a crowded field, plagued by global over-capacity, but Lee was a powerful chieftain and a passionate car buff, and none of his subordinates questioned his strategy.

A year after the first cars rolled off the line in 1999, however, Samsung Motors sold its assets to Renault. Many of Samsung's top managers had silently opposed the investment and Lee later told them he was puzzled why none had openly expressed their reservations. By then, though, Lee had reached into his own pocket for $2 billion to placate his irate creditors.

COURAGE TO LEAD UP

A common element among those who successfully lead up is a driving urge to make things happen on high, an unflinching willingness to take charge when not fully in command.

The exercise of upward leadership has been made easier by contemporary expectations in many companies that managers learn not just from their superiors, but also from all points of the compass. The phrase "360-degree feedback" has come to mean a manager's annual task of gathering reaction from direct subordinates and immediate bosses. So it is with leading up: instead of just motivating those below, managers must also muster those above; instead of just learning from those above, managers need to listen to those below.

Such leadership can be inspired when executives are willing to take the time to create the right culture. Once established, a company-wide emphasis on leading upwards serves as a kind of inertial guidance system, continually reminding everybody that they are obliged to stand up without the need for superiors to ask for them to do so. Figure 9.1 provides some of the cornerstone principles for company managers in leading up.

7. Ibid.

Figure 9.1 – Principles of leading up for KM managers

Leading Up Principles for KM Managers

✓ Building superiors' confidence in you requires giving them your confidence.

✓ The bond between manager and executive should be a relationship based on an open flow of information and respect.

✓ The more uncertain or irresolute your superiors are about achieving a goal, the more clear-minded and determined you must be in formulating and executing your strategy.

✓ If your superiors do not appreciate a grave threat, transcend the normal channels of communication to drive home the message.

✓ Persistence often pays but it requires determination to stay on a rocky path when you have persuaded those above and below you to follow.

✓ However hostile your superior, however harsh your message, the well being of those in your hands must remain foremost.

Figure 9.2 provides some of the cornerstone principles for chief "x" officers (in particular CEOs and CKOs) in leading up.

Figure 9.2 – Principles of leading up for chief "x" officers

Leading Up Principles for Chief "x" Officers

✓ If you want subordinates to offer their best advice, you must value and make use of it.

✓ Stay tuned to what your subordinates are implying or communicating through other means. Because their personal stake in you and the company is large, they may appreciate your situation better than you do yourself.

✓ If you expect those below to support your leadership and step into the breach when needed, they will need to understand your strategy, methods and rules. That requires repeated restatements of your principles and consistent adherence to them.

✓ Downward leadership and upward leadership reinforce one another; if you are effective at the former, it will encourage the latter; if you are adept at the latter, it can inspire the former.

In addition, CKOs must be builders and strategists. So if you want to be a successful CKO you must be a self-starter who is excited by business development and by growing something. A critical attribute of such entrepreneurship is being a strategist who can grapple with the implications of using KM as a tool for corporate transformation.

To a degree, as discussed earlier in this chapter, by being a CKO you should also be a visionary, able to see the big picture that the CEO has in mind, but also able to translate it into action, to think of new ways of doing things and yet focus on deliverable results. CKOs are thus entrepreneurs inside organizations. However, vision and determination are not enough. The CKO is also a consultant, bringing in ideas and seeding them, listening to other people's ideas and backing them if they make sense and fit the knowledge vision.

THE CKO'S JOB DESCRIPTION

The position of CKO and its job description will vary according to each organization, depending on corporate culture, industry, organizational structure, and business strategies. Sometimes, in particular within the government sector, the CKO position may be one of a few other "Chiefs" for knowledge, IT, human resources, and finance, assuming, therefore, a key leadership position in the particular agency he/the CKO is associated with. Nonetheless, the CKO should typically operate within a broad mandate to maximize the organization's intellectual capital, and manage knowledge to the benefit of its mission and employees.

More broadly, a CKO's job description should reflect their accountability for the knowledge management of an organization, as someone responsible to champion the concept and spearhead the enormous effort needed to overcome inherited obstacles to the free flow of information within the organization.

Therefore, CKOs must have a working knowledge of several disciplines, such as information systems, business economics and management, law, research, and communications. Although the job description tends to be nebulous, that is because the duties must be highly tailored to the individual company's needs. Thus, CKOs must draw their skills set and knowledge from a wide range of disciplines and technologies, including:

- business process improvement to include process modeling, analysis, costing, process simulation, functional economic analyses, etc.

- change management

- cognitive science

- computer science

- computer user interface design

- computer-supported collaborative work (groupware)

- data administration/standardization

- decision support systems

- document management

- expert systems, artificial intelligence and knowledge base management systems
- library and information science
- organizational science
- relational and object databases
- semantic networks
- technical communications

Regardless of the organization, public or private, the CKO must become a vital and dynamic force in the organization rather than the figurehead of yet another corporate change program. Leadership must be dispersed and accountability for the success of knowledge initiatives widely held.

Duties and Responsibilities

Typically, the CKO is responsible for ensuring that the organization's employees have the right information at the right time in the right place. Knowledge lives in people, while data and information reside in computers. The CKO provides the leadership required to successfully transform organizations into learning organizations that are flexible, agile, and open to change.

Working cooperatively with the CFO, CTO, and CIO, the CKO builds collaborative work environments, infrastructure, resources, and skills to provide the necessary enterprise architecture for knowledge management within the organization. In addition, the CKO must serve as chief advisor to the CEO, board of directors, and other members of the executive staff on all matters pertaining to knowledge management, including the identification of goals, strategy, tools, measurements, targets and project management. Typical tasks that should be part of a CKO's job description include, but are not limited to:

- Developing program management structure to support the major corporate business mission and goals through selective pilot and demonstration projects related to knowledge management. CKOs should encourage, coach, steer, and direct, where necessary, the corporate initiatives to deliver positive and measurable results to the organization.

- Serving as primary spokesperson, both within and outside of the organization for the company's knowledge management program. The CKO should be able to represent the organization at conferences, forums, consortia, and academic seminars, as well as to the print media, and should serve as the chief corporate expert, the evangelist, on knowledge management.

- Developing knowledge and skills of corporate audiences at all levels, including the leadership, middle management, knowledge workers, and entry-level workers in the full range of knowledge management and development.

- Identifying highly knowledgeable and skilled employees, and ensuring that they maximize their skills in their jobs and careers. The CKO should provide guidance and encouragement to these valuable employees.

- Working cooperatively with the CEO on business strategies, as they should have a good knowledge of the organization's work force, the technology, and the corporate business goals. The CKO should also be able to redirect training to more actively support the knowledge management agenda: for example, expanding the company's distance learning capabilities, reinventing the company's library as a knowledge management center, etc.

- Working cooperatively with the CIO and/or CTO to ensure an adequate electronic knowledge environment at the corporate and organizational level.

- Working cooperatively with the CFO to identify resources to support knowledge management efforts.

- Providing predictive KM strategy based upon research of state-of-the-art business practices in the private and public sectors, benchmarking with both sectors' entities to ensure that the company stays on the cutting edge.

- Developing and maintaining a knowledge management portal for the company, including Web services and interfaces, interactive groupware, enterprise resource planning (ERP) and customer relationship management (CRM) applications, databases, data warehouses, and educational links.

- Facilitating the growth of communities of practice, and identifying knowledge sharing needs throughout the organization, while fostering learning and knowledge creation.

- Providing access to knowledge-sharing tools, evaluating their effectiveness, and recommending leading-edge tools as standards for the agency.

- Representing the company committee and standards events, sharing best practices, new techniques, technologies, and information, and working collaboratively with colleagues in similar positions throughout the public and private sectors.

- Identifying skills and knowledge gaps in the company's workforce, and working collaboratively with the company's CEO, developing strategies to enhance the organization's skills set.

- Visioning the future, and articulating strategies for the company to meet its goals in a rapidly changing environment, while developing measures of effectiveness and results.

- Maintaining working relationships with senior and executive staff in other groups within the organization, subsidiaries, supply chain, distribution channels, and partners to keep abreast of KM and business developments. The CKO should exchange information with the company's leadership, and foster an atmosphere of growth and openness for the agency.

- Communicating the company's commitment to knowledge management and leading by example.

In addition, enabling technologies for KM should be part of a CKO's skills set, including: object-oriented information modeling; electronic publishing technology, hypertext, intranet, extranet, and Internet; help-desk technology, full-text search and retrieval, decision support systems (DSS), and performance support systems (PSS).

CKOs and Start-ups

CKOs are very rare in start-ups. However, they can be instrumental in making sense of all the vital signs of an early-stage company, due to their multi-disciplinary background. From being instrumental in the evolution of a business and advising on the funding dilemma, through providing interpersonal, technical and managerial skills on evaluating the management alignment process and the organizational design and analysis, CKOs can act as co-leaders, along with the CEO, in managing early stage companies.

In this case, the CKO's main mission is to identify knowledge within the company, be it documented or in the heads of employees, explicit or tacit, and to encourage workers to share it, as they would in any other organization. But, in addition, the CKO should have an active role in detecting changes in the market, technology, and business environment that could potentially affect the organization or create new business opportunities. That is why they should work very closely with the CEO and the CTO (and the CIO, if there is one), as well as the whole executive staff and groups within the organization.

More specifically, there are three areas of responsibility that CKOs can contribute to in early-stage companies.

1. Knowledge Management
   - Responsible for internal knowledge management such as care of patents, ongoing research and development (R&D) documentation, technical contents, and verbatim of memorandum of understanding (MOU) between strategic partnerships and alliances
   - Technology evangelist for company's products, proprietary technology, and awareness programs. Examples would be keynote speaking in trade shows, expositions, user groups, forums, partners-sponsored technical meetings and/or boards, etc.
   - Dissemination of technical-oriented articles and white papers about the

company's technical/technological achievements, products, partnerships/ alliances, successes, etc., in the media (magazines, trade journals, electronic boards, etc). These activities are aimed to develop public awareness about the company and its products/services, as well as branding development and overall exposure.

- Identify knowledge within the company, be it documented or in the heads of employees, and to encourage workers to share it.
- Promote the development of knowledge, imagination, and new ideas within the company aimed at promoting continuous growth of the company, its staff, and renewed goals.

2. Technology and New Trends Strategies

- Develop a network of technical/technological relationships with the supplier, vendor, and user community, always searching for business opportunities, R&D synergy and new business/technology trends
- Research and educate groups within the company on new technology trends and their impact on company's products and services
- Act as the technical liaison, along with the CTO and development group between the organization and business partner's technical counterparts
- Help to identify new technology trends that could promote new products and business opportunities for the company.

3. IT and Emerging Technologies Advisory

- To advise the board of directors, company's executives, and business partners on the impact of new technologies, standards, and schemas on product development, market, and existing competing product/ technologies.
- Participate on organized workgroups helping to define new standards and schemas, with the objective of promoting company's awareness and developing competitive advantage.
- Recommend and help to establish new partnerships and alliances with companies and organizations that can provide the company with competitive edge, new business/technology opportunities, product awareness, and market share.
- Help (by overseeing or advising, depending on CEO's/CTO's guideline) to develop an e-business strategy, which should include e-tailing, e-fulfillment, and e-chain and e-commerce strategies, to address branding, pricing, partnerships, creation of value, and overall company's goal and values blueprint.

Knowledge Manager's Job Description

Knowledge managers work very close, and tend to report, to CKOs. In many companies, the CKO is the knowledge manager, or there is no CKO, but a knowledge manager. Typically, both positions will exist in larger organizations only.

The purpose of this position is to provide CKOs, or the organization as a whole, in the absence of a CKO, with program management and senior staff level support to KM programs. When the organizational currency is ideas, sophisticated approaches must be employed to foster the creation, evolution and communication of those ideas. Thus, knowledge managers strive to improve the organizational environment for valuing, generating, sharing, and applying knowledge. The value must be translated into business value – neither too broadly nor too narrowly defined. Difficult questions must be answered such as: "How does a company measure and manage intellectual capital?"

Such requirements are necessary because, as Tim Van Gelder of Indiana University once stated, "cognitive agents are better understood as continuous dynamic systems that evolve in real time. In a stroke, this shifts the emphasis from static structures and discrete operations to continuous change, puts cognition in the same dynamic domain as the brain, body, and environment, and makes contact with principles of self-organization."[8] Therefore, it will require more than simply deploying technology for knowledge to be successfully organized and shared. Provisions for change, speed, and agility will be critical in everything a knowledge manager (and a CKO for that matter!) accomplishes.

Responsibilities

The following are some of the main responsibilities of a knowledge manager (notice the similarities of these roles with of a CKO):

- marketing the importance of knowledge that allows both internal and external users to use it

- ensuring that KM efforts are structured, funded, created, implemented, and maintained

- leveraging knowledge in building the structure to take advantage of technology, using it as an enabler

- creating the KM architecture with strategic goals in mind

- developing the organization to manage knowledge in order to improve

---

8. T. Van Gelder, "A 'Reason!Able' Approach to Critical Thinking" *Principal Matters: The Journal for Australasian Secondary School Leaders*, May 2002, pp. 34–6.

processes and increase efficiency, and decrease time spent in research/ development, while cutting costs

- creating the KM database despite any barriers, including cultural, technical, and logistical
- providing support to users so they and the database will succeed, including training
- identifying which knowledge is more important; setting priorities
- capturing the information and maintaining it
- distributing information in a manner that is most effective for users, allowing some personalization techniques
- developing and maintaining intranet and Internet – picture, bio, vision statement, etc. (possible venues for highlighting successes)
- posting calendar and other recent or upcoming events of note on the web (intranet and/or Internet) including speeches, etc.
- maintaining electronic files on latest speeches, briefings, etc. given by high-level managers among others
- capturing presentations for reuse
- indexing information so it is easily accessible.

Finally, I believe one of the major counterproductive habits CKOs and knowledge managers should aim to break is with regard to the technical groups within organizations and their customers. Often technical groups tend to spend time not with customers, but with each other, discussing the technicality of their problems (the customers that is!). Even within the organization, this pattern among technical groups is very common. They tend to gather in common areas, like in the cafeteria or kitchen, hang around the coffee pot, and swap stories from the field, or their own development practices. Although managers may adopt a posture of a garden-variety reengineer, looking at these groups as a low-hanging fruit, easy pickings for immediate productivity gains, they would attempt to simply reroute the group, cut out the conversation, eliminate the dead time, and pocket the savings.

   However, what should be realized here is that, aside from the alienation of the customer, which should be included in those dialogs, the time spent at the cafeteria or coffee pot is anything but dead. These technical groups are not really slacking off, but doing some of their most valuable work, even if they do not realize it. Field service, for example, is no job for lone wolves. It is a social activity. Like most work, it involves a community of professionals. Thus, rather than eliminating informal conversations in pursuit of corporate efficiency, a KM approach would expand them in the name of learning and innovation.

CHAPTER 10

The Need for Gaps: Trusting the Corporate Instinct

Swift instinct leaps; slow reason feebly climbs.[1]

Opinions vary regarding the best ways to manage during hard times. Some say a downturn is a great time to consider outsourcing, while others say it is the worst. Some argue for immediate cuts across the board; others suggest it is better to examine processes and projects in order to trim fat, not internal organs. Interestingly enough, hard times are always characterized by the presence of many gaps in the organization, the market, the economy, management, and so on. The harder the times, the more the gaps and the greater their impact. The following are examples of such gaps:

- gaps in the excess of inventory, compared to demand

- gaps in profitability, compared to levels of investment

- gaps in creativity, compared to fierce competition

- gaps in skilled personnel and management, compared to eminent need for downsizing, layoffs, and employee loyalty – and the list goes on…

Corporate gaps, no matter their nature, are always a challenge for management and the organization as a whole. However, for learning organizations, gaps can and should be opportunities to transcend, to renew, and to reinvent themselves. As discussed throughout this book, although organizations must learn to deal with the constant "move of the cheese," they will be better off learning to constantly reinvent, recreate their own cheese. By doing so, learning organizations will be actually moving the market's cheese – its competitor's cheese. Call it disruptive technology, or strategy, in the twenty-first century economy, organizations must be ready to view the everyday business challenges coming their way as a necessary gap. After all, such gaps are inevitable.

This chapter introduces the concept of twenty-first century learning

---

1. E.L. Young and D.L. Schallert, "The Influence of Personal Intentions and External Constraints on College Students Writing". Paper presented at the meeting of the Southwest Educational Research Association, San Antonio theme Written Language.

organizations feeding on gaps such as the ones listed above, and many others, as a necessary competitive advantage, as a way to transcend them and disrupt the status quo of their competitors and the business landscape. In the process, due to its very disruptive and unprecedented nature, the only way organizations can deal with gaps is by trusting their very own corporate instinct. If they were to rely on any other form of information other than that, they would only be repeating the so-called "reengineering cycle." As a result, instead of transcending their corporate culture and know how, they would be simply readapting to whatever model is known as "best practices" at the time, losing their edge, becoming conformant.

THE VERSATILE CORPORATION: ACTING ON INSTINCTS?

When I think about how important versatility is for any organization in the twenty-first century economy, I remember Richard Talaber, VerticalNet's CIO. Challenged to run a fast-paced business-to-business (B2B) marketplace for Vertical Industry's IT organization, Talaber knew that the most efficient way to handle staffing was to focus on training and retention. But not only that, I believe versatility was the magic ingredient!

At some point during the economic downturn of the late 1990s in the US, VerticalNet had to lay off 150 people, but the cuts did not significantly affect Talaber's department, primarily because by then the company had acquired more than twenty other companies, which kept him and his staff still busy. Nonetheless, such economic downturn, especially after the September 11 terrorist attacks on New York's Twin Towers of The World Trade Center, not only created a very sad gap in Manhattan's skyline and the hearts of most of the civilized world, but also a huge one in IT spending.

For Talaber, of course, dealing with IT budget cuts was by no means an easy ride, but he took advantage of such a gap, not by reducing work force and shrinking back, but, on the contrary, by spending some more on IT, by focusing on working with his staff to optimize their skills and reduce redundancy. For instance, help-desk professionals were trained to fill in, if necessary, better yet, when necessary, as Web engineers or even as systems administrators. By preparing the original help-desk employee to become a problem solver, and a skilled networking professional, including a Microsoft certification, Talaber was not only increasing the value of such an employee to the company, but also making a very versatile professional, ready to deal with and confront at least three potential organizational gaps in the future. By promoting such a level of versatility inside the organization Talaber was moving from being oriented towards break-and-fix kinds of situations to planning strategically for things like change management. Versatility enables the optimization of what you have, and gaps are the catalysts.

Outsourcing: Are You Creating Another Gap?

Outsourcing can bring tangible benefits to any organization. It is typically the quickest response to any non-anticipated new gap in the organization, as well as the most efficient in quickly addressing and (hopefully!) closing a gap. But opting for outsourcing too quickly has a lot in common with taking a painkiller when something hurts, without bothering to identify the real source of the problem. Unfortunately, if not carefully considered, outsourcing promotes a lack of trust in the organization's instinct.

Any organization, like any human being, has its own instinct, something we Christians call spirit. To ignore such corporate instinct is the same as Christians ignoring the spirit: it means you are definitely in danger and heading for trouble. Outsourcing has too many issues around it for any CIO/CTO to do it quickly and correctly. If management does not stop and listen to the corporate instinct, the odds are that if they go through with it, they will not be able to outsource in a time frame that is meaningful. Once they do the due diligence and think it through, they will be about one year down the road, by which time the economy, and gaps, will have changed. They may find themselves ready to outsource at just the wrong time, just as those Christians who do not rely on the spirit find themselves in the wrong path only because it was easier to enter the broad road than walk the narrow one. In business, just like in Christian life, the danger of outsourcing is that it often becomes a "quick fix," a "quick hit solution," that often produces adverse consequences. The odds are high that if a CIO/CTO tries to rush through this kind of major decision, they will end up paying for it in the long run. Even if they do it right, they might not get the savings, or results, they want in the time frame they need.

Using Corporate Instinct: Strengthening Your Processes

Using the above example of an economic downturn, the tendency of management tends to be in cutting cost, in an attempt to reduce, or eliminate, the budget gap. Delays in project development or layoffs are very common, and are the result of conditional behavior, and not corporate instinct. But isn't that what any competitor will typically do? However, if you were to use your corporate instinct, your gut feelings, you could instead begin preparing your transition to economic recovery and boom. The challenge in tapping into corporate instinct is not intuitive and requires some level of paradox thinking. The challenge in "listening" to corporate instinct is that it invariably requires improving processes and automation. By improving processes you are making an investment during a downturn to prepare for an upswing. Otherwise, when it comes, you may find your company very inefficient.

Trusting corporate instinct, as Koulopoulos and Spinello[2] point out, enables

---

2. T. Koulopoulos, W. Toms, and R. Spinello, *Corporate Instinct: Building a Knowing Enterprise for the 21st Century,* New York, John Wiley & Son, 1997.

companies to be successful time and time again. It is a result of deliberate action and can be developed. Actually, it must be! If you begin to rely on your organization's instinct you will find your organization acting beyond the confines of rational control, beyond memory and systematic analysis. In this case, strategies are created out of a collective reflex. It is important to always improve efficiency and plan ahead, as traditional IT gurus will tell you, but, more importantly, you should help your organization to tap into and intensify its corporate instinct, by enabling everyone to access this *collective corporate wisdom.*

Building on Koulopoulos and Spinello's concept, corporate interviews, and my own Knowledge Tornado concept, I confirm that such collective corporate wisdom is an entity of the organization that can be negatively distinguished from an organization's memory by the fact that is does not, like the latter, owe its existence to corporate professional experience and consequently is not a corporate acquisition. That is why many companies do not react to fatal market shifts and sadly crash and burn: management tend to reject the collective corporate wisdom and oppose anyone that promotes or points it out, and instead waste their time on committees and PowerPoint presentations.

While the corporate memory is made up essentially of professional knowledge, best practices, and other contents, which have at one time been conscious to the organization and its staff, but which have disappeared from corporate consciousness through having been forgotten or repressed, the collective corporate wisdom has never been in any database or KM system. Therefore it has never been individually acquired by anyone in the organization, but owes its existence exclusively to what I call *corporate heredity.*

Whereas the corporate memory consists for the most part of complexes, the content of the collective corporate wisdom is made up essentially of knowledge. Koulopoulos and Spinello confirm this, as they point out the importance of understanding that the knowledge on which corporate instinct is based is essentially mistaken by corporate memory. They go on to say that in a corporate setting, memory is most often associated with informal means of information capture and retrieval, a far less reliable basis of decision making than knowledge. Memory is selective and subjective. Knowledge, or, more specifically, a knowledge base, provides specific mechanisms by which to objectify, capture, and make available the collective experience of an organization.[3]

The concept of knowledge, which is an indispensable correlate to the idea of the collective corporate wisdom, indicates the existence of definite forms in the corporate culture that seem to be present always and everywhere in the organization. In addition to corporate memory, which is of a thoroughly knowledge base gathering nature, every organization also has a second

3. Ibid., p. 6.

knowledge system, an instinctive one. Such an instinctive system is collective, universal (every other corporation has it too!), and impersonal in nature. It is a collective corporate wisdom. This collective corporate wisdom is not developed individually, by each professional in the organization, but is inherited. It is created by everyone in the organization but is not owned by anyone. It consists of pre-existent data, the capital knowledge, which can only be turned into action secondarily and which provides definite data to certain knowledge contents.

DISRUPTIVE KNOWLEDGE: CREATING THE GAP

Corporate instincts, as any human instincts, are highly conservative and of extreme antiquity as regards both their dynamism and their collective reflex. Such a reflex, when represented to the organization, appears as an idea or strategy which expresses the nature of the instinctive impulse visually and concretely, like a picture. Now you know why after a new concept or idea is presented the presenter typically asks if you "got the picture."

In order to take advantage of corporate instinct you must understand that instincts are anything but blind and indefinite impulses, since they prove to be attuned and adapted to a definite external situation, beyond the corporate walls. This latter circumstance gives it its specific and irreducible structure. Just as instinct is original and hereditary, so too its structure transcends current management, market conditions, or knowledge base.

These considerations naturally apply also to the corporation as a whole, which still remains within the framework of general business practices, despite the possession of knowledge, decision-making, and rationale. The fact that corporate business, in particular in the twenty-first century, should be rooted in instinct and derive from it its dynamism, as well as the basic features of its innovation strategy, has the same significance for corporate business practices as for all other competitors in the marketplace.

The dynamic nature of instinctive organizations allows for the free flow of new ideas. These organizations focus on their core competencies and not their core products, thus constantly competing not against their competitors, but against themselves. They do not allow the market or the competition to create a gap in their business goals, product/technology roadmap, or revenues. The paradox is, these companies compete against themselves, creating the gaps before them and striving to overcome them before the competition does it. A great example of such a company is Microsoft, which drives the competition insane with the many products, versions, and renewed feature sets they release over and over again, several times a year.

Disruptive knowledge, a powerful strategic tool for the twenty-first century enterprise, consists essentially of the constant adaptation of the primordial knowledge (or technology) pattern that was instituted in the organization.

Disruptive knowledge creates gaps, challenges in the organization, as it introduces certain modifications or insights into the original organization's knowledge. If the flow of instinctive dynamism into the organization is to be maintained, as is absolutely necessary for its existence in this new knowledge economy, then it is imperative that learning organizations remold their knowledgebase into new and disruptive ideas that are adequate to the challenge of the ever-present market.

Organizations that are confronting gaps (changes) must first determine that they have the resources required to succeed. They then need to ask a separate question: does the organization have the processes and values to succeed? Asking such a question is not as instinctive because the processes by which work is done and the values by which employees make their decisions have served them well (corporate memory). Thus, disruptive knowledge can turn the very capabilities of an organization into its own disabilities as well. Relying on corporate instinct in such a situation can pay off handsomely. Collective corporate wisdom should be able to know if the process by which work habitually gets done in the organization is appropriate for the new problem.

Understanding what the gaps created by a disruptive knowledge are is a very important step in solving them. Not relying on the collective wisdom of the corporation can set teams charged with developing and implementing an innovation on a course fraught with roadblocks, second-guessing, and frustration. The reasons why innovation often seems to be so difficult for established firms is that they refuse corporate instinct (or do not tap into it!), employ highly capable people, and then set them to work within processes and values that were not designed to facilitate success with the task at hand.

Tapping into corporate instinct, especially when dealing with disruptive knowledge, is not an easy task. Nothing estranges a corporation more from the ground plan of its instincts than its learning capacity, which turns out to be a genuine drive towards progressive transformations of corporate culture modes. The creation and recreation of such disruptive knowledge, more than anything else, is responsible for the altered conditions of successful organizations and the need for new adaptations the marketplace brings. It is also the source of numerous organizational disturbances and difficulties occasioned by corporate progressive alienation from its instinctual foundation, i.e. by its affinity and identification with its corporate memory, by its concern with corporate memory at the expense of the collective wisdom. The result is that most of today's corporations can know themselves only in so far as they can become aware of themselves.

Corporate Instinct is Old

Has corporate instinct always existed? Yes! Although some believe that corporate instinct is new, and that only individual instincts driven by their vision existed before, corporate instinct has more influence over individual's instinct than the other way around. It is true that corporate instinct can only be leveraged fully when the tools and technologies for its development are readily available. But every corporation always had at its disposal tools and technologies, as those define the very nature of a corporation.

What does happen today that did not happen before is that businesses are conducted at the speed of thought, as Bill Gates defines it. The advent of e-mail, enterprise workflow, and other collaboration tools enables changes that used to take a full year to occur (i.e. manufacturing procurement) to be implemented in less than a few minutes (through e-procurement exchanges, such as eSteel, eChem, and ANX), through the use of collaboration tools, partnerships, and alliances. Actually, the twenty-first century is being characterized by alliances and partnership, as no organization can succeed on its own.

But collaboration always existed, even if through primitive means such as interoffice memos or telex. The issue is that organizations never had the need to tap into corporate instinct, because there was time for fully rational decisions. But as the wheels of progress, in particular technological progress, increase in speed and availability, corporations are being forced to tap into their corporate instinct in order to compete in time, to innovate, and to adapt to new market demands. One way to keep up is through the development of communities of practice.

Communities of Practice: Coping with Disruptive Knowledge

The concept of communities of practice is relatively new and has been used to describe loosely structured groups of people that share knowledge in areas of common interest. Innovative organizations have adopted this model to position themselves for leadership in the knowledge economy and to expand the benefits of corporate collective wisdom.

Often, communities of practice do not operate on an explicit agenda. Instead, communities of practice members tend to share their experiences and knowledge in free-flowing, creative ways that foster new approaches to problems and promote collective wisdom.[4] At Virtual Access Networks I organized a community of practice around the needs of the industry the company was in. I decided to call it a Technology Advisory Group (TAG), and it was composed of members that exhibited a wide range of sizes, structures, and means of communication, including companies such as IBM, Oracle, Nokia, Motorola, and a few other Fortune 1000 companies. Despite this diverse group, we all shared a few common traits that, besides dealing with disruptive knowledge, included:

4. W.M. Snyder and E.C. Wenger, "Communities of Practice: The Organizational Frontier" *Harvard Business Review*, 78(1), January 2000, p. 139.

- Common interest or goal: TAG was organized around topics that were important and meaningful to our membership.

- Common means to stay connected: TAG stayed in frequent contact using e-mail listservs, webcasting, or conference calls, as well as more traditional approaches, such as face-to-face meetings.

- Facilitated, not dominated: the role of the facilitator was important as it focused on recruiting and engaging members, not dictating content, which would completely block any instinctive activity.

- Management support, not control: management provided tools and a supportive environment that included providing members the time to participate, and recognized those that demonstrated an exemplary attitude for community and sharing. TAG set its own agendas based on the needs of members as they did their jobs.

- Voluntary participation: members choose to participate due to the "value added" in performing their jobs. Communities complement existing functions and organizational structures; they do not create additional ones.

- Willingness to share knowledge: members were willing and able to share what they knew, respond to requests, and collectively solve problems. They built trusting relationships.

SUSTAINABLE INNOVATION THROUGH GAP GENERATION

Successful use of corporate instinct enables sustainable innovation in the sense that what gets produced or created by the organization is sustainable. For instance, in the late 1980s, I used to be the CEO of an IS&T consulting firm in New Hampshire, TechnoLogic. After the crash of the stock market in 1987, the US experienced an economic downturn, so business was not easy and gaps were being generated almost daily. We decided to devote our human resources to innovating new products and services with office automation and Internet working in mind. While the rate and quality of innovation exceeded my expectations, the innovation regimen, *per se*, was hardly sustainable.

Despite the merits of *collective wisdom* (the term did not actually exist back then, since the Delphi Group had not yet coined it!), with everyone engaged in product and service development, the more we exercised corporate instinct, the less we had people to take care of the day-to-day needs of the corporation, such as making products, filling orders, or dealing with customers. In other words, we were all willing to think-out-of-the-box, but no one knew what to do with the ideas and projects that resulted from such brainstorming, as they were all new to everyone, not present in the corporate memory or part of the skill set of the staff, which made the insights even more amazing as no one had any idea of how we got to them.

Clearly, there is a difference between the notions of sustainable innovation in the organization, and innovation that is sustainable in the work process. Thus, the challenge to any organization tapping into its corporate instinct is that as a gap is filled (need for innovation), another one emerges (how to implement such innovation). As you rely again on corporate instinct and tap into corporate memory to resolve the challenge of implementing an innovative product/service, a new gap is created, as innovation then begins its institutionalization, thus no longer so innovative. The cycle continues. The first stage deals with innovations and the corporate instinct in which they are produced, while the second deals with the innovation process itself, as a component of the value chain, tapping into corporate memory, independent of products produced or the sustainability of a firm.

Therefore, sustainable innovation must promote the sustainability of business; otherwise, innovation becomes only a great idea. The concept not only applies to outcomes in the product or organization sense of the term, but also to the process through which innovations are created. Thus, in my view, sustainable practices in business are utterly dependent upon whether or not sustainable innovation processes are in play, where the former cannot exist without the latter. Nonetheless, sustainable innovation programs do not always lead to sustainable businesses; organizations that practice sustainable innovation will not always be sustainable in their business affairs. The bottom line is that sustainable business is very unlikely in the absence of sustainable innovation.

NURTURING COLLECTIVE WISDOM: ATTEMPTING TO FILL THE GAP

Collective wisdom, as discussed earlier, can be an effective tool for solving the problem of knowledge deficit, or the underutilization of organizational knowledge. Hence, strategy meetings and other forms of brainstorm meetings where employees across the organization are encouraged to freely share their own ideas are powerful tools in nurturing collective wisdom that transcends the corporate memory. These meetings should cover areas that are largely determined by the specific needs (gaps) of the organization and may range from developing a corporate quality mission statement to establishing practical methods for empowering employees, creating a new concept for a product or service, and so on.

The main idea is to tap into the collective knowledge of the organization as a whole (memory) and its members, inheriting the tacit knowledge that they carry with them. Unfortunately, most of the knowledge contained in an organization goes unused, and often gets lost through employee layoffs and resignations, even before it is acknowledged and captured, generating knowledge deficits (another form of gap!).

According to a study by the Delphi group, less than 20 percent of knowledge available to an enterprise is actually used. Furthermore, IDC predicts that Fortune 500 companies are currently operating at a $25 billion knowledge deficit, increasing to $31.5 billion by 2003, as shown in Figure 10.1.

Figure 10.1 – Fortune 500 companies are losing millions in underutilized knowledge

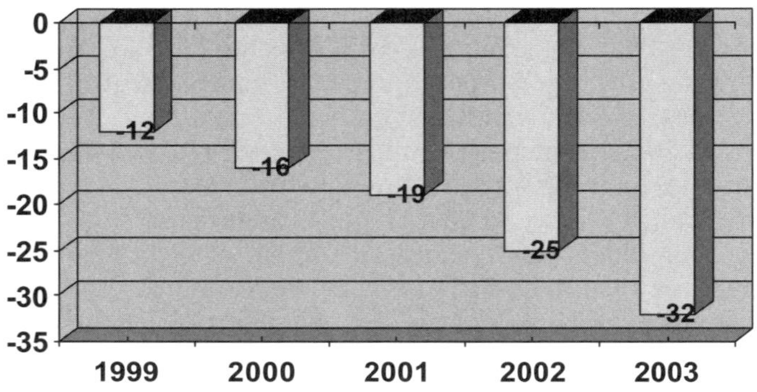

Source: IDC

According to TMP Worldwide,[5] it takes 1.5 times an employee's annual salary to replace that employee. This is due to several factors, one of which is the loss of unrecorded information and data. Lost information may include internal business processes, external contacts/relationships, and proprietary data. Knowledge deficit refers not only to know-how, but to codified data as well. Knowledge deficit is caused when employees cannot access:

- databases
- documents
- e-mail communications
- expertise of other employees/outside sources
- Internet content

Therefore, as gaps are created and the organization attempts to fill them, employees should have at their disposal searching capabilities that enable them to search for codified data, as well as unrecorded tacit knowledge. Such a process fosters collective wisdom, which in turn fosters innovation, one of the

5. http://www.tmpsearch.com.

prime goals in tapping into corporate instinct. Expertise management, as *Information Market* accurately contends, enables the creation of knowledge superconductivity. For instance, strategy meetings can enable employees with business problems to tap into the minds of those experts who can at the very least add to their knowledge, and may even be able to solve the business problem at hand. However, these meetings should be moderated and include a variety of themes and dynamics that encourage free thinking, commitment, loyalty, and willingness to create. Hence, these meetings play an important role in ensuring that any effort in developing new concepts, in innovation, is supported by the entire organization, top to bottom. These meetings can include topics such as:

- achieving unanimous agreement and commitment to a new concept from executives and senior management

- creating a comprehensive plan by which a new product or service concept can be implemented and become sustainable (remember, without sustainability, the new concept is only a great idea)

- crisis/contingency systems (dealing with major gaps in times of chaos)

- developing specific tactics by which new concepts and respective plans are to be realized

- establishing appropriate goals and benchmarks.

As well as these strategic and planning meetings, there are also some less apparent but equally important communication issues which can be addressed during the quest for collective wisdom, including:

- developing high-profile actions that communicate management's commitment to change (creation of gaps) and innovation (bridging the gaps)

- developing ongoing means for communicating progress of the strategy meetings and developing a collective wisdom process for both internal and external customers

- effectively communicating the collective wisdom to managers, staff, and the entire organization as a whole.

A FEW FOCUS AREAS WHERE CORPORATE INSTINCT PAYS OFF

Corporate instinct is key in crossing new gaps and bridging them. It enables companies to unlearn as quickly as they relearn, thereby pushing aside their own best ideas for new ones that meet the rapidly changing markets they inhabit. There are some areas, however, where corporate instincts can really pay off, including the ability to:

- recover from mistakes, both quickly and creatively
- take considered risks and facilitate organizational change
- communicate conviction
- balance conflict tensions
- promote intellectual prowess.

Recovering From Mistakes, Both Quickly and Creatively

If well cultivated, corporate instinct enables the organization to handle ambiguity, allowing it to recover from mistakes both quickly and creatively. Taking Wal-Mart as an example, going global is not always a smooth process. In fact, some blunders are inevitable. So the real measure of success becomes how, and how quickly, mistakes are detected and then fixed. Wal-Mart excels in this area, and the result has been a reawakening of the kind of entrepreneurship and experimentation Wal-Mart has been known for in the early days under Sam Walton. In an instinctive corporation, the moment you let avoiding failure become your motivator, you lose.

Taking Considered Risks and Facilitating Organizational Change

Competing in the global knowledge economy is a risky business. Today's global companies are trailblazers, with entrepreneurial pioneer (instinctive!) executives who are propelling themselves and their companies into the business frontier, and taking tremendous risks at every turn. Therefore, corporate instinct is one of the few tools these executives have to help them take considered risks and facilitate organizational change. Today, and into the foreseeable future, it is not enough to have a revitalized business organization. The organization itself must be able to be reinvented.

A great example is Alex Trotman's "Ford 2000" initiative. His idea was to save Ford billions of dollars a year by standardizing (and going global) the company's product development and production. Instead of producing different cars for different markets – and bearing the high cost of redundancy – Trotman envisioned world cars for a world market. It was a bold move, a risky move, and one that caused a fair amount of turmoil throughout the company. But by 1997, a few years into Ford 2000, the company had cut a record $3 billion in costs and was targeting another billion in 1998.

Beyond being bold and risky, Ford 2000 is pure Trotman. The initiative was molded from Trotman's core belief that success can only be achieved by driving down costs and becoming more efficient.

Communicating Conviction

Tapping into corporate instinct without communicating conviction predicts how likely to succeed the organization is, as well as how prone it is to derailing. Thus, as flag holders of corporate instinct, senior management must consider whether their organization fosters this competence, communicating conviction, or discourages it. To the degree that the organizational climate nourishes this competence, it will be more effective and productive, as group intelligence[6] is maximized, that is, the synergistic interaction of every individual's best talents in the organization.

Take the example of GE's leadership development center, GE Crotonville, embodied by Jack Welch's vision for GE. Welch effectively communicated the conviction about his vision for GE, and the results are unquestionable to this date as we look at GE's performance year after year, and the caliber of its management staff. But looking at Welch's example, how can we break down his communicating conviction? Through a number of qualities that together inspire others to take risks, to trust their core competencies, and so on. It means a number of things, chief amongst them being confidence, clarity, and charisma.

Today, more than ever before, executives in learning organizations must ride the knowledge tornado ever present in a knowledge-based economy. As a requirement, they must posses the confidence to make a difference. And they must be able to make critical decisions on the spot, sometimes in far-flung corporate outposts. They must trust the corporate memory and the collective wisdom of the organization, in particular of the senior staff. The ability to articulate a powerful vision for the company's future, to motivate others to put it into action and to act decisively is absolutely vital to any organization's success. But in a global organization, it is no less than a requirement.

Looking at how Welch reshaped GE over the past eighteen years is a good example. He has done it through more than 600 acquisitions and a powerful push into the world's emerging markets. But he has also done it through the sheer force of his personality – and his conviction. No corporate memory could have provided data and enough conviction to achieve such a goal. It was, for the most part, the fruit of innovation, and corporate instinct at its best.

The mastering and leveraging of technology for business success is essential when competing in global markets and in a knowledge-based economy, in particular knowledge technologies. But it is not enough. Despite the wonders of today's electronic communications, technology is no substitute for face-to-face interaction, emotional intelligence, and corporate instinct. That is why Jack speaks to every class at GE Crotonville and gathers his top executives there every quarter to review company strategy. It is also why he is known to fax off handwritten notes to his executives throughout the world. Beyond his unwavering conviction, Jack is also a master at balancing technology and technique.

---

6. D. Goleman, *Working with Emotional Intelligence*, New York, Bantam Books, 2000.

Balancing Conflict Tensions

The ability to balance conflicting tensions is a balancing act. Senior staff, in particular CEOs, are increasingly being pressured to find new ways of organizing and managing the tensions between:

- achieving growth organically and through acquisitions
- centralized and decentralized structures
- competing alone and in tandem with partners
- global and local interests
- product or market-oriented organizations and geographical organizations
- short-term and long-term perspectives
- the rights of parent corporations and those of subsidiaries

Clearly, these are thorny issues with no simple solutions, and a challenge in turning such an organization into a knowing organization for the twenty-first century. In fact, some of these issues may defy solution. The challenge for the knowing organization, one that relies on corporate instinct, then, is not to solve these conflicts, but to acknowledge them and operate from within them. This means making a shift from *either/or* thinking to a broader, bolder both/and perspective. Again quoting Welch, from a *Business Week* article a few years ago, he said that "Anybody can manage short. Anybody can manage long. Balancing those two things is what management is really all about."[7]

Managing a business structure that addresses the challenges listed above will always be prone to failure. In order to be able to adapt to the ever-shifting challenges (gaps!) so present in a knowledge economy, executives must organize without structure. When executives become aware of the corporate instinct, they morph their organization into a knowing organization, thus shifting its organization structure paradigm into a fluid organizational structure. They would have developed and honed its instinctive power of adaptability and versatility through a heightened internal awareness that is not locked into rigid organizational structures.

Promoting Intellectual Prowess

To accomplish these aforementioned complex balancing acts and trust the corporate instinct also requires intellectual prowess. In the knowledge economy, being both smart and highly focused is no longer enough. Executives must be able to increase velocity – by cultivating a versatile knowing organization –

---

7.   J. Welch, "The New Global Executive: What it Takes to Succeed" *Business Week*.

and also what Koulopoulos calls return on time (ROT).[8] Koulopoulos defines ROT as the financial return for a given period of time invested. This is not something that is used in place of return over time or return on investment (ROI), which are both important metrics of an investment's performance.

Unlike a few years ago, when CEOs could rely on their keen insights into their workforce and consumers, coupled with a solid understanding of their local, national economy, they are also required to know Wall Street and Main Street. But in the twenty-first century economy, business acumen alone is not enough and there is a lot more ground to cover. Knowing organization executives not only need a solid grasp of Wall Street and Main Street, but also Tiananmen Square and the Left Bank, Bovespa (Sao Paulo's-BR, stock exchange), and so on. To successfully compete on multiple fronts across the globe, today's executive must comprehend the concepts of the Knowledge Tornado, as well as a myriad of international approaches to public relations, the media, Internet technology, and public speaking. I call it "the fox trot act."

---

8. T. Koulopoulos, W. Toms, and R. Spinello, *Corporate Instinct: Building a Knowing Enterprise for the 21ˢᵗ Century,* New York, John Wiley & Son, 1997, p. 91.

CHAPTER 11

The Science of Bridging the Gap: The Leader's Dilemma

There is only one truth, steadfast, healing, salutary, and that is the absurd.[1]

We would all like to think that business affairs are essentially rational; that they work like any other tangible interaction in this world, and that we should therefore be able to gain from them, as they work to our benefit. However, we just need to take a look at the financial section of any newspaper, the TV news, the financial bulletins, Wall Street, to realize that business, in particular in the twenty-first century, is anything but rational.

This chapter discusses exactly that, the leader's dilemma in making sense out of something that makes no sense at all, the business world. In having to rely on their own instincts, and the corporation's instinct as the only tangible source of information to address the gaps and the challenges of business strategies and practices, leaders are, more than ever before, faced with the imperative need to understand what I call the *science of bridging the gap*. In other words, they need to understand how the way they think shapes what they see, and how paradox and absurdity inevitably play a major part in their every action.

MANAGING CHAOS: A SEA OF GAPS

As discussed in chapter ten, in order to innovate and effectively compete in the knowledge economy, learning organizations must become knowing organizations; they must rely on the corporate instinct and tap into their collective corporate wisdom. The bottom line is, organizations must generate as many gaps as possible. After all, gaps are the seeds of innovation. But by the same token, organizations must bridge such gaps as quickly as possible, otherwise chaos emerges.

Poor working relationships, internal and external strife, conflicts, misunderstandings, low productivity, and decreased customer satisfaction, lack of referrals, poor communication, and low sales are all symptoms of chaos, all

---

1. A. Salmon, http://www.southerncrosscoaching.com.au/AboutUs%206.01htm.

symptoms of gaps that are not being bridged, be it intentionally or not. The knowledge economy is characterized by constant and fast changes. To be successful, organizations and professionals must embrace change as quickly as it comes.

To prevent chaos, or proliferation of gaps, executive leaders must embody the science of bridging gaps, of dealing with ever-changing environments and business landscapes, by developing a productive, team-oriented, positive atmosphere where good communication is paramount. In the twenty-first century economy, executives and the organization as a whole must not only learn to manage time, but to manage themselves. Rather than focusing on tasks and time, managers must focus on preserving and enhancing relationships, and on accomplishing results.

The reality is, there will always be more to do than can be done by one person. If you are only doing the work of two people, you are loafing in your company. It does not matter whether it is two, four, or twelve full-time jobs that you have to do. Your organization's productivity is the result of the trust the members of the organization have in each other. If you have the right trust, working relationship, and environment, the work gets done!

As a lecturer at Boston University's (BU) graduate program,[2] I have the opportunity to interact with management and computer sciences students. I am pleased to recognize that, unlike many programs in management at other universities and colleges today, BU's program is keen to educate management professionals not to take for granted the complex and paradoxical nature of human organizations. In my own lectures I am quick to point out that thinking loses out to how-to formulae, which is one of the issues the Knowledge Tornado concept deals with in turning know-how into how-to, knowledge into action. Considering the task-oriented nature of MBA candidates, it is not surprising that these students and the majority of business managers and executives still find themselves prone to accept a definition of management that makes it seem as if it could be simply learned.

Chaos, the end-result of gaps, is a wonderfully evocative word: a formless void of primordial matter, the great deep, or, if you prefer, the abyss out of which the cosmos or order of the universe evolved. Can you think of anything that could be better calculated to set the creative energies of executives going than the challenge of forming order from the chaos eminent changes in their business and organization will bring? A challenge, a gap, it certainly is. Many management and technology icons have responded to it and made remarkable progress in the last few years, but much remains to be done. The word on the street was that MBAs and other advanced management studies were redundant, that anyone could be a CEO and successfully run a company. Since the burst of the dotcom bubble the opinion is not encountered as often now. Overnight,

---

2.   At the Metropolitan College.

executives learned that, in the business world, especially one characterized by virtual enterprises and goods sold, executives, in particular CEOs, must also be information professionals, with demonstrated ability to build a meaningful business within the void.

One of the most important lessons the dotcom era taught their executives was that you do not build a company in five days; you do not go IPO in a couple of months. For those companies that survived the first impact of the stock market crash in 2000, initially it was very hard to know how to break through the chaos barrier. Where could they begin? Savvy and successful executives answered by taking one first small step: developing a business strategy for what they would want to collect and preserve from their business, a laser-beam focus approach...if they could only find the wherewithal to do so!

You see, there was no corporate memory that could lead them in the right direction, and, sadly, most of them did not know or rely on their corporate instinct. Thus, they started on a long steep learning curve. As of today, summer of 2002, the great majority of the dotcom corporations that survived (98 percent of them died)[3] are still spinning, burning cash, and trying to figure out where to go next. Take a look at Wall Street and you will find companies like CMGI, Internet Capital Group, Mercator, and many others that are still around, but have no clear perspective of where to go next. They are still in the gap, in the chasm I should say, enduring their everyday chaos, waiting for a clear strategy to surface. If it ever does.

Unfortunately, schools are not teaching managers to deal with gaps, never mind bridge them when they occur. While business is booming, great; but when a hiccup in the economy happens, then it is doomsday. The problem is, managers, in particular in the US and other developed countries, have become accustomed to believing the familiar bromides. When a manager, or any leader or executive believes that their responsibilities can be discharged adequately by attending seminars or following simplistic formulae, then we have a problem. When such formulae fail them, not only do they get discouraged and frustrated, but sometimes they totally derail.

What is it about the twenty-first century economy that makes executives feel that it is so chaotic? Is it the sheer volume of information that needs to be absorbed? Is it the lack of quality assurance we have been used to in the financial literature and media? Is it the uncertainty about the authority of many business concepts and theories – mine included? Is it not knowing what is out there, especially beyond our international borders? Is it the unmanageable number of materials, experts, gurus, and consulting practices when you attempt to seek advice or professional service? Is it the lack of expertise? Perhaps it is the difficulty of establishing a business strategy, a business goal, one that you

---

3. According to ARC Advisory Groups' report.

are sure will not get you fried by the board. Perhaps it is the ephemeral nature of being an executive in the twenty-first century – here today, but changed or gone tomorrow? Or is it the dilemma for executives trying to keep up with both the business goals and the intra-organizational challenges, and attempting to provide the best solutions for both to the board and stockholders? Maybe it is the fast-changing business practices and technology, which demand continual upgrade of IS&T, management skills, and expertise for continued success. Most probably it is many or all of these things.

These gaps are largely beyond anyone's control; they are part of the chaos, or the eye of the tornado, as I define it, and there is no golden rule for addressing them. Although gaps can be bridged, no bridges are created equal, and one must build one's own organization bridge. Further, as Richard Farson so eloquently points out:

> [Y]ears ago we talked about 'leadership,' then the byword became 'morale,' then it was 'motivation,' then 'communication,' then 'culture,' then 'quality,' then 'excellence,' then 'chaos,' then back again to 'leadership.' Along the way we were buffeted about by buzzwords like 'zero defect,' 'management by objectives,' 'quality circles,' 'TQM' (Total Quality Management), 'paradigm shift,' 're-engineering,' 'six-sigma,' and now 'knowledge tornado.'[4]

The confused executive, careening from trend to trend, cannot be an effective leader while believing in simplistic formulae and models, mine included!

Complexity science suggests that paradoxes are not problematic. Rather, they create a tension from which creative solutions emerge. This realization can shake someone at the core of his being. Charles Handy for example, writes, "the important message for me was that there are never any simple or right answers in any part of life. I used to think that there were, or could be. I now see paradoxes everywhere I look. Every coin, I now realize, has at least two sides." Others see the concept of paradox as so important that they now define leadership as essentially the management of paradoxes. Paradoxes are defined as simultaneous or interdependent opposites.

WHAT BRIDGES A GAP IS A NEW GAP

Rational and logical thinking has been responsible for most of all achievements in life. However, as these achievements were archived and access to them became possible, answers to previously unknown problems became searchable, thus limiting and constricting our ability to think creatively, to innovate. Just

---

4. R. Farson, *Management of the Absurd: Paradox in Leadership*, New York, Touchstone, 1997, p. 87.

think about the automobile industry. Nothing really has changed, except for the first foray of hybrid cars, since the invention of automobile. Cars are still running on wheels and burning fossil fuel. Yet, from the invention of the wheel, cars pushed by horses, the first steam cars, and finally the first engine-powered car, not many years had gone by, but each of those stages transcended the next. The same holds true for the architecture and building construction.

I believe, the problem is that we have grown unsecured. Unfortunately, the price of relief from anxiety is the loss of creative ability. This is surely why we lost innovative teachers who felt there was no room for creativity, with the latest decade of change. At the beginning of the twentieth century, inventors were bold risk takers, and had to rely a lot on their own instincts, as there was not much memory (libraries, knowledge resources) available other then their own experimentation.

The concept of dealing with gaps did not exist, as life in itself was a big gap – no wonder the many philosophic schools, in particular the existentialist. Today's executives, for the most part, are not willing to take risks. After all, many of them are afraid of what the board will say, how Wall Street will judge them, what will happen if they are wrong, and so on. Instead of bridging gaps with another gap, they get immobilized. They become victims of their own contradictory impulses.

Back in 1988, while delivering a workshop for a group of banking executives and senior technical managers in Brazil's capital, Brasilia, I talked with at least three executives that clearly wanted to succeed in their business, but at the same time showed all the signals of wanting to fail as well. Everything they did carried both messages. One of them, from a major bank in Brazil, would be very excited about the prospect of automating certain decision-making process within his organization. However, at the same time, all he did all day long was to cripple the project, by refusing to delegate, undermining his newly formed taskforce committee, failing to meet deadlines, and stalling on crucial decisions.

Although back then I could not understand the situation – I too was a victim of not wanting to fill my own gaps by just accepting the most plausible excuse – what I realized over and over again throughout the years was that his behavior was not so unusual. Contradictory impulses, and Farson discusses the phenomenon extensively, are present in every project, every team. Thus every situation, every outcome, every achievement, can be both good and bad. That is why the science of bridging the gaps is essentially a challenge every leader has, the management of dilemmas, coping with contradictions while appreciating the coexistence of opposites is crucial to the development of a different way of thinking.

ALL THINGS ARE IMPERMANENT: BRIDGES DO NOT LAST FOREVER

It is evident that all things are impermanent, including the bridges used to overcome gaps. But used they not fade or change more slowly? Not long ago, businesses were experiencing massive restructurings, reengineering, and redirection. Skills and tools were needed for response to various impacts, to help us create rather than react. But now we are spinning faster, and the group change tools do not always seem to work. The reason is twofold: mistakenly identifying problems and believing that once a gap is bridged it will always be bridged. Both these assumptions are incorrect.

First, many executives have difficulty distinguishing a problem from a predicament. Problems can always be solved, while predicaments can only be coped with. Spending time and energy on a predicament will only bring frustration, discouragement, and desolation. Most issues one faces in life, from marriage, family affairs, business affairs, and so on are complicated and inescapable dilemmas; they tend to be predicaments that make no single option the best option, where all tend to be relative. Business in the twenty-first century is a lot like that. In this new economy, MIS, or management of information systems, most often will not serve the executive management, either because these systems will be inadequate, or because the executive will be computer naïve. Besides, how good is stored data if it is not real-time?

By accepting that all things are impermanent, executives can take advantage of business tools that help them solve problems and accept predicaments, actually taking advantage of them, as those are very possibly the only consistent data they will have. Thus, some strategies to cope with the paradox of bridging gaps are outlined below.

Get Familiar with the Eye of the Knowledge Tornado Concept

Consider for a moment the outer limits of the tornado as one goes through its outer stages of growth. It is chaotic, as it causes great devastation and change to everything it touches in the organization. Then think of the center of the tornado, the eye, where all is calm, peaceful, and quiet. Think of it as your present organization status. For sure you will not be able to stop or even control the wind and the noise around the organization, be it competition noise, market shift winds, and so on.

While you can retain your own center, and flow with the wind, with the tornado, that is the obvious thing to do. However, doing so only postpones the inevitable, when the periphery of the tornado comes crashing down on your organization, as in the example of the movie *The Perfect Storm*. This is not a predicament, and has a solution. The solution requires courage and willingness to fail and die, crash and burn, as the fishermen did in the movie. But it is a calculated and well-thought-out strategy that transcends the corporate memory and taps into the corporate instinct. Keep in mind that doing little other than that which seems absolutely safe could run much bigger risks than taking a chance. Risks are how we learn from our successes (not mistakes!).

Know What Matters

Michael Korda once said, "[T]he first rule of success, and the one that supersedes all others, is to have energy. It is important to know how to concentrate it and focus it on the important things, instead of frittering it away on trivia."[5] The most powerful thing you can do at any moment is re-focus. Ask yourself: What do you want to achieve? Why is this important?

Keep in mind that gaps are inevitable; you will always have to deal with consequences of changes in the organization. And the fact that your organization is learning only makes the advent of changes even more obvious, as awareness is part of the process. Once you learn that there is no face lost in abandoning all hope of completely avoiding gaps, you can much more comfortably get down to the task of managing how to decide which bits of it are worthy of your attention, and, more importantly, which are not.

Your goal should always be to bridge the gap, which is the same as transcending, not adapting. Many people come to this epiphany when they have their second child. All the angst spent worrying about potential crises with the first child turns into considered risk management. With the first one it's "Gee – keep him away from that – it's got dirt on it!!" and panic sets in. With the second one it's "Well, it's only dirt," and serenity flows. Once you learn that gaps are part of business and transcending them part of the thrill, you then become a knowing organization, dependent on the next gap, so you can learn one more time and set a distance from your competitors. Much like surfers, you should look at gaps as the waves, the necessary element for a fun ride, full of emotions, accomplishments, and lessons learned.

The trick is continually to assess issues on the amount of influence you have in determining their outcome. If you have no influence, your worrying is not going to help, so don't worry. If you have a moderate amount, do what you can and be satisfied that you have done your best. If you have great influence, then set it as a priority and influence away. No time to worry.

Maintain Your Network

No organization is an island, and the twenty-first century will be characterized by partnerships and alliances. Any organization operates best when interdependent – not leaning, but supported. It may be time to revalue partners, to reassess alliances, and to reenergize team consciousness in the workplace and communities of practice.

---

5. M. Korda, *Another Life*, New York, Delta, 2000, p. 32.

One of the keys to bridging gaps is the ability to tap into support facilities. Productivity almost invariably increases when it is delegated, leveraged, and pulled together. Thus, maintain your network of contacts:

- begin using a contact manager
- keep all of your contacts – business, school friends, acquaintances
- be a source of referrals
- let organizations know you do not mind being referred
- build a select distribution list of supply chain, distribution channels, and partners that you want to keep posted on what you are doing.

Effective Leadership Does Not Avoid Conflicts

I believe that most executives may not have a problem with this, but as Wall Street gets more and more sensitive about the financials of any organization, there are executives that waste an enormous amount of time and energy developing and maintaining a peachy mask. Today's business environment allows no time for that! It is time for empowerment. Some areas you should be aware of include:

- protecting the organization's interests from unscrupulous profit-making gigs
- protecting organizations from unscrupulously employing tax shelter schemes
- addressing privacy issues generated by the Internet and other new technologies
- monitoring the stewardship of the organization's assets.

Learn to Live with Less

This is a strange concept for many of us in business who have spent much of our working lives running after more physical assets for the corporation. When the economy moves fast, the less baggage and overhead an organization has to carry the better; after all, everything is impermanent! Look what happened to Digital Equipment Corporation and Data General, to cite only a couple of examples. Traveling light – in many ways – becomes more effective. KPMG is an example of such a premise, which in several centers uses the hotel system to accommodate many times double of the number of consultants it has in the same facility.

Choose Care Over Fear

Marianne Williamson, who wrote the words Nelson Mandela used in his inaugural address, was the first to suggest the choice of care over fear. There are only two fundamental emotions – love and fear. Anything that isn't one is the other. Until recently, we did not talk about this in the corporate arena. Now we know, tough love builds good teams, and gaps are exacerbated by fear. This is not about being soft and gooey – you know that. It is about finding a way to address issues head on with an intelligent mix of courage, commitment, and compassion.

Gaps are inevitable. In the sense that perturbation is evolutionary, it is also desirable. But managing it is essential. It is no use for any of us to hope that someone else will do it. Do you have your own personal strategies in place? Therefore, any executive staff, when acting in that capacity, should have two general but very important duties:

- to ensure that they have an adequate information flow regarding all the activities and affairs of the organization, especially with regard to finances

- to act solely on what they believe is in the best interest of the organization and not in their personal interest, their private business interests, or their associates' interests, including avoiding conflicts of interest.

A MATTER OF COMMUNICATION: AVOIDING PREDICAMENTS

Richard Farson encourages leaders to think "beyond the conventional wisdom...to understand how the ways we think shape what we see, and how paradox and absurdity inevitably play a part in our every action."[6] According to him, we think we want creativity or change, but we really don't. We stifle creativity by playing intellectual games, judging and evaluating, dealing in absolutes, thinking stereotypically, and not trusting our own experiences (and training our employees not to trust theirs).

Nonetheless, although it is true that leadership is trapped by many paradoxes, communication can be an important vehicle to bridge gaps and management of gaps. Communications provide the link through which information is shared, opinions are expressed, feedback is provided, and goals are formulated. Work cannot be done without communication. It is necessary to communicate in order to advise, train, and inform. Members of an organization must translate corporate goals into action and results. In order for this to happen, all forms of correspondence must flow freely throughout the organizational structure.

There is also a correlation between the willingness of every level of the organization to communicate openly and frequently and the satisfaction expressed by the workers. Most organizational predicaments from mis-understandings to disasters; from small frustrations to major morale problems

---

6. R. Farson, *Management of the Absurd: Paradox in Leadership*, New York, Touchstone, 1997, p. 89.

can be traced back to either a lack of communication or ineffective technique.

Communication does not take place unless there is understanding between the communicator and the audience. Simply learning to write, read, or speak is not enough. Does one make music by merely striking the keys of a piano? The difference between making noise and making music is study, understanding technique, and practice, practice, practice. The same is true for communications. The difference between talking, reading, writing, or hearing and communicating is study, understanding technique, and practice, practice, practice.

Therefore, executive staff should examine the process of communication within the organization and strive to increase their propensity for successful communication. Messages must be clearly stated, brief, and well planned, and must answer the questions who, what, when, where, and why.

The sending modes of communication are speaking, writing, and nonverbal messages. The receiving modes are listening, reading, and observation. Each of these modes is used in the process of getting work accomplished. Improvement in the effectiveness of any one of these modes will result in higher productivity and increased satisfaction. It is not simply a matter of how much one communicates, but how well.

BRIDGING THE GAP FROM THE TOP DOWN OR FROM THE BOTTOM UP?

Organizational leaders are perpetually faced with a series of questions:

- In bridging a major gap (a change effort), should they drive the change, or build the bridge, from the top down, or must it have bottom up leadership?

- How would you make sure your organization is constantly innovating and at the same time delivering a standardized level of service?

- How would you encourage your senior management group to work as a team and at the same time not lose your star performers?

As discussed earlier in this chapter, what these three questions all have in common is that they cannot be answered using solely logical methods. Yet, one of the bedrock principles of science is the universal applicability of logic. But an understanding and a facility with paradoxes is as important as, if not more important than, understanding logic.

Although leadership is defined above as the management of paradoxes, paradoxes are not managed in the way that problems are. Paradoxes have to be constantly managed, for they are never "solved" like problems. Additionally, paradoxes can be a critical concept to integrity. If a concept is paradoxical, that itself should suggest that it smacks of integrity, as it gives off the ring of truth. Conversely, if a concept is not in the least paradoxical, you should be suspicious of it, and suspect that it has failed to integrate some aspect of the whole. Such a premise is very important in generating and evaluating Koulopoulos' concept of collective corporate wisdom.

It is common today for CEOs to report that "all management is people management." Given that Christianity, also, could be described as being about "people management," it is not surprising that the work world and the religious world would share the phenomenon of paradox.

CHAPTER 12

Knowledge Management in Government

Knowledge management initiatives are on the upswing as managers at all government levels face mounting pressure to work smarter and faster while wrestling with the demands of electronic government and a shrinking work force.

Practices developed when governmental agencies had more workers and fewer and far less demanding constituents do not cut it in today's fast-paced environment, where nearly every worker has access to rapid-fire e-mail, the work force is more transient, and the inflow of information is almost uncontrolled. The Internet revolution has brought with it the mandate of speed, service, and global competitiveness. Government agencies at national, state, and local levels are rising to the challenge by leveraging knowledge management techniques and modern thinking.

The demands of the public sector mimic those experienced in the private sector. Habituated by Internet-based "round-the-clock-retailing and commerce", the pressure is now on governments to offer services 365 x 24 x 7. But, more importantly, governments are moving to simplify interactions between citizens and government agencies, providing services and information that streamline and improve the delivery of services to citizens and the business community. Considering that voter approval will follow easy-to-use government services, governments at all levels are looking at ways to leverage models and techniques successfully employed in the commercial world to gain advantage. These models and techniques, such as knowledge management, are driving innovative service models in government agencies such as education, healthcare, law enforcement, and industry.

NEED FOR KNOWLEDGE MANAGEMENT IN GOVERNMENT

Why the sudden emphasis on knowledge management? Following the lead of the private sector, governments, which are usually slow adopters of best practices and revolutionary technologies, are beginning to see the light and are willing to undergo change in ways not heard of earlier. They are increasingly focusing energies on responding to public demands for faster and more efficient services, thus leading to the development of new models for implementation and best practices. On a similar note, the citizens are beginning to expect more from their governments as consumers become accustomed to the quality of service offered by the private sector. They are beginning to expect always-on availability and convenience, fast delivery, customer focus, and personalization. As these practices and standards set by the private sector seep into the general population not only will it make life easier, but it will also bring about fundamental changes in the people's perception of government.

One of the greatest challenges in dealing with government agencies is the complexity and redundancy of day-to-day procedures. It is estimated that the average government has between 50 and 70 different departments and agencies. It is not uncommon for citizens to experience difficulty finding the right governmental agency for a task in hand. For routine matters such as the sale of a house, or obtaining immigration and travel permits, several different agencies may be involved, each agency having its own requirements, procedures, regulations, and forms. Further, departments are vertically organized such as the department of agriculture or the department of immigration and naturalization. Many of the services that these departments have to deliver require complex collaboration across departments/agencies. For example, immigration agencies require frequent interaction with law enforcement agencies, employers, and private or public educational institutions.

As is evident, the potential to streamline processes and interdepartmental communication is enormous, but governments will need, along with the right technology, a committed leadership, in-depth understanding of knowledge management principles, partnerships with public and private sectors, and a well-defined strategy for overcoming the barriers to change: the departmental rivalries, the hostility of unions, the fears of individuals, and the sheer size of the undertaking. The technology although crucial to making it all possible is the least of the challenges outlined above. Employing the appropriate KM techniques can help agencies at all levels to improve their services to members of the public by responding quicker and more efficiently to the changes that take place within the government. It is critical for agencies to define their needs, refine the information required to support these business processes, and consolidate the knowledge assets.

Governments typically have tremendous amounts of data gathered over several centuries. Unless all this data is put into context, appropriate benefits will not ripple to the constituents. In the words of one US county executive, "We have 316 years' worth of documents and data and thousands of employees with long years of practical experience. If we can take that knowledge, and place it into the hands of any person who needs it, whenever they need it, I can deliver services more quickly, more accurately and more consistently."[1]

In the twenty-first century, the US Federal government faces serious human resource issues as it strives to improve services and be more accountable to its

1. In T. Newcombe's "Knowledge Management: New Wisdom or Passing Fad?" *Government Technology Magazine*, Folsom, 1999.

citizens. The average age of a federal worker is 46 years. Approximately 71 percent of federal senior executives will be eligible to retire by 2005. It must compete for workers, as its workforce grows older with the anticipated mass exodus of baby boomers. And unless the tacit knowledge of those retiring is captured and appropriately documented, service to citizens will suffer. Thus, KM attracted the attention of the federal government. Towards fostering best practices and the capture of knowledge, the government enacted management reforms and expanded the use of information technology to improve performance and services to its people.

The past decade has seen significant development in technology and business process reengineering concepts. All of this has had tremendous impact on the manner in which organizations (primarily commercial) conduct business and gather information using new and innovative means. The Internet revolution set new trends in e-business and it was only a matter of time before governments began seeing value in promoting e-government initiatives. Just as for businesses, governments need to be effective and the clear challenge is to employ better, faster, and smarter ways to learn and work. As mentioned earlier, customers accustomed to e-business services now expect information and services to be "always-on" and tend to be frustrated if the information or products they want are not easy to find and purchase.

A strong analogy can be drawn between companies that risk losing customers to competitors and governments losing constituent confidence and voter disapproval if they do not provide the desired services in a reliable and easily accessible manner. Increasingly, governmental agencies will need to learn, manage knowledge, apply constantly changing technology, streamline processes, integrate external and internal computer systems, plus share and use knowledge both within the organization with its employees, and externally with other agencies, governments worldwide, customers, and, most importantly, its people. For most nations, the economy is shifting away from the production of tangible products, such as steel, oil, or automobiles towards services. A government's requirements for KM are in many ways similar to those of a successful service-oriented business.

A recent survey conducted by business process consultant Kepner Tregoe, Inc. found that although workers and managers claimed that the number of decisions they have to make daily has increased over the last three years, 82 percent of workers and 85 percent of managers said that the average time they have to make those decisions had stayed the same or decreased. The most common negative result was, "We do a poor job of sharing information." Thus, the need for better knowledge management and information sharing is very evident.

In a global environment, in a knowledge-based economy, the government is expected to bring cultural and social change through knowledge and know-how. It is expected to be a model learning organization, capturing and disseminating knowledge and converting it to value for its people. These new roles require new skills in project management, people management, knowledge management, networking, facilitation, negotiation, partnering, as well as leadership and taking initiative at all levels. A learning organization is much more than training and development. It understands that learning is central to its mission and essential to its ongoing relevance. A learning organization is characterized by its ability to continually improve performance through new ideas. It is able to anticipate. It finds new and better ways to fulfill its mission. Governments, in order to be successful will need to effectively employ the "learning-organization methodology" and understand that their success is built around people, their culture, knowledge, know-how, and ability to innovate, not around the rule of law! Implementing state-of-the-art technologies or cool business processes are not the only or by any means the most important factors in facilitating a "Knowledge-Based Society."

CURRENT KM EFFORTS IN GOVERNMENT

E-business has spawned e-government. Many governments around the world have realized the importance of managing knowledge within their organizations and have initiated KM efforts at varying levels. Many of these efforts are very comprehensive, recognize the importance of KM, and follow well-defined methodologies, procedures, implementation guidelines, and evaluation metrics (as outlined in this book). Others have focused on technology implementations as the solution to KM. Further, KM efforts have been adopted at all levels of government: national, state, and local. This section outlines some instances of KM employed by governments at different levels in different parts of the world.

Starting in the 1990s with the US Federal government's use of e-commerce to reduce the cost and time of procurement, it has come a long way. The Federal government has taken it upon itself to expand the delivery of services electronically over the next several years. The promise of e-government was also one of the high points of the Bush presidential campaign. Thus the importance of bringing together knowledge and utilizing that information for the betterment of governmental processes and the life of citizens is well acknowledged. The Government Paperwork Elimination Act of 1998 requires federal agencies to provide electronic services to citizens by October 2003. As it stands today, the government operates some 20,000 sites to share information with members of the public including one for knowledge management (www.km.gov). The most notable of all such efforts is firstgov.gov, a portal to provide citizens with simpler and quicker access to information.

As in the case of firstgov.gov, the "portal strategy" is gaining a foothold among governments across the world to provide access to valuable government-related information to citizens and members of the public. KM efforts in most cases result in the providing of online services, and hence are often put on par or even confused with e-government. Speaking of portals, many types of portals have been associated with government functioning primarily based on the interfaces to the government. Although mere implementation of these portals does not constitute the entire solution to KM, it serves as an important component in the delivery of information to the right person(s) at the right time to facilitate timely decision making. Some examples of these types of portals include:

- *Citizen Portals.* Also termed Citizen-to-Government (C2G), some initiatives in this direction include services provided by federal, state, and local agencies to allow citizens to pay taxes, dues, fines, and renew drivers' licenses.

- *Industry Portals.* Electronic procurement portals are among the most widely adopted e-business processes because they can bring about significant efficiencies and cost benefits. E-Procurement Portals dramatically lower the cost of doing business with government suppliers, partners, and customers. These marketplaces allow the exchange of goods and services with suppliers, partners, and other agencies via Internet-based communities. Several governments are collaborating with the private sector to create commerce portals to stimulate local economies, making it attractive for companies to stay or increase local investments. Noteworthy examples are the world's first bilingual Hong Kong portal and the new e-commerce hub, dubbed "ePort," in China's landlocked province of SiChuan.

- *Government Portals.* Also termed Government-to-Government (G2G), these portals may facilitate intra/inter-departmental communication or communication between agencies of different governments. Intranets often fall into this category and supply customized information to agency personnel on data, regulations, reports, and metrics. They also provide the capability to conduct online secure transactions, such as submitting requests and receiving responses from other agencies.

Increasingly, governments are eager to take advantage of technology and are looking for smart ways to invest. They recognize that they will need to construct Internet portals, similar to consumer portals such as MSN and Yahoo!, that can provide a one-stop shop for all a citizen's needs. A central government portal of this kind has just been launched in Singapore; another is being developed in Austria. In Britain, BT has recently won the contract to build UK Online, a portal to offer government services that should, in a basic form, start up in the autumn. In the words of UK Prime Minister Mr. Tony Blair, "By 2002, 25% of all government will be online."[2] Other governments such as those of the US and Canada have similar plans. The Canadian government

---

2. In "Prime Minister Launches Major Campaign to get UK Online" *10 Downing Street Newsroom*, London 2000.

estimates that by 2004, Canadians will have access to government information and services online at the time and place of their choosing.

As the use of information technology becomes more widespread and accessible to the general public, portals will increasingly connect citizens with their governments and serve as windows into the functioning and services offered by the government. A recent study has shown that more than half of Americans with access to the Internet have visited a government website in the past year. According to the National Technology Readiness Survey,[3] 21 percent of adults with access to the Internet had conducted an online transaction with a government over the past year, while only 15 percent had paid a credit card bill, and 10 percent had traded stocks. Overall, 55 percent of adult Internet users said they had visited a government site in the past year.

In the state and local marketplace, knowledge management is gaining a foothold in specific public policy concerns. There have been a number of initiatives at the state level involving large medical assistance programs, such as Medicaid, that would provide public officials with more insight into how to improve their services. Consistently, large projects are also being undertaken by the Defense Department. Lack of information sharing between law enforcement agencies nationwide is often a major problem for countries in bringing criminals to justice. As is very commonly claimed by governments and organizations worldwide, "We don't know what we know," "We don't know what we need to know," and "We don't know what information we have (or need), where it is, or how to find it." The seriousness of the problem is highlighted in the example of the police: often police from one jurisdiction are unaware of a burglary ring operating in a neighboring city; or sometimes police do not know the true identity of a suspect because there is no way to share information easily with another state where the suspect resided under an alias. To improve how it shares knowledge about crimes, criminals, gangs, and ongoing efforts in other jurisdictions, Florida's Brevard County is using a knowledge management system of integrated databases of knowledge about criminal activity within the county. Called "The Bastille", the system enables smaller police departments to tap into the wealth of knowledge Brevard County has assembled from its records-management system, photo-identification database, and crime-mapping system. In addition, officers and detectives can define characteristics in a search and have The Bastille continually probe the network using an intelligent agent that reports back when it finds a match. At this time, Brevard County is the main source of the knowledge in The Bastille, but as other counties add their knowledge, the goal is to build up a vast repository of criminal knowledge to improve the way crime is fought in Florida. Eventually, police officers will know what they want to know, when they want to know it.

---

3. Survey results can be found at http://www.rhsmith.umd.edu/ces/National Technology Readiness Survey.htm.

At a different level, the US State Department is looking at ways it can make its country teams work more effectively at two of the nation's larger embassies, India and Mexico. The issue of interoperability is one of the big drivers in this case. Officials from the US departments of Agriculture, Commerce, and State are represented on country teams that have a lot of different interests, and they have not been working with one voice very effectively. Knowledge management is one tool they can use to try to provide a single voice for the officials on these country teams.

Another pioneer in the use of KM techniques and principles to foster change, growth, and innovation is the UK Government. Governments like that of the UK have been steadily proclaiming the need for "joined-up" government,[4] and are working to foster and build the foundations required and overcome entrenched habits and procedures that conspire against such a goal.

Joining up is a mind-set and a culture. It is not a system or a structure. The concept of joining up recognizes that no one has all the knowledge and resources, or controls all the levers to bring about sustainable solutions to complex issues. The key to "joined-up" government is to learn about shared purpose, teamwork, partnerships and building relationships. Joined-up organizations are built around the knowledge and know-how of people. This differs from the organizational model of the past, which was built around tasks, units, and titles.

As stated earlier on, a typical government has between 50 and 70 agencies, each dealing with a vertical segment. One of the most difficult problems citizens face in dealing with governments is getting sent from one place to another without a clear plan of the steps involved. To overcome this difficulty, governments have recognized the need to map the overall workflow/transaction flow for a citizen interaction or life event. This can be a great help to automation, and a correspondingly great opportunity for government to seize control of these workflows, codify them, and document them in the best way possible – and perhaps offer online services too.

The UK government, for example, as a part of the "joined-up" government, took a very innovative approach to researching people's experience and analyzing such workflows by selecting seven of the most common "life episodes." The government asked groups of public sector volunteers called "Integrated-Service Teams" to put themselves in the position of a member of the public experiencing one of the life events. Team members contacted the relevant departments and agencies direct, and utilized that insight to identify problems resulting from the way services are organized at the moment, and what might be done to improve things. These life episodes included: leaving school, becoming unemployed, changing address, having a baby, retiring, needing long-term care at home, and bereavement. One of the main aims of

---

4. See http://www.servicefirst.gov.uk/2001/joinedup/joinedup.htm for more information on this program.

the government is to encourage and facilitate more joined-up working between government departments and agencies, and also with the rest of the public sector, like local government. All of this leads to better management of knowledge thus resulting in high quality, modern, accessible, and responsive services.

As stated by the cabinet office of the UK government, the "true" levers are to be found in the art of leadership:

- the power to convene
- the power of ideas
- the power of initiative
- the ability to capture and share knowledge
- the ability to explain and to teach
- the ability to speak with one voice
- the ability to be in tune with the different voices of the public service as a whole.

In another instance of organization learning, the South Australian Government Education department used a Microsoft Outlook-based knowledge-management application to track project details, and to share information and learning. Information technology professionals face many challenges regarding IT development and deployment. For some, it might be the daunting task of introducing a computer system into a workgroup that has never used technology before. For other agencies, it is the constant challenge of upgrading existing systems to keep up with ever-increasing needs and technological improvements.

A new solution lets the South Australian Education Department share knowledge across all its physical sites, utilize its trained experts more broadly, raise everyone's knowledge level, and reduce the project time. The solution allowed the department to shorten the time needed to roll out new computer equipment to 630 schools. Dubbed CLASS (Client Liaison and Support System), the system records collective learning from every installation and every problem solved. The department gets smarter with each task completed. As soon as an issue is dealt with and a decision made, the details are automatically recorded and used to support future decision-making. Thus the department is not wasting time solving the same problems over and over. Also, the school staff are now smarter through collective learning and are avoiding many problems altogether.

The creation of reusable knowledge assets is vital to achieve the department's goal of consistent performance on large-scale projects. Facility tracking, trend analysis, response-time analysis, and knowledge sharing have become the basis for future decisions and methodologies. Also, any work performed by the department or by outside vendors on behalf of the department needs to comply with mandated policies and objectives. CLASS provides built-in policy-compliance checking by continually comparing actual activities with required activities. If a policy is ignored or abridged, it shows up on a CLASS exception report.

Within the Canadian government, many agencies are now addressing KM and a recently established Corporate Renewal and Knowledge Management Office within the Treasury Board Secretariat, confirms that KM is becoming part of the strategic thinking of the Federal government. The October 1999 Speech from the Throne stated that the Public Service has a key role in helping Canada stay at the leading edge of the knowledge revolution. The February 2000 budget then provided the financing for the Government On-Line project. A Federal Government Learning and Development Committee was subsequently established and now has two publications. Each considers the Public Service of Canada as a learning organization. From the publication *Directions for the Future*:

- A learning organization is characterized by its ability to continually improve performance through new ideas, knowledge and insights. It is able to constantly anticipate, innovate and find new and better ways to fulfill its mission. It is continually changing its behavior to reflect new ideas and insights.

- It is built around people. People, their knowledge, know-how and ability to innovate, are at the heart of the learning organization.

- It recognizes that learning is a collective undertaking involving the exchange of knowledge and ideas among people working together in teams and networks. Just as the machine in the industrial age expanded our physical capacity, the learning organization relies on teams and networks to expand our intellectual capacity.[5]

Other efforts within the Canadian government include The Inter-departmental Knowledge Management Forum (IKMF), which is an inter-departmental community of practice brought together by the common need to understand and apply the new and emerging issue of knowledge management for the public sector. The importance of KM as a governmental strategy is evident from the Speech from the Throne that said, "our human talent, our values and our commitment to working together will secure Canada's leadership in the knowledge-based economy."[6]

Further, it recognized that "in the global, knowledge-based economy, the advantage goes to countries that are innovative, have high levels of productivity,

5. In "Application of Knowledge Management to NTC" from the National Research Council Canada, 2000 (http://www.nrc.ca/corporate/vision06/pdfs/km.pdf).
6. Speech address by the 26th Governor General of Canada in 2001 (http://www.sftddt.gc.ca/sftddt_e.htm).

quickly adopt the latest technology, invest in skills development for their citizens . . ."[7]

A Canadian government effort that has received acclaim is that of Health Canada. Health Canada analyzes, creates, shares, and uses knowledge strategically to maintain and improve the health of the people of Canada through its knowledge management processes and strategies, which are tailored to advance the business lines of the department both as a model knowledge organization, and as a leader, facilitator, and partner in the development of a Canadian health infrastructure. Health Canada defines knowledge management as a departmental strategy for ensuring that health knowledge and information are identified, captured, created, shared, analyzed, used, and disseminated to improve and maintain the health of Canadians.

The strategy acknowledges and builds upon the need for Health Canada to assist in improving and to interact as a valued partner in the health system through influence and outreach, through world-class analysis and research products and capacity, and through connecting and empowering employees via IT infrastructure, tools, and services. Working within an intricate policy and legislative environment, the strategy supports departmental priorities and business lines, recognizing that in one way or another, all branches and the department as a whole are in the health knowledge business. The strategy also relies upon and builds from professional and societal values to nurture and sustain a learning and knowledge culture. The Committee recommends the following principles as the foundation upon which the strategy is built:

- Committed leadership must be exercised in valuing, analyzing, creating, sharing, and using knowledge.

- Health knowledge must be: analyzed, created, and captured wisely; easy to access; shared thoughtfully; and managed well.

Thus, Health Canada recognizes the central role of knowledge in improving the health system, and is committed to investing in learning and development, IM, and IT to build and maintain business-driven knowledge management infrastructure, tools, and services. This commitment is consistent with the three priorities of the Clerk of the Privy Council: to strengthen policy capacity (in our case, by creating, sharing, and using health knowledge strategically and across departments); to modernize service delivery (by developing a national health infostructure);[8] and to build a vibrant national public service adapted to future needs (by developing health knowledge workers).

---

7. Ibid.
8. See the document titled "Vision and Strategy for Knowledge Management and IM/IT for Health Canada" located at http://www.hc-sc.gc.ca/iacb-dgiac/km-gs/english/ vsmenu_e.htm for definition of InfoStructure and detailed information about this program.

Similarly the Workplace Safety and Insurance Board's (WSIB) successful knowledge management practice, which started in the summer of 1994, is today highly regarded in Canada, and is considered an early adopter of KM, and a KM leader and practitioner in the industry. At the Workplace Safety and Insurance Board of Ontario, technology, IBM's Lotus Notes/Domino solutions, was employed to build an effective KM system. Referred to internally as ASK, an acronym for "Ask Seek Knock," the board's system includes repositories of best practices, company policies, links to subject experts, and chat rooms for live, online collaboration. Employees can access these repositories, which are all interlinked, through an intranet portal. A querying mechanism allows searches by topic and provides such valuable information as definitions, examples, lists of experts in a particular area, and even a potential list of questions and best practices. Since it was first created in 1994, ASK has grown from sixteen repositories to more than 200 today.

Although technology is an important component of KM, it is even more important for every agency to invest resources in determining the organization's ultimate objective, knowledge proponents and workers within the organization and potential projects that could help meet the desired goals and objectives. Over and above the technology in place, the success of such initiatives is based on each member's recognition for the need to create a culture of information sharing, including broad accessibility to knowledge across departments. CLASS and ASK are clearly early but innovative examples of how knowledge management systems can support a state or local government. These agencies must in turn have strong mandates to share information such that even the most unlikely pieces of information and tacit knowledge get captured. Government is competing with the private sector for quality staff as people are leaving government in greater numbers. Thus, KM can help governments leverage what they already have.

For systems such as CLASS and ASK to be effective, the users must not only be encouraged to search the system for what they need, but to also contribute their own knowledge, including best practices. A growing number of agencies already have the tools (such as KM software, databases, search-and-retrieval tools, document management systems, and process automation software) essential to making knowledge management an active part of the practice. As stated earlier, a challenge for governments is the classification and organization of the ever-growing repository of documents so that employees and members of the public can easily find what they are looking for and then use that information for value-added functions. Tagging information with metadata (information about information) and developing software components (often called "spiders") that constantly seek and collect metadata about documents stored in information repositories are solutions that are already being deployed effectively as KM solutions to address the challenges raised by constant information and data overload.

All of the above examples have focused on KM initiatives primarily in developed countries and may lead you to think that KM is not the foray of developing nations. Consider the case of an effort code-named SMART (Simple, Moral, Accountable, Responsive, and Transparent government) in the southern state of India, Andhra Pradesh. The state's dynamic leadership launched an initiative called eSeva. eSeva, the first such service to be launched in the country, is focused on providing a wide spectrum of citizen-friendly services that will provide value-added services to citizens and save them the anxiety of dealing with various government departments for such routine tasks as payment of utility bills, reservations, permits, licenses, and certificates.

These services are delivered through eSeva centers located at strategic locations in cities, towns, and villages. In addition, many of these services are also available via a web-based portal operated by the government. The government has launched other initiatives too, such as MPHS (Multi-Purpose Household Survey), which aims to build a comprehensive database of households for the purposes of accurately targeting economic and health schemes; FAST (Fully Automated Services of Transport), which computerizes issuance of driving licenses; and SKIM, a project to manage the information and knowledge resources of the Secretariat and enhance decision-making efficiency. To support all these initiatives, the government is relying heavily on information technology solutions.

Although India is among the élite league in the development of information technologies, making such technology accessible to the masses can be very challenging considering the constraints imposed by the infrastructure, and the economic and social conditions. In the case of Andhra, the introduction of these e-governance systems is not taking place due to either public pressure or grass-root level demand. In fact, many critics even consider such initiatives ahead of their time. In this particular case, the government firmly believes that a "Push approach" must be employed in the development and deployment of e-governance systems if the vision of transforming the state into a knowledge economy is to be achieved. Much like the "joined-up" government initiative in the UK, it is believed that these e-governance initiatives will eventually provide economic and social stimulus. The government, however, realizes that pushing e-governance is not easy or even straightforward. In the words of one government official:

> It is not simply a matter of introducing technology into the system. Indeed, technology is only 20 percent of the task. The big part is really managing the resistance and inertia of the existing system and of altering existing procedures to make them compatible with e-governance systems. These are management tasks which cannot be accomplished overnight. They take time.[9]

---

9. N. Chandrababu Naidu, Chief Minister of Andhra Pradesh, Secretariat (http://www.ap-it.com/egovernway.html).

Andhra's e-governance initiative is impressive and well positioned for success. Led by a very dynamic and cyber-savvy Chief Minister, Mr. Chandrababu Naidu, the government has spelt out a clear vision for this state called *Vision 2020* (seems to indicate 20/20, perfect vision), which includes a mission statement for e-governance and information technology, and focuses on transforming the state into a leading knowledge-driven economy. With the belief that strategy has to be driven by vision, the plan comprises a detailed road map outlining specific projects and timetables for each project, and flexible and innovative ways to fund each of these projects. In the words of the Chief Minister, Mr. Naidu:

> Andhra Pradesh will leverage information technology to attain a position of leadership and excellence in the information age and to transform itself into a knowledge society. The state will use information technology to improve the quality of life of its residents and help them achieve higher incomes and employment. It will also aggressively promote the pervasive use of IT to achieve higher levels of efficiency and competitiveness in both public and private enterprises.[10]

Since rapid deployment of such KM and e-governance initiatives can impose severe monetary constraints in a developing economy, the state adopted such novel financing models as BOO (Build-Own-Operate), BOOT (Build-Own-Operate-Transfer), and PPP (Public-Private-Participation).[11] Further, critical to such success and innovative development is a team approach. Towards this end, the leadership has assembled some of the best minds in KM and information technology to plan, execute and measure the progress and efficacy of the e-governance programs.

Based on the initiatives outlined above, it is obvious that governments around the world are realizing the importance of KM and adopting it as a time-tested strategy to deliver quality services and streamline operations. In fact, those like Mr. Kenneth Duncan (Centre for Management and Policy Studies, Cabinet Office, UK) view KM as an approach to deliver "Value for money." He says:

> For Government to deliver user focused, value for money, high quality public services, Knowledge Management is a key organizational and cultural issue. Sharing knowledge and working collaboratively is critical to improving public service delivery. Knowledge Management strategies within Government have enabled the public sector to communicate more and more effectively, reducing duplication and wasteful practices,

---

10. R. Sudan, IAS Special Secretary to Chief Minister, Government of Andhra Pradesh, "Towards SMART Government: The Andhra Pradesh Experience" 2001, p. 3.
11. More information on Andhra's KM and e-governance initiatives can be obtained from http://www.ap-it.com and <http://www.esevaonline.com>

but perhaps most important of all, giving value for money by enabling them to work smarter.[12]

Governments to address a variety of issues are increasingly adopting KM, but all these efforts are only the tip of the iceberg. There is still tremendous opportunity and room to innovatively employ KM to solve many of the challenges faced by governments and society.

ROLE OF THE CKO IN GOVERNMENT

So, you may ask, what are the roles of a CKO in the public sector? How are they different from those in the private sector? Ash Sooknanan, a Senior KM Consultant for the Bank of Montreal Group of Companies and the former Corporate Knowledge Officer of the Ontario Workplace Safety and Insurance Board (WSIB), Canada says, "The differences in roles and responsibilities between the public and private sectors are not so much in the function of the CKO as it is in the KM drivers."[13] Launching an effective KM program in both sectors require a well defined strategy and rollout plan, with tangible metrics to measure the success or failure of the initiative. Sooknanan says:

It's the drivers that are different. Knowledge management in the private sector is primarily driven by adding tangible value. There's a tremendous focus on using KM to increase profitability, to increase shareholder value and thus return on investment. The clientele being served are seeking a return on their investments. In the public sector, the reasons to employ KM are more often than not, service oriented and driven by a desire to improve the life of the people the organization or government body serves.[14]

For KM to succeed, the CKO must ensure that all programs are tied to the organizational mandate – what the organization is in the business of – why it exists. In the case of WSIB, managing knowledge needed to be handled in fundamentally new and innovative ways when the WSIBs moved away from "compensation and rehabilitation" to "prevention and health and safety" with its mandate being "the elimination of all workplace injuries and illnesses." In a financial organization like the Bank of Montreal Group of Companies, KM

---

12. In "Prime Minister Launches Major Campaign to get UK Online" *10 Downing Street Newsroom*, London 2000.
13. A. Sooknanan on KM in the Public Sector, from *destinationKM.com* by Michael Robbins, 2001, p. 1.
14. A. Sooknanan on KM in the Public Sector, from destinationKM.com by Michael Robbins, 2001, p. 2.

might be used to help the organization focus on increased shareholder value.

KM initiatives in both sectors face very similar challenges. The CKO needs to develop programs that impact the bottom line, produce tangible results, and thus get buy-in from all stakeholders. Sooknanan says:

> KM doesn't happen overnight. At the WSIB, it took 5 years for the initiatives to gain strong hold. The ultimate recognition for KM came only in 1999, when the WSIB catapulted KM as a corporate priority and incorporated KM as part of its 5 year plan, and identified it as one its four 'key pillars' moving forward...the staff began to feel that KM was the right thing to do. They took control, felt a deep sense of ownership and eventually it became an integral part of their daily routine. We knew that our KM initiatives were beginning to yield results when we saw a change in culture; in the way staff accessed and shared information and knowledge. And while we believe that the KM Practice at the WSIB still had a fair way yet to go, we knew we were on the right track by the results and success we had, when clearly, we could see the value in how KM was changing our culture and the way we worked.[15]

FUTURE KM EFFORTS

Governmental agencies are just now beginning to build knowledge bases that help them get a better understanding of things, such as who are the recipients of those services, who are the providers, and where is there room for improvement and cost control. In order for governmental agencies to realize the benefits of such initiatives as the "joined-up" government, they will have to identify, adopt, and implement new and innovative ways in the most unlikely places to streamline processes and manage knowledge within their organizations. In doing so, governments need to ensure that their services reflect real-life situations, are value-added, and meet the demands of their people. Such efforts must be initiated at all levels of government and all places that impact public life: health care, educational institutions, law enforcement, public transport, housing, social security, employment, media, and even security, to name a few.

Further, it is important for governments to recognize that populations are increasingly becoming heterogeneous. There is increased migration of people, and societies all over the world are becoming increasingly diverse culturally, economically, and socially. Each person or group of people in these heterogeneous societies has differing needs, aspirations, and goals. Then, across all segments, people fall into different age groups, have varying degrees of

---

15. A. Sooknanan on KM in the Public Sector, from destinationKM.com by Michael Robbins, 2001, p. 2.

skills, have differing education levels and even multiple levels of abilities or disabilities. Thus, the success of a government lies in understanding its people, their preferences and unique needs, and in working towards building a framework that can provide services at a more personalized level. Formulating "one size fits all" policies, procedures, regulations, and guidelines is a sure way to disaster. By the same token, developing customized policies is not easy and could cause more chaos in the functioning of the government than good. An optimal solution for governments to "understand" its people is to develop knowledge bases of information that capture such data as age, preferences, education levels, crime rates, and employment, and develop policies that are in line with the statistics and current trends. Governments, like the private sector, need to be increasingly agile and adapt to the changes impacting society and the global village at large.

Most governments around the world expect to see significant investment in education driven by a nationwide push among school systems to learn about best practices that can lead to improved test results, thus leading to a more "well-learned" population. A "well-learned" and "well-informed" population can in turn bring about increased innovation that creates knowledge, generates economic stimulus, and thus more stable societies. It is not surprising at all that there has been an increased thrust to manage knowledge in the education sector. The concern is not just with retaining knowledge resources, but also with leveraging intellectual investments to improve the economic and educational quality of life in the state. Further, it is very important to clearly outline how to capture the intellectual capital in our universities in ways that would benefit government and industry.

Another area that has begun to increasingly focus on KM is criminal investigation. These knowledge bases allow law enforcement officials to track terrorists, share information in real time, and also conduct pattern analysis. Case in point, the Central Intelligence Agency (CIA) sponsored venture capital firm In-Q-Tel has been investing heavily in Enterprise Knowledge Management, Visualization, and Data-mining technologies that can lead to enterprise search/retrieval, indexing, access management, personalization data warehousing/mining, and collaboration environments. The firm has already invested in companies such as Mahomine, Stratify, Tacit Knowledge Systems Inc., and Traction, all of which develop Knowledge Management solutions. Since the unfortunate incidents of September 11, 2001, the Federal law enforcement and security agencies such as the FBI are looking at ways to use the very same KM technologies to identify terrorists, track and interpret messages, identify patterns, analyze historical data, and build intelligence that will enable the agencies to be proactive rather than reactive.

However, technology is not the ultimate solution and security cannot be assumed by putting technology solutions in place. What is required is a more deep-rooted and well-articulated effort that brings about more general awareness in the people and the government officials that are in charge of playing such roles. Agencies must be willing and able to share more data about suspicious activities, potential terrorists, and lessons learned.

The process of sharing information is not as simple as sharing or integrating information between databases. More often than not, there have been cultural and statutory barriers and the situation is further complicated by turf wars. With the incidents of September 11, the world has seen an upsurge of nationalism and a greater respect for life and human values. These incidents have also led people to view knowledge sharing in a new light, and have forced both cultural and legislative change in a way that had not happened previously. A greater degree of communication and coordination is now taking place and people are more willing to undergo change (and better still point out areas that need change) than they were previously. People seem to realize that battling an enemy that is widespread, has access to a wealth of destructive power, little regard for human values, and, above all, is amorphous, requires us, as people and governments, to be much more closely integrated than we have been in the past. In the "war against terrorism," technology is only one component. The more important challenges are definitely collaboration, knowledge sharing, and overcoming cultural and statutory barriers.

Dealing with terrorism requires more than just state-of-the-art weaponry or a large armed force, since terrorism by definition strikes at the most unlikely places at the most unlikely moments; it is always unexpected. Bio-terrorism is a looming threat to the world and among the many anti-terrorism strategies, governments must focus on building reliable health communication networks. These networks must connect and facilitate information sharing between agencies, schools, drug manufacturers, pharmacies, emergency response teams, and even research labs. Knowledge bases must contain information on all existing harmful agents, their effective ranges, potential damage to life and property, short and long-term health hazards, immediate neutralizers, nearest treatment centers, best practices, and even contact information of the renowned experts in that domain. Unless such information is readily available and effectively shared, humanity's war against terrorism is incomplete. The threat to human life will continue to loom over our heads.

In this direction, a key report by the Gilmore Commission (instituted by the US Defense Authorization Act) on government capabilities necessary to counteract terrorism highlights the need for improvements to the health communication networks. As a result, federal, state, and local health departments and emergency management agencies would be better prepared to share information. For boosting cyber security, the commission recommends the involvement of the Critical Infrastructure Protection Board at all levels of government. The report also expresses concerns about the National Infrastructure Protection Center, saying its placement within the FBI inhibits data sharing. The commission also recommends the creation of a federally funded body consisting of representatives from both public and private sectors to address cyber detection, alert, and warning functions. It is very easy to visualize how these health communication networks can play a significant role in preparing for and recouping after natural calamities such as earthquakes, floods, volcano eruptions, hurricanes, and droughts.

At present, most of the government initiatives focus on the front-end delivery of services. The critical infrastructure issues are, to a large extent, still back-office operations. In the private sector, many of the greatest benefits in the application of KM and technology have come from applying the principles to back-office. Thus, it is critical for government to focus on enhancing back-office performance and reengineer processes in a manner that leads to better KM and longer-term benefits.

Among the many hurdles towards implementing strong and successful KM initiatives are the lack of knowledge about the importance of KM, lack of a well-defined strategy, absence of leaders, volatile governments, or merely ill-trained executioners/practitioners. As it stands today, there are not many companies or individuals that understand the complex problems posed in the public sector. As governments increasingly realize the importance of KM in the delivery of quality public services, a multibillion-dollar market for knowledge management in government is bound to open up.

KM is often associated and even perceived to be closely intertwined with e-government initiatives. Although such assumptions may not always hold true, an interesting trend is beginning to emerge from data gathered from very recent world indices. According to the second World Globalization Index, a recent compilation by AT Kearney and the US journal *Foreign Policy*, the top ten most globalized economies are: Ireland, Switzerland, Singapore, Netherlands, Sweden, Finland, Canada, Denmark, Austria, and the UK. Another very comprehensive attempt, a 2001 study of 196 nations, carried out by the World Markets Research Center outlines the world's top e-government countries: the US, Taiwan, Australia, Canada, the UK, Ireland, Israel, Singapore, Germany, and Finland. Among these lists, the overlap (Ireland, Singapore, Finland, Canada, and the UK) – five out of ten – is strong. Further, this overlap seems to indicate a relationship between the world's most globalized economies with those of the most developed e-governments. Although these trends seem too good to be ignored and can be assumed to make a case for KM, there is no evidence that one directly influences the other, or that KM is the reason for the success of e-government.

Realizing the digital government presents great technical and intellectual research challenges, but it also promises great value and can provide valuable new insights and interesting new applied research problems, leading to deployable new systems. Thinking of Federal Information Services as a laboratory means that a huge variety of sources and systems are available to invent new and very advanced applications. Typically, academic research laboratories do not have sufficient tools or sources of information and data to explore real-world problems. Instead, abstractions are studied in closed, controlled environments.

Figure 12.1 – KM framework in public sector

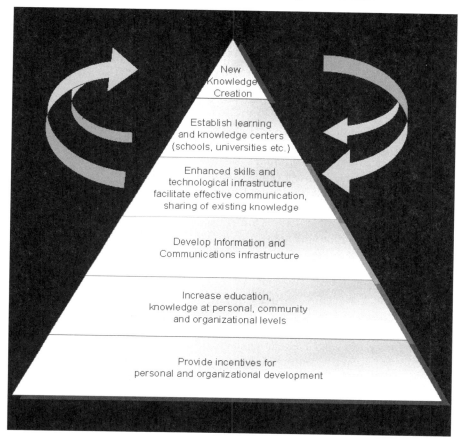

Research that considers real-world operating constraints can lead to new insights that reduce the complexity of real-world problems. Students immersed in a real world context can learn how to apply the knowledge acquired from their academic studies to large problems of great potential impact, thus helping to ensure the next generation of knowledge workers can impact the Federal enterprise. In summary, applied research in Federal Information Services offers some unique challenges unavailable in basic theoretical research. Building, nurturing, and leveraging relationships with Federal Information Service providers and the research and education community supported by sufficient long-term funding for applied research, training and advanced education, is key to developing a critical mass of researchers and students to work on truly large-scale demonstrable applications of benefit to the public.

CONCLUSION

Developed and industrialized nations are rapidly adopting KM and migrating towards "knowledge economies." However, a significant part of the globe is composed of developing and Third World countries where poverty, health, and the well being of people are the major concerns, let alone good infrastructure. Much like the developments of the past decade have attempted to bridge the digital divide, we need to move towards bridging the "knowledge divide" that is so prevalent today.

Currently, the knowledge divide between the rich and poor, urban and rural, educated and uneducated communities is significant, primarily in developing countries where these communities lack access to basic amenities such as education, healthcare, power, and telecommunications. Such a knowledge divide can be effectively bridged through education and knowledge sharing between the developed and developing nations. Case in point, diseases such as malaria or even malnutrition are practically non-existent in developed nations, but millions around the world (in Africa, for example) continue to die because of lack of access to treatment facilities, medication, and, even more importantly, due to lack of "know-how" and "how-to" about the cure for such common ailments.

Education, knowledge sharing, learning communities, and information and communications technologies are the engines for social and economic development. The rapid development, proliferation, and adoption of information systems and telecommunication technologies are making the world truly a global village by mitigating time and distance barriers. The advantages of greater knowledge and superior ability to learn are now greater, as people around the world have access to richer information resources. According to the World Bank statistics, 40 years ago Ghana and the Republic of Korea had virtually the same income per capita, but by the 1990s Korea's income per capita was six times Ghana's. More than half of that difference is attributed to Korea's greater success in acquiring and using knowledge.

In 1996, the World Bank undertook a strategic initiative to become a Knowledge Bank that could initiate the knowledge revolution in developing countries and serve as a global catalyst for creating, sharing, and applying the cutting-edge knowledge necessary for poverty reduction and economic development. Towards achieving these goals the bank underwent significant restructuring and invested in knowledge networks, communities of practice, and information technology within the organization to enable better internal and external knowledge sharing. Further, the bank has launched several new global knowledge initiatives in partnership with the private sector, international and bilateral agencies, nongovernmental organizations, and others to tackle the key social, financial, and technological challenges of the new knowledge economy. These new partnerships lie at the heart of the bank's vision of knowledge for all, since effective global action depends on the global community working together to leverage the bank's collective resources, experience, and expertise.

KM when implemented with strategic vision has the potential to foster innovation, competitiveness, economic development, jobs, better access to basic services, tangible benefits from education and health initiatives, and, most importantly, enhanced empowerment of local communities and stronger voices for poor people. Nongovernmental organizations such as Sakshi (India) and the CDIT (Committee for Democracy in Information Technology, Brazil), with assistance from international groups, have played significant roles in the promulgation of national and local laws relating to sexual harassment and community associations that run computer science and citizenship schools, respectively. Many more examples of such organizations exist which have been successful due to effective knowledge sharing between the experienced and inexperienced.

In the public sector, it is very important to place higher emphasis on community development with the focus on raising education standards, experience, and individual knowledge levels. Without such grass-root level development, most technological infrastructure will be out of place and probably even useless to a population that does not have operational skills or knowledge of its capabilities and potential.

Organizations such as the United Nations have adopted new global frameworks to bridge the information and knowledge divide through economic and structural reforms to stimulate competition and innovation. These frameworks rely on stakeholder collaboration to optimize global networks and investments in people, as well as the promotion of global access and participation. International organizations, governments, private sector, academic and research institutions, nongovernmental organizations, and the common people all have significant roles to play in the development of a new global economy.

Governments must provide enabling policies and regulatory frameworks, taking the lead where markets will not provide adequate infrastructure investment. The private sector must develop infrastructure and disseminate information and communications technologies. International organizations and bilateral development aid must help generate, share, and apply critical development knowledge on the ground, and support the massive capital requirements of the knowledge revolution. Academic and research institutions must continue to create and disseminate new knowledge critical for development. And nongovernmental organizations and civil society need to help bridge the knowledge gap between global agencies and local community organizations and use the potential of information technology to spread the voices of poor people.

Managing knowledge management projects is an iterative process. Therefore, focusing on end results, with a clear picture of existing knowledge is important to determine the knowledge gaps. Only with such information can a clear KM project plan be put in place that identifies knowledge attributes, key influencers, stakeholders, processes, actors, and technological requirements. Such analysis is critical for e-government initiatives due to the abundance of unorganized information. The abundance of information also leads to another key issue: knowledge prioritization. Such prioritization is very important to develop lean and agile processes that are responsive, efficient, and facilitate value-added decision making.

Knowledge is best harnessed and yields true benefits only when it is shared openly and not contained for personal gain. Knowledge between people, communities, states, and nations must be shared towards the advancement of the human race at large. Knowledge exchange between these entities can include best practices, lessons learned, and effective problem-solving techniques. Such knowledge sharing avoids effort duplication and yields tangible, predictable results in a more efficient and cost-effective manner. It is, however, important that such knowledge transfer and/or sharing not be conducted at a "spoon-feed" level as that tends to inhibit innovation in communities. Lesser advantaged communities must utilize knowledge gained from more advanced communities towards the development of local infrastructure, as a means to quickly ramp up the learning curve and stimulate innovation. When such relationships become parasitic rather than symbiotic, the benefits of knowledge transfer are clearly being undone.

About the author
Viijay Gummadi is currently the Vice President, Product Development at Campfire Interactive, Inc, a technology company in Ann Arbor, Michigan, USA that is involved in the development of Collaborative Product Development solutions for the Manufacturing sector. He possesses unique expertise in visualizing and architecting leading edge technology solutions. His extensive experience encompasses design of electro-mechanical devices, complex software systems, and Manu-facturing.

He also has interests in diverse areas such as Knowledge Management, Governance, International relations and Accessibility for people with limited abilities. Particularly, he is interested in the application of pioneering concepts and technology to solving real world problems at individual, organizational and community levels.

Mr. Gummadi serves as an Invited Expert to the World Wide Web Consortium's (W3C) Web Accessibility Initiative and the Object Management Group's (OMG) Manufacturing Domain Task Force. He has a Master's degree in Manufacturing Engineering and Information Systems from Wayne State University, Detroit, MI and a Bachelor's degree in Mechanical Engineering from the University of Mysore, India.

He can be reached by e-mail at vgummadi@cfi2.com

Glossary

API	Application Program Interface
BI	Business Intelligence
BOO	Build-Own-Operate
BOOT	Build-Own-Operate-Transfer
BPR	Business Process Reengineering
C2G	Customer to Government
CAGR	Cumulative Average Growth Rate
CEO	Chief Executive Officer
CFO	Chief Financial Officer
CIO	Chief Information Officer
CKO	Chief Knowledge Officer
CLASS	Client Liaison Support System
CLO	Chief Learning Officer
COO	Chief Operating Officer
COM/DCOM	Distributed Component Object Model
CORBA	Common Object Request Broker Architecture
CRM	Customer Relationship Management
CTO	Chief Technology Officer
DARPA	Defense Advanced Research Projects Agency
DBMS	DataBase Management System
DEC	Digital Equipment Corporation
DNA	Distributed InterNet Architecture
DSS	Decision Support System
PSS	Performance Support System
DTP	Dynamic Transcoding Proxies
EAI	Enterprise Application Integration
EAP	Enterprise Application Process
EDI	Electronic Data Interchange
EIP	Enterprise Information Portals
EJB	Enterprise JavaBeans
ERP	Enterprise Resource Planning
FDA	Food and Drug Administration (US Government Agency)
FORCE	Framework for Open Redirecting Content Exchange, coined by Marcus Goncalves in September of 2000.
G2G	Government to Government
GAO	General Accounting Officer

GB	Gigabyte
GUI	Graphical User Interface
HDML	Handheld Device Markup Language
HMI	Human Machine Interface
HTML	Hyper Text Mark-up Language
HTTP	HyperText Transport Protocol
IC	Intellectual Capital
ICA	Independent Computer Architecture
ICD	International Code Designator
ICE	Internet Content Extraction
ICOC	International Churches of Christ
ICT	Information and Communication Technology
IKMF	Interdepartmental Knowledge Management Forum
IP	Intellectual Property
IPO	Initial Public Offer (event when a company goes public)
ISV	Independent Software Vendors
IS	Information Systems
IT	Information Technology
JDK	Java Development Kit
KB	Kilobyte
KCV	Knowledge Capital Valuation
KE	Knowledge Ecosystem
KM	Knowledge Management
LAN	Local Area Network
MAN	Metropolitan Area Network
MIS	Management of Information Systems
MOU	Memorandum of Understanding
M&A	Merging and Acquisitions
NCF	Network Computer Interface
OASIS	Organization for the Advancement of Structured Information Standards
OLAP	Online Analytical Processing
OLE DB	Object Linking and Embedding Database
OLAP	Online Analytical Processing
OO	Object Oriented (technologies)
PAN	Personal Area Networks
PDA	Personal Digital Assistants
PIM	Personal Information Manager
PPP	Public-Private-Participation
RAINBOW	Remote Agent for Intelligent Normalization for Bytes over Wireless
RDF	Resource Description Framework
ROA	Return on Assets
ROE	Return on Equity

ROI	Return on investment
SAP	Service Access Point (Also the name of a leading German ERP company)
SHD	Smart Handheld Devices
SHTML	Secure HyperText Markup Language
SI	System Integration
SOAP	Simple Object Access Protocol
SPUD	Skill Planning "und" Development
SRM	Supplier Relationship Management
SW	Semantic Web
TB	Terabyte
TCO	Total Cost of Ownership
TCM	Total Customer Management
TQM	Total Quality Management
UDA	Universal Data Access
UDDI	Universal Description, Discovery, and Integration (protocol)
VAN	Virtual Access Network
VAPOR	Virtual Agent for Parsing of Objects and Records
VC	Venture Capitalist
W3C	World Wide Web Consortium
W3H	Who, What, Why, and How
WAN	Wide Area Network
WAP	Wireless Application Protocol
WSDL	Web Service Description Language
WSIB	Workplace Safety and Insurance Board
XHTML	eXtensible HyperText Markup Language
XML	eXtensible Mark-up Language
XSLT	eXtensible Stylesheet Language Template
XSP	XML Server Pages

Bibliography

Abecker, A., Aitken, S., Schmalhofer, F., and Tschaitschian, B. "KARATEKIT: Tools for the Knowledge-Creating Company" in *Proceedings of KAW 1998: Eleventh Workshop on Knowledge Acquisition, Modeling and Management*, Voyager Inn, Banff, Alberta, Canada, 18–23 April 1998.

Abecker, A., Bernardi, A., and Sintek, M. "Enterprise Information Infrastructures for Active, Context-Sensitive Knowledge Delivery" in *ECIS 1999: Proceedings of the 7th European Conference on Information Systems*, Copenhagen, Denmark, June 1999.

Abecker, A., Bernardi, A., and Sintek, M. "Towards a Technology for Organizational Memories" *IEEE Intelligent Systems and Their Applications*, 13(3), May/June 1998.

Abecker, A., Bernardi, A., and Sintek, M. *Developing a Knowledge Management Technology: An Encompassing View on Know-More, Know-Net, and Enrich.* Paper presented at IEEE WET-ICE 1999 Workshop on Knowledge Media Networking, Stanford, 16–18 June 1999.

Allee, V. *An Emerging Model of Intellectual Capital (or Intangible Assets)*, Boston, Butterworth-Heinemann, 1997.

Allee, V. "eLearning is not Knowledge Management" *LineZine*, Fall 2000.

Allee, V. "New Tools for a New Economy" *Perspectives on Business and Global Change*, 13(4), December 1999.

Allee, V. "Reconfiguring the Value Network" *Journal of Business Strategy*, 21(4), July/August 2000.

Allee, V. *The Future of Knowledge: Increasing Prosperity Through Value Networks*, Boston, Butterworth-Heinemann, 2002.

Allee, V. *The Knowledge Evolution: Building Organizational Intelligence*, Boston, Butterworth-Heinemann, 1997.

Allee, V. *The Knowledge Evolution: Expanding Organizational Intelligence*, Boston, Butterworth-Heinemann, 2002.

Amidon, D. *Innovation Strategy for the Knowledge Economy: The Ken Awakening*, Boston, Butterworth-Heinemann, 1997.

Applehans, W. and Globe, A. *Managing Knowledge: A Practical Web-Based Approach*, Reading, Addison-Wesley, 1998.

Bair, J. "Knowledge Enabled Enterprise Architecture" *White Paper*, http://strategy-partners.com

Baron, D. *Moses on Management*, New York, Pocket Book/Simon & Schuster, 1999.

Becker, K. *Culture and International Business*, Binghamtom, Haworth, 2000.

Bennis, W. *Organizing Genius: The Secretes of Creative Collaboration*, Reading, Addison-Wesley, 1997.

Bolman, L. and Deal, T. *Modern Approaches to Understanding and Managing Organizations*, San Francisco, Jossey-Bass Inc., 1988.

Bookstein, A. "Information Coding in the Internet Environment" in chapter 19, T. Kanti Srikantaiah and M. E.D. Koenig (eds) *Knowledge Management for the Information Professional*, ASIS, 2000

Bossidy, L., Charan, R., and Burck, C. *Execution: The Discipline of Getting Things Done*, New York, Crown, 2002.

Bounds, G., Yorks, L., and Ranney, G. *Beyond Total Quality Management*, New York, McGraw-Hill, 1994.

Bourdreau, A. and Couillard, G. "Systems Integration and Knowledge Management" *Information Systems Management*, 16(4): 24–32, 1999.

Brandenberger, A. and Nalebuff, B. *Co-Opetition: 1. A Revolutionary Mindset That Redefines Competition and Cooperation; 2. The Game Theory Strategy That's Changing the Game of Business*, New York, Doubleday, 1997.

Briggs, D. "Maximizing the Knowledge Asset Value Within the Enterprise" *DM Direct*, 21 April 2000.

Brooking, A. *Corporate Memory: Strategies for Knowledge Management*, London, International Thomson Business Press, 1999.

Brooking, A. *Intellectual Capital: Core Asset for the Third Millennium*, London, International Thomson Business Press, 1996.

Brooking, A., Board, P., and Jones, S. *The Predictive Potential of Intellectual Capital*. Paper presented at the National Business Conference, Hamilton, Ontario, 22–4 January 1997.

Browne, J. "Unleashing the Power of Learning" *Harvard Business Review*, September/October 1997.

Brown, J. and Duguid, P. *The Social Life of Information*, Boston, Harvard Business School Press, 2000.

Bukowitz, W. and Williams, R. *Knowledge Management Fieldbook*, London, Financial Times/Prentice Hall, 2000.

Bukowitz, W. *Knowledge Measurement: Phase Three, Global Findings Report*, Boston, Arthur Andersen, 1998.

Burstein, D. and Kline, D. *Road Warriors: Dreams and Nightmares Along the Information Highway*, New York, Penguin Group, 1996.

Cabrera, A. "Making Sharing Good for All" *Financial Times*, 2 October 2000.

Capshaw, S. and Koulopoulos, T.M. "Knowledge Leadership" *DM Review*, May 1999.

Charan, R. *Boards at Work*, New York, Jossey-Bass, 1998.

Charan, R. "Simplicity, Speed and Self-Confidence: An Interview with Jack Welch" *Harvard Business Review*, October 1989.

Charan, R. *What the CEO Wants you to Know: How Your Company Really Works*, New York, Crown, 2001.

Charan, R. and Tichy, N. *Every Business is a Growth Business*, New York, Times Books, 2000.

Christensen, C. *The Innovator's Dilemma*, New York, HarperBusiness, 2000.

Cohen, D. and Prusak, L. *British Petroleum's Virtual Teamwork Program.* Case study, Ernst & Young Center for Business Innovation, June 1996.

Collins, J. *Good to Great: Why Some Companies Make the Leap and Others Don't*, New York, HarperCollins, 2001.

Collison, C. "BP Amoco's Knowledge Repository – Connecting the New Organization" *Knowledge Management Review*, March/April 1999.

Comeau-Kirschner, C. and Wah, L. "Who Has the Time to Think?" *Management Review*, January 2000.

Cortada, J. and Woods, J. *The Knowledge Management Yearbook 1999–2000*, Boston, Butterworth-Heinemann, 1999.

Cortada, J. and Woods, J. *The Knowledge Management Yearbook 2000–2001*, Boston, Butterworth-Heinemann, 2000.

Craig, Lt Col Robert G. "Quality in the Operational Air Force: A Case of Misplaced Emphasis." Maxwell AFB, AL.: Air War College, May 1994.

Cross, R. and Israelit, S. *Strategic Learning in a Knowledge Economy: Individual, Collective and Organizational Learning Process*, Boston, Butterworth-Heinemann, 2000.

Cuthbertson, B. "Tacit Solution Puts Users in Charge" *Knowledge Management Magazine*, January 2000.

Dao, J. and Kristof, N. "Bradley's Fatal Mistakes" *New York Times*, 8 March 2000.

Davenport, T. *Mission Critical: Realizing the Promise of Enterprise Systems*, Cambridge, Harvard Business School Press, 2000.

Davenport, T. and Prusak, L. *Working Knowledge: How Organizations Manage What They Know*, Boston, Harvard Business School Press, 1998.

Dennison, R. "Bacon, Eggs and Knowledge Management" *Virtual Business*, 5(1): 12–14, November 2000.

Despres, C. and Chauvel, D. *Knowledge Horizons: The Present and the Promise of Knowledge Management*, Boston, Butterworth-Heinemann, 2000.

Dixon, N. *Common Knowledge: How Companies Thrive By Sharing What They Know*, Cambridge, Harvard Business School Press, 2000.

Drennan, D. *Transforming Company Culture: Getting Your Company From Where You Are Now To Where You Want To Be*, London, McGraw-Hill, 1992.

Drucker, P.F. "Knowledge-worker Productivity: The Biggest Challenge" *California Management Review*, 41(2), 1999.

Drucker, P.F. "Managing Knowledge Means Managing Oneself" *Leader to Leader*, 16, Spring 2000.

Edvinsson, L. and Malone, M. *Intellectual Capital: Realizing Your Company's True Value by Finding Its Hidden Brainpower*, New York, Harper Business, 1997.

English, L.P. "Information Quality in the Knowledge Age" *DM Review*, October 1999.

Farson, R. *Management of the Absurd: Paradox in Leadership*, New York, Touchstone, 1997.

Ferrusi Ross, C. "The Role of IT: Subtle Changes Afoot for IT" *Information Week*, 26 April 1999.

Fisher, K. and Fisher, M. *The Distributed Mind: Achieving High Performance Through the Collective Intelligence of Knowledge Work Teams*, New York, Amacom, 1998.

Fowler, A. "The Role of AI-Based Technology in Support of the Knowledge Management Value Activity Cycle" *The Journal of Strategic Information Systems*, 9(2–3): 107–28, 2000.

Freedman, D. *Corps Business: The 30 Management Principles of the US Marines*, New York, Harper Business, 2000.

Freese, E. "Harvesting Knowledge from the Organization's Information Assets" in *Proceedings of XML Europe 2001, 21–5 May 2001, Berlin, Germany*, Alexandria, VA, Graphic Communications Association, 2001.

Garratt, B. *The Learning Organization: Developing Democracy at Work*, London, HarperCollinsBusiness, 2000.

Garratt, B. *The Twelve Organizational Capabilities*, London, HarperCollinsBusiness, 2000.

Garvin, D. *Learning in Action: A Guide to Putting the Learning Organization to Work*, Cambridge, Harvard Business School Press, 2000.

Gates, B. *Business @ the Speed of Thought*, New York, Warner Books, 1999.

Gersting, A., Gordon, C., and Ives, B. "Implementing Knowledge Management: Navigating the Organizational Journey" *Knowledge Management*, March 1999.

Goleman, D. *Working with Emotional Intelligence*, New York, Bantam Books, 2000.

Goncalves, M. "The Power of Cocoon for Knowledge Technologies" in *Proceedings of XML Europe 2001, 21–5 May 2001, Berlin, Germany*, Alexandria, VA, Graphic Communications Association, 2001.

Graham, A.B. and Pizzo, V.G. "A Question of Balance: Case Studies in Strategic Knowledge Management" *European Management Journal*, 14(4): 338–46, 1996.

Grammer, J. "The Enterprise Knowledge Portal" *DM Review*, March 2000.

Gray, P.H. "The Effects of Knowledge Management Systems on Emergent Teams: Towards a Research Model" *The Journal of Strategic Information Systems*, 9(2–3): 175–91, September 2000.

Grushkin, B. "Context Dependency" *Intelligent Enterprise*, 3(15), 29 September 2000.

Halal, W.E. *The Infinite Resource: Creating and Leading the Knowledge Enterprise*, San Francisco, Jossey-Bass, 1998.

Hamel, G. *Leading the Revolution*, Boston, Harvard Business School Press, 2002.

Hamel, G. and Prahalad, C.K. *Competing for the Future*, Boston, Harvard Business School Press, 1994.

Harris, K. "Transforming the Way Organizations Work" *White Paper* in *Strategic Directions: Knowledge Management and e-Learning, CIO Magazine* supplement, New York, CMP, 2001.

Hately, B.J. and Schmidt, W. *Peacock in the Land of Penguins*, San Francisco, Berrett-Koehler, 2001.

Hatten, K. and Rosenthal, S. *Reaching for the Knowledge Edge: How the Knowing Corporation Seeks, Shares and Uses Knowledge for Strategic Advantage*, New York, Amacom, 2001.

Heenan, D. and Bennis, W. *Co-Leaders: The Power of Great Partnerships*, New York, John Wiley & Sons, 1999.

Hickins, M. "Xerox Shares its Knowledge" *Management Review*, September 2000.

Hildebrand, C. "Making KM Pay Off" *CIO Enterprise Magazine*, 15 February 1999.

Jensen, B. *Simplicity: The New Competitive Advantage in a World of More, Better, Faster*, Cambridge, Perseus, 2000.

Johnson, S. *Who Moved my Cheese?* New York, G.P. Putnam's, 1998.

Joia, L.A. "Measuring Intangible Corporate Assets: Linking Business Strategy with Intellectual Capital" *Journal of Intellectual Capital*, 1(1): 68–84, 2000.

Kelley, T. *The Art of Innovation*, New York, Random House, 2001.

Klein, D. *The Strategic Management of Intellectual Capital*, Boston, Butterworth-Heinemann, 1998.

Korda, M. *Another Life*, New York, Random House/Dell, 2000.

Kotter, J. "Leading Change: Why Transformation Efforts Fail" *Harvard Business Review on Change*, 1998.

Koulopoulos, T. *Smart Company, Smart Tools: Transforming Business Process Into Business Assets*, New York, John Wiley & Son, 1997.

Koulopolus, T. and Frappaolo, C. *Smart Things to Know About KM*, Dover, Capstone, 1999.

Koulopoulos, T. and Palmer, N. *The X-Economy*, New York, Texere, 2001.

Koulopoulos, T., Toms, W., and Spinello, R. *Corporate Instinct: Building a Knowing Enterprise for the 21st Century,* New York, John Wiley & Son, 1997.

Kransdorff, A. *Corporate Amnesia*, Boston, Butterworth-Heinemann, 1998.

Lawler, E.E. "Adaptive Experiments: An Approach to Organizational Behavior Research" *Academy of Management Review*, 2: 576–85, 1977.

Lawson, I. *Fast Track: Leadership*, London, The Industrial Society, 2001.

Leonard-Barton, D. *Wellsprings of Knowledge: Building and Sustaining the Sources of Innovation*, Cambridge, Harvard Business School Press, 1995.

Leonard-Barton, D. *When Sparks Fly: Igniting Creativity in Groups,* Cambridge, Harvard Business School Press, 1998.

Liautaud, B. *e-Business Intelligence: Turning Information Into Knowledge Into Profit*, New York, McGraw-Hill, 2000.

Lowe, J. *Jack Welch Speaks*, New York, John Wiley & Sons, 1998.

Malhotra, Y. *Knowledge Management and Virtual Organizations*, New York, Idea Group Publishing, 2000.

Malhotra, Y. *Knowledge Management and Business Model Innovation*, New York, Idea Group Publishing, 2001.

Maurik, J. *Writers on Leadership*, London, Penguin, 2001.

Nonaka, J. *Knowledge Emergence: Social, Technical and Evolutionary Dimensions of Knowledge Creation*, London, Oxford University Press, 2001.

Pascale, R.T. *Managing on the Edge*, New York, Simon & Shuster, 1990.

Peppers, D. and Rogers, M. *The One to One Future: Building Relationships One Customer at a Time*, New York, Currency/Doubleday, 1993.

Pfeffer, J. and Sutton, R. *The Knowing-Doing Gap*, Boston, Harvard Business School Press, 1999.

Prusak, L. *Knowledge in Organization*, Boston, Butterworth-Heinemann, 1997.

Ruggles, R., Meyer, C., and Holtshouse, D. *The Knowledge Advantage: 14 Visionaries Define Marketplace Success in the New Economy*, London, Capstone, 2001.

Schein, E. *Organizational Culture and Leadership*, New York, Jossey-Bass Business and Management Series, 1997.

Schrage, M. *No More Teams! Mastering the Dynamics of Creative Collaboration*, New York, Currency/Doubleday, 1995.

Schwartz, E. *Digital Darwinism*, New York, Broadway Books, 1999.

Selby, R.W. *Microsoft Secrets: How the World's Most Powerful Software Company Creates Technology, Shapes Markets, and Manages People*, Louisville, Touchstone, 1998.

Senge, P. *The Fifth Discipline*, New York, Currency/Doubleday, 1994.

Skyrme, D. *Knowledge Networking: Creating Collaborative Enterprise*, Woburn, Butterworth-Heineman, 1999.

Snyder, W.M. and Wenger, E.C. "Communities of Practice: The Organizational Frontier," *Harvard Business Review*, 78(1) January 2000.

Stevens, M. *Extreme Management: What They Teach at Harvard Business School's Advanced Management Program*, New York, Warner Books, 2001.

Strassmann, P. *Information Productivity*, New York, Information Economics Press, 1999.

Strassmann, P. *The Squandered Computer*, New York, Information Economics Press, 1997.

Toffler, A. *The Third Wave*, New York, Bantam Books, 1991.

Tzu, S. *The Art of War*, Oxford, Oxford University Press, 1984.

Useem, M. *Leading Up: How to Lead Your Boss So You Both Win*, New York, Crown, 2001.

Useem, M. *The Leadership Moment: 9 True Stories of Triumph and Disasters and Lessons for Us All*, New York, Times Book, 1998.

Van Krogh, G., Ichijo, K., and Nonaka, I. *Enabling Knowledge Creation: How to Unlock the Mystery of Tacit Knowledge and Release the Power Innovation*, Oxford, Oxford University Press, 2000.

Ward, R. *21st Century Corporate Board*, New York, John Wiley & Sons, 1997.

Welch, J. *Excellence in Management and Leadership Series*, MICA Group, Canada, 2001.

Wheelwright, S. and Clarke, K. *Revolutionizing Product Development: Quantum Leaps in Speed, Efficiency and Quality*, Free Press, 1992.

Yang-Ming, W. *The Philosophy of Wang*, trans. Frederick Goodrich Henke, The Open Court Publishing Co., 1916, *passim*.

Yoffie, D. and Kwak, M. *Judo Strategy: Turning your Competitor's Strength to Your Advantage*, Cambridge, Harvard Business School Press, 2001.

Index